Single, Spiritual...
AND Sexual!

(A Black Woman's Quest for 'the Truth')

Cezanne Poetess

© Artisan Impression (Publishing) Ltd. 2012

The moral right of the Author has been asserted in accordance with the Copyright, Designs and Patents Act, 1988.

All rights reserved. No part of this publication may be reproduced, stored in a retrieval system, or transmitted in any form or by any means, electronic, mechanical, photocopying, recording or otherwise, without the prior permission of the Publisher.

Email: artisanimpression@gmail.com

ISBN: 978-0-9576969-0-7

PUBLISHER'S NOTE:
This is a work of (fact-based) fiction. Names, characters, places, and incidents are either a product of the author's imagination, or are used fictitiously. Any resemblance to actual persons, living or dead, are purely coincidental (!).

Dedicated to my three 'suns'
Zaviere, Sanchez and Azagba
And for the Love of 'my people'

Contents   Page

Foreword		1
Year One:	The Truth?	6
Year Two:	Who Am I?	51
Year Three:	Mind…the Gap!	81
Year Four:	Finding Her Self	109
Year Five:	Be Careful What You Wish For!	135
Year Six:	Trust the Process	150
Year Seven:	Love Attraction	164
Year Eight:	In Deep	190
Year Nine:	Another Level	208
Year Ten:	A Spiritual Union	228
Year Eleven:	Double Celebrations!	246
Afterthought…		269
Book Two		272
Acknowledgments		273
References		278
About the Author		280
'Seeds of Love' CD		282

Foreword

"When was the last time you had sex?"

This might be a question you would ask someone you're considering sleeping with if you are single, but *not* if you are religious – you're not meant to be *having* sex!

Are you?

'Fornication' (sex outside of marriage) is one of the most common sins committed in church, yet probably the least talked about.

Has your sexuality been suppressed by your religious beliefs?

If you are a woman, are you concerned about your biological clock ticking away while you 'wait on the Lord' for a husband?

Do you wish you could be more sexually liberated but fear retribution from God, your religious community, or your own guilty feelings?

If so, this book is for YOU!

If you were *not* brought up in any religious institution and celebrate your sexuality openly, this book if for you too!

I was raised in the Christian faith, and as an adult, found that I was still able to develop my relationship with God despite my weakness of 'Sexual Sin'. Yet my relationship with God kept on developing, to the point where I began being inspired to write poetic 'messages from God'. The very first one I wrote "Look to Me!" features in Year One. You can hear the rest of them at: **www.myspace.com/poetryspokenword/music**.

Yet despite my *spiritual* growth, I had made little progress in my *personal* life. Feeling frustrated, I wrote what some might call 'an angry letter to God'. In it, I asked God all the questions I wasn't supposed to ask because I was questioning 'the infallible Word of God', including the idea of having to wait until I die to get to 'heaven'. One thing I'd just like to say is that I don't actually remember writing it! It wasn't something I sat, planned and pieced together – it was an inspired piece of writing. When I found it on my computer a year later I thought "This is good!" and gave it the title *'The Rebellion'*. I had no intention of ever publishing it, but when I was inspired to start writing *this* book I was led to include it – it now forms the foundation to the whole story! (You can hear the audio version of 'The Rebellion' at **www.singlespiritualandsexual.com** under 'Extracts')

Mind you, I could have been suffering from depression at the time I wrote it, since I *did* battle with feelings of hopelessness from time to time – that is, until I learnt that 'depression' is just a fancy word for 'negative thinking patterns'!

One of my favourite sayings now is;

"Whatever the mind can conceive,
it can achieve –
I can CREATE whatever I can IMAGINE!"

And I am. Why don't you join me in creating *heaven on earth*?

In the past, my imagination has often worked against me; I would conjure up all sorts of 'vain imaginations' and then wonder why my life was in such a mess. So when I discovered that I have the power to create *whatever I can imagine,* I decided to use this novel to stretch my imagination to its limit – and then I discovered it didn't have any!

By taking the limitations off my imagination and learning to 'think outside of the box' I have unblocked as a writer and artist, and am well on my way to creating the life of my dreams. My aim is not to lead 'my people' astray, but to lead them to the *light* and bring them out of mental bondage. Come to think of it, I was probably inspired to write this book to get people to start *thinking for them Selves*!

Most people no longer use the faculty of their Creative Imagination because they're too busy allowing their minds to be controlled and distracted by other things; tell-lie-vision, radio, newspapers, *anything* but 'the Silence'. One of my tasks in writing this story was to paint vivid pictures with *words* that would enable you to exercise *your* imagination.

Creative Visualisation is the mental tool that enables you to bring things from the *non-physical* realm into the *physical*. I very much live between two parallel worlds; this *physical* world, and the *spiritual* world. When I first started learning how to meditate in order to control my negative thinking patterns, I found a whole new world within! You can see from what I produce that I very much live in a fantasy world of my own creations. But is it fantasy, or am I actually *creating* what I am visualizing? Which is the real world, this world, or the spiritual realm? Let's not go there (yet!).

This book explores the theory that each person has two selves; the *Higher Self* and the *lower self*; the Higher Self relates to spiritual matters, while the lower self relates to 'carnal', or physical matters. When referring to the Higher Self, I have capitalised the word 'Self'. When referring to the lower self, I have kept the word how you would normally see it written, e.g. 'herself'. To lead a balanced life, you should be able to operate from both.

I've used my painting *'Black Butterfly'* to illustrate the front cover design of this book because it's symbolic of 'Transformation of the Mind'. (The Adinkra symbol used throughout the book is also a symbol of Transformation). My poem *'The Black Butterfly Effect'* on my next CD *'Rise of the Phoenix'* is a metaphoric explanation of the transformational process a caterpillar goes through before it becomes a beautiful butterfly. It is likened to the process we have to go through in transforming our *mind*.

Back in the early 90's, I used to play the song 'Black Butterfly' by *Sounds of Blackness* constantly as I found it very inspirational. I didn't realise it had sunk into my subconscious mind until *after* I completed the painting in January 2009, then I realized the song complimented my painting perfectly!

'Black Butterfly
You can do 'most anything your heart desires
Freedom comes with understanding Who You Are
It's time to reclaim your place among the stars
Spread your wings and fly!'

For the last ten years I have been 'cocooned' away from the outside world (as best as I could be with three children!); no tell-lie-vision, no radio, no 9-5 job, while I went through the process of 'transforming' my mind. It felt slow, but when I really thought about it, I was undoing thirty plus years of negative programming and indoctrination!

Through this story, I will share everything I've learnt since asking God for 'the Truth' in 2007.

It is aimed at Truth-seekers; those who like me have been taught one thing, but deep down *know* that there's 'more to life' than what we've been led to believe. Throughout this book all I'm doing is planting Seeds of Love that *should* make you want to go and do the research to find out 'the Truth' for your Self.

If you don't have this book's accompanying CD **'Seeds of Love'**, you can listen to/download all the poems featured in the story at **www.reverbnation.com/cezannepoetess**.

Join Suzanne on her 11-year transformational quest for 'the Truth' about sex before marriage, the creative power of her thoughts, Universal Laws, her African ancestry, and the his-story of the religion she had been indoctrinated into.

'You will know the Truth, and the Truth will set you FREE!'

Start the journey...

'Sesa Wo Suban'
The West-African Adinkra Symbol for 'Transformation'

Year One: The 'Truth'?

"What is the real meaning of life?" I ask my Self as I lay here, eyes closed, in deep contemplation.

"Why am I here?"

I am a deep thinker. I'm always trying to get to the bottom of things, instead of looking at them from a surface level.

Born in the UK of Jamaican parentage, I was raised in the Christian faith. My deepest desire has always been to develop a relationship with my Creator, and to discover my 'destiny'. So I continue to attend a non-denominational church as an adult, and have been led to believe that going to church, reading my bible, praying, denying myself of life's pleasures and accepting Jesus Christ as my Lord and Saviour is the only way to God.

So I have diligently followed the teachings set out in the bible and church, to the best of my abilities.

The problem is, I could be described as a 'non-conformist free spirit', which makes it somewhat difficult for me to always abide by their rules and regulations. My biggest weakness is 'Sexual Sin'. Although I sincerely desire to serve God 'in spirit and in truth', my *natural* desires to be with a man do, every now and again, get in the way of my spiritual progress.

"But everybody has a weakness, don't they? With some people it's over-eating, with others, it's addiction to alcohol, or smoking, some people even have a habit of telling lies, or *gossiping* – what's the difference? They're all sins according to the bible, and no sin is greater than the other" I often reason with my Self.

Still, the bible makes it very clear that sex before marriage is wrong, and so it's almost a taboo subject in my church. Everybody appears to be so spiritual.

I remember the time when I discovered I was pregnant with my first son nine years ago; I had been in turmoil. What should I do? What would people in the church *think* of me? Now *everyone* would know I'd had sex! Distraught, I had confided in a church sister who advised me to terminate the pregnancy; "Loads of girls do it" the 'friend' had said. But that seemed even worse than having the baby! According to the bible, (all) 'children are a heritage from the Lord'.

And what if I ended up being one of the women who never *got* married, since there weren't enough men to go around? God knows, I'd seen enough women in the church shrivel up like a prune 'waiting on the Lord' to provide them with a husband before they had children. Many reached menopause with still no sign of a husband *or* baby – I didn't want to be one of *them*!

The ones who *weren't* 'waiting' were secretly having their needs met. I fell into the second category, and had paid the price dearly. I'd gone from being a career woman to a 'single mother on a low income'.

My change in status left me feeling like a second-class citizen in God's kingdom. It seemed to me that church folk look down on me for having had my two children 'out of wedlock'. Not that my Self-esteem had been too great to start with; in my *heart* I had wanted to marry a God-fearing man like my Self, but in the back of my mind, I didn't really believe I deserved it. The demons in my head were always telling me I wasn't good enough, pretty enough, successful enough, or worthy of such a nice man. So instead, I had settled for what I subconsciously believed I deserved.

My two sons, Micah and Elijah, are now aged six and eight. My relationship with their father broke down when they were only three and five; it took me over two years to heal emotionally from the break-up. We'd never really been in a proper couple to be honest, not in the sense that I would have liked. When I told him I was pregnant with our first son, he'd done a disappearing act for months, only re-emerging when I was due to have the baby. Suddenly, he wanted to play the proud father, but after a few short months the novelty of the new baby soon wore off, and he was off again. I hadn't relied on him for anything, buying everything I needed for the baby myself. Then just as I was getting my life back on track he'd come back, wanting to start over. Before I knew it, I was pregnant again. This time, he tried to stay, but it wasn't long before he started playing away. Having two young boys to look after *had* ruined our sex-life somewhat, but the message he'd sent out to me was that our relationship was only built on sex. That was my punishment for getting involved with a non-believer, no doubt.

Now aged almost 28, all I have to show for my life are two children and a few poems. I don't own my own home, I don't have a job – well, I believe it's more important to be committed to my two sons than to any employer – I have no car, no savings, and no man.

What I *do* have though, is a dream.

****

"What if…"

It was a warm spring evening in 2001, and the boys were away for the weekend with their father. Suzanne was feeling more sensual than usual. As she lay on the sofa contemplating life, she slid her hand up her skirt, down into her panties, and began massaging her clitoris slowly. With her eyes still closed, she wondered why God had put it there in the first place; "Is it there for me to gratify *myself*, or for my 'husband' to satisfy me?"

According to her church, it was even a sin to masturbate, since the mind is likely to start creating images of a sexual nature. If you so much as *think* about having sex, it's just as 'bad' as *doing* the act. "But how many men actually know how to stimulate a woman's clitoris enough to bring her to orgasm?" with all these thoughts going through her mind, she continued to pleasure herself. She couldn't help *re-creating* the image of her 'phantom lover' who visited her whenever she needed a release. She could almost *feel* him as he rode her silently back and forth; she increased the pressure and speed of her finger as she simulated sex in the sofa. With every withdrawal, she let out a sigh, and with every penetration, a deep moan. Before long, they both came to climax, and he had slipped away before she even opened her eyes.

Suzanne felt like she was *always* sinning, and this just left her in a perpetual state of 'unworthiness'. She just couldn't seem to stay on the narrow path! Her *spirit* was willing, but her *flesh* was weak.

Suzanne couldn't understand *why* God would give her sexual desires, and then demand that she ignore them until she got married. "What if I end up being one of the women in the church who never *get* married, since there aren't enough men to go around?"

The thought of never having sex again didn't appeal to Suzanne! She wondered why God hadn't just programmed her to only desire a man *after* she got married. But whenever she asked God directly about this, He always remained silent.

So despite her weaknesses, she continued going to church every Sunday, paying her tithes, reading her bible, praying and developing a relationship with her Creator, to the point where she couldn't wait to rise early in the morning to spend time in God's presence before the boys got up.

In fact, it was only through having children of her own that Suzanne really began to understand God's Unconditional Love for her. There seemed to be nothing she could do to make God stop loving her. No matter what she did, God always did something to let her know He still loved her, much like a spiritual Father. As such, He would give her instructions on how to live her life, but if she chose to 'do her own thing' and 'fell', He would only pick her up, dust her off, and stand her back on her feet again. And that's how she developed her relationship with God; His strength really *was* made perfect through her weakness.

But the more Suzanne studied the bible, the more questions arose for her, and lately she had found her Self questioning everything she'd been taught to believe:

"There are *so many* different religions, and they all think *they*'re the right one! What if Christianity *isn't* the only right religion? Would God really be so narrow-minded as to only create *one* possible path to Him? How could all the different types of people God has created possibly fit into *one box*? And will all those people who live good, clean righteous lives, but who are not *Christians* still get thrown into the lake of fire along with the devil, just because they hadn't accepted Jesus Christ as their Lord and Saviour? And what about all the billions of people who lived *before* Jesus came 2,000 years ago?" The thought of all those people perishing based on one scripture; *'no man can come to the Father but through me'* didn't even *sound* like the God she knew loved her.

Suzanne also questioned the 'no sex before marriage' rule: "Who created the 'institution' of marriage anyway, God or man?" she challenged.

In her mind, 'the wedding' was a man-made concept: walking down the aisle in a white dress with 'a veil over your eyes', exchanging rings, signing a register (or *contract* as she preferred to think of it), the wedding reception and honeymoon were all creations of man, not 'of God'. So is it possible for God to be in the centre of a union if the couple *aren't* married, and does a marriage certificate *guarantee* that God had blessed the union? Suzanne wondered how many couples in church were currently going through 'hell' in their marriage.

She came to the conclusion that since 'the wedding' is a man-made concept, she wanted to find out what is *God's* idea of marriage.

Another thing Suzanne wanted to know was *why* she wasn't supposed to study Astrology as a Christian, when she felt so drawn to the stars and the universe. She somehow believed that learning more about her Star Sign might help her navigate her way through life. Even the three *wise* men followed a star! But her church was strictly against anything to do with Astrology, calling it 'witchcraft'. She had once asked a pastor why there were so many planets out there, and *what if* we aren't the only species that God created; he could only reply "Maybe they're just there for us to look at". To her, this answer was totally inadequate.

Suzanne had reached a point in her spiritual journey where she could no longer continue walking in 'blind faith', believing everything she had been taught without *proof*. Was she supposed to ignore science, historical evidence and hard facts, and just accept everything written in the bible without questioning anything? But *Faith* and *Intellect* do not mix. She had been taught not to question the 'infallible Word of God'. Yet why would God bless her with intelligence and then tell her to ignore it – only where His Word is concerned?

Is that what faith really is – *ignorance*?

Potential

Despite becoming another statistic, deep down Suzanne knew she was more than that; that she had real potential.
When her boys had reached the ages of two and four, she had started attending college part-time. She knew she couldn't go back to working full-time, and that she had to do something that would fit around them, so she had decided to look into starting her own business. But doing what? The only thing she was really good at was writing poetry, but friends and family were always telling her "writing poetry won't pay the bills" and that she should just treat it as a hobby. But somewhere deep inside, Suzanne believed she *could* make a living doing what she loved – *how* she was going to achieve this goal though, she didn't know.

She felt like a caterpillar, crawling through life, but even caterpillars still have the *heart* of a butterfly, and still aspire to fly.

...But they were right – writing poetry *wasn't* paying the bills. So eventually Suzanne took a Part-time job doing Administration, only to find out that she had joined the rat race of just working to pay the bills. She still couldn't afford to buy a car, take the boys on holiday, or even save.

But she continued to write whenever she felt inspired, and was compiling her first collection.

****

The Rebellion

After a day at work and picking up the boys from school, Suzanne returned home and instructed the boys to change out of their uniform while she started the dinner. She took the chicken she had seasoned the night before out of the fridge, stuck it in the oven, and put the rice on to cook slowly. Returning to the living room, she sat on the sofa and switched on the telly. As usual, all the news reported were the bad things going on in the world. As she watched images of starving children in Africa, listened to the latest report of another 'black on black' murder, and heard about the state of the country's economy, fear and anxiety began to set in.

Feelings of hopelessness overwhelmed her as she wondered if the point of her life was to just live a meaningless existence, get saved, and spend the rest of her life waiting to go to heaven?

"There's got to be more to life than this!" was the mantra that seemed to play over and over again in her head.

Was there 'more to life'?

On a conscious level, Suzanne believed that as a 'child of the King' she was entitled to the best of everything. She wasn't meant to live a sub-standard life; *'The earth is the Lord's and the fullness thereof'*, the bible said. So if the earth is abundant (which it is) what was stopping her from claiming her piece of the pie?
The *devil*. That's what the bible told her. The 'devil came to kill, steal and destroy' anything good that was due to her. The only way to stop him from stealing her good was to fight him every day. *'Put on the whole armour of God, so that you can withstand the fiery darts of the devil'*, that's what she'd been taught to do. But she was tired of fighting. She was tired of always having to worry about what the devil was going to do to her next. Why wasn't God, her 'spiritual Father' protecting her from the devil anyway? And with all the studying of the bible she was doing, going to church every week, paying her tithes, praying in Jesus' name and even fasting sometimes, she still didn't seem to be any better off than a non-Christian! The only people *she* knew living the 'abundant life' promised in the bible were pastors of the big churches.

"All I want is RESULTS!" she would often say out loud. What was the point in being a Christian and dedicating her life to God if she wasn't going to live a better life *here on earth* than a non-Christian? Why did she have to wait until she got to heaven?

So that evening, feeling depressed, Suzanne decided to confront God directly with all the questions that the church couldn't, or wouldn't answer. If it wasn't for the devil she wouldn't be going through all these challenges in life. So sitting up in bed with a heavy heart, she reached for her trusted notepad and pen on her bedside table and wrote what some might call 'an angry letter to God'. She started off by informing God that she was going to be open and honest with Him, since He could see what was in her heart and thoughts anyway. She was going to 'tell it as it is' from her point of view, regardless of the consequences. Besides, she was sure many more of her church brothers and sisters wanted to ask these same questions, but were too scared for fear of His wrath, so she decided to stand in proxy for them.

She started off by asking God why He had allowed the devil to run wild on the earth that *He* had created, and to corrupt His creation, making *her* life a misery. She questioned whether God really *could* kill Satan because if He could, surely He would have done it by now? *"...after all, You were quick to punish man when WE rebelled!"* she reminded Him – she even accused God of showing favoritism!

She then proceeded to analyze 'The Fall of Lucifer' story, aiming to get to the *root cause* of all the world's problems: she relayed the story back to God as *she* understood it; that Lucifer – God's 'Lead Worshipper', the most beautiful angel of them all – got a bit egotistical and decided that *he* was worthy of some of this praise too; *"He obviously didn't understand why You Alone should be worshipped, and why everyone else has to bow to You! This is where all the trouble started..."* She continued sarcastically re-telling the story of how Lucifer managed to get a third of the angels to join him in rebelling against God, resulting in God booting them out of heaven. She questioned God why He hadn't banished them to one of the far distant planets in the galaxy and put some kind of force-field around it so that they couldn't reach His creation on Earth. Instead, He had allowed them to corrupt His creation, as if He had no control over what Lucifer and his posse did!

She then proceeded to scrutinize 'The Fall of Adam and Eve' story, again trying to get to the *root cause* of all of the world's (and her) problems. She reminded God that after making Adam and Eve in His *very own image* and creating a beautiful garden for them to inhabit, He gave them free access to all the fruit of the garden – except from the tree right in the *middle* of the garden; the 'Tree of the Knowledge of Good and Evil'. She pointed out that Satan *also* had free access to the Garden of Eden, and was allowed to go in and out as he pleased, tempting Adam and Eve over and over again until eventually they gave in – inevitably! Instead of God taking responsibility and admitting that it was *His* mistake for giving Satan access to the garden in the first place, God cursed His creation, evicted them from their home, and sent them out into the Big Wide World only to be tempted and corrupted by the devil even more! He THEN placed the Guardian Angel at the entrance of the garden to stop Adam and Eve from going back in to eat of the *Tree of Life* (which by the way, was situated *right beside* the Tree of the Knowledge of Good and Evil).

None of this made any sense to Suzanne. Was the Tree of Life more important to God than the human race? She then questioned God *why* He had placed the Tree of the Knowledge of Good and Evil right in the *centre* of the garden, if Adam and Eve weren't supposed to eat of it – had He deliberately set them up to fail? Suzanne believed that even if Satan *hadn't* come along, *curiosity* would have got the better of them sooner or later anyway; *"...As a mother, I know that if I placed a handful of sweets in the middle of a table, in the middle of the sitting room and then told my children "Don't eat those sweets!" and just left them there for weeks and weeks, I guarantee You that it would only be a matter of time before those sweets started disappearing down their throats!"* Suzanne knew *her* children would eventually take the risk of whatever punishment they would have to suffer later, just for that moment of pleasure. She continued; *"...Now what if I then said to my children; "Right, because you ate those sweets, I'm not going to give you any dinner for a week!" Wouldn't You think I was being a bit – harsh?"*

Suzanne's argument was that instead of making Adam and Eve feel as if it was *their* fault that Satan came to tempt them, God should have *apologized* to them for putting them in such jeopardy in the first place! But instead, He cursed the whole of the human race, and now generations later, we are *still* suffering because 'Adam and Eve ate of the forbidden fruit'.

The intensity of her Scorpio energy flowed onto the pages; she could feel the frustration building up inside of her as she wrote furiously, continuing her critical examination of what she had learnt from years of studying the bible. By now, she was past caring what the consequences of her outburst would be. All she wanted was answers to her questions – and she didn't stop there! She went on to point out to God that when He sent his *only son* Jesus Christ to redeem the world of our sins, his message was only to the Jews – anyone else was considered a Gentile, or worst still, a 'dog'! And maybe *that's* why she was having so much trouble 'entering the kingdom'; maybe she simply wasn't 'worthy'…well at least that's what she'd been led to believe.

She then pointed out to God that the world has been in a state of anarchy literally since the beginning of time; *"The bible has barely begun, when already there's disobedience, damnation, murder, incest, war, famine and woe! But who's really to blame here; man, the devil, or dare I say it – YOU?"*

At this point she cringed as if waiting to be struck by a bolt of lightning…when it didn't happen, she carried on more boldly. She asked God *why* He had instructed in His Word that she should not react to people who acted wickedly towards her, but to see 'past' the flesh, and deal with it in the spiritual realm, since they were just 'pawns in the devil's game'. She told God she had a problem with that, because from what she had read, God had consistently throughout the bible reacted to flesh and blood people, destroying them when He could no longer stand their wicked ways! She reminded Him of Sodom and Gomorrah and The Flood, two occasions where God, in His anger, had wiped out whole populations:

"…But You didn't kill SATAN, the ORIGINATOR of the corruption, so when the earth became re-populated, the whole cycle just started all over again!"

Pausing to think about this, she wrote;

"In fact, I'm not sure I even believe this story, as I don't think You would be so naïve as to believe that by wiping out the whole of humankind without destroying the ROOT CAUSE, you would ERADICATE the problem? You are far too wise a God to not see that…"

For a moment she seemed to come back to her senses as she stared up at the blue-red sky, watching the sun set through her window. But returning to her notepad, the doubts instantly resurfaced, and she continued to question *why* God had allowed Himself to be portrayed as a Jekyll and Hyde character (loving us one minute, then cursing us the next) and then challenged God as to whether He had looked at His *own* faults!

"...How many mistakes have You made in YOUR lifetime? I'd say that putting Your adversary right on the same planet as Your new creation has to be the BIGGEST MISTAKE OF ALL TIME! What did You expect Satan to do? Leave us alone, knowing we were made in the image of the person he hated the most – YOU?"

She may have been 'having a go at God', but her intention was to simply 'keep it real' with her Creator. She wanted to understand God's thinking *behind* His decisions, so she implored *"...I know Your Ways are not my ways but please, help me to understand..."*

After reminding God that the battle was in fact between *Him* and the *devil* and didn't really have anything to do with *US*, His creation, she pointed out to Him that the war was getting *worse* and *worse*; *"This isn't the world that You created for me to live in, I was meant to live in peace, and harmony, and joy and happiness with You and my fellowmen...the fact that there's some devil making my life a living hell isn't MY fault, I didn't create him, YOU did! So why don't You take responsibility, and protect me when You see him coming for me, like the Loving Father you're meant to be?"*

Stopping for a moment to reflect on what she had just written, a shiver ran up her spine at the thought of the scenario she had just created. If she had allowed *her* children to be abused by some crazy tyrant, wouldn't she be held accountable? So why not God, the Ultimate Heavenly Father? How could she trust a character like that with her life?

Returning back to her notepad, she continued to write; *"according to the bible 'the battle is already won' but it doesn't seem like it to me, I'm still living in defeat; I still worry about how*

I'm going to pay my bills, feed the kids this week, get to church on Sunday, pay my tithes... I've sowed, believing, and I'm STILL waiting for my harvest – Oh, I forgot to water and nourish my seed!

Well I was never good with plants anyway.

That's the other thing; we're expected to 'wait on You' and we have no way of knowing when You're going to come up with the goods! So many times I've 'waited on You', believing and praying for my miracle, and when it doesn't happen, we're expected to resort to the conclusion that it was just 'not God's timing'. You seem to play with us like we're a chess game, only moving when it suits YOU!"

She again implored God; *"I want to know and understand You more; I want to understand Your ways".*

She recalled the times when she had walked closely with God, thinking they had been the most beautiful; *"...I mean, there's nothing like waking up in the morning and feeling Your presence all around me, or being inspired to write a piece of poetry... But I want more: I want a big house! I want nice clothes! I want to be able to go on holiday yearly with my family, buy myself a decent car, have plastic surgery to correct all those things You got wrong with me..."*

She acknowledged that it was probably due to her own rebellious attitude and lack of the 'Fear of the Lord' why she was *not* walking in His blessings, but wanted to know *why* she was expected to do God's will without questioning His Word; *"...What good is a 'free will' when You demand that I do things YOUR way? What kind of a free will is that, anyway?"*

She demanded the answers to her questions through her sheer *will power*.

In all honesty, Suzanne loved the Lord and really wanted to serve Him 'in spirit and in truth', but the truth was, she was finding it hard to put her trust in Him totally and follow His ways: *"...I know*

*Your Word; I've read it, spoken it, confessed it, meditated upon it, memorized it, and I still have **so many needs**!*

Is it because I didn't BELIEVE enough, or perhaps I didn't PRAY enough, or maybe I just didn't have enough FAITH?

...All I want is to live the life of my dreams, is that asking too much?

Why can't I just live in heaven – on EARTH?"

Suzanne yearned to be At One with her Creator; she had experienced His pure, unconditional Love, and was finding it difficult to equate the character in the bible with the God she had built a relationship with.

When she really thought about it, Suzanne realized that even though Satan had taken a third of the angels with him, there was still two thirds left in heaven with God. She told God she believed He was mightier than the devil, and that since He also had twice as many angels, where was the battle, really? So writing her last lines she ended; *"...You know, the more I think about all of this, the more I realize that these stories just don't sound true, nor do they reflect the character of You,*

So now what I really want is...the TRUTH!"

Feeling pleased with her Self, she entitled her letter to God 'The Rebellion'. Writing it had felt cathartic. She had put it 'out there', and now she would wait for God's response.

****

God's Reply

The following morning as soon as Suzanne woke up, she felt inspired to write. So picking up her notepad and pen still lying on the bed beside her, she turned over to a fresh page and wrote:

Think on My Love,
Think on My goodness,
Think on My grace,
And all the things I've done for you.

When you think on these things,
Your problems will become small
Your mountains will become molehills
And everything you aspire to WILL become reachable.

Don't look at your situation,
Look to Me.
You can do all things, through Me.
I Am the Way that makes crooked paths straight
I Am the Key that unlocks the doors
I AM the Great I AM.

Do not fear when trials come your way
Do not bend when temptation is at your door
Always remember that in trials there are testimonies
And no <u>test</u>imony without a TEST.
So don't be discouraged,
Don't feel downhearted,
Be of good cheer
And always remember that in Me
There is victory.   (Track 1 on the CD 'Seeds of Love')

God responded to her promptly, and in a language that she could relate to – poetry! As she was writing, she could feel God's presence surrounding her, as if comforting her. Tears rolled down her cheeks as she wrote a letter of apology back, for allowing her Self to lose focus.

****

Synchronicity

Later that morning as Suzanne was washing the dishes, she had an inspired idea to design some backdrops for her poems. She had done a photography course at college some years ago and was proficient in Photoshop, so she had a go at creating layers of photographs, and adding her text on top. She was pleasantly surprised at the results. "I can sell these!" she thought.

Quite by chance (or should we call it 'synchronicity?') she was at a community event the following day where she met a local councillor. She told him about her new poster designs, and he informed her about an International Caribbean Trade Expo happening the following weekend. He gave her a number to call to book a stand, and said to mention his name.

When she called, she was offered a stand for only £50 for the 3 days. She didn't have a spare £50, so she asked her sister Janice if she wanted to share the stand. Her sister was also entrepreneurial; she would travel to places like Egypt, the West Indies and Ghana, and bring back items of black interest to sell.

Suzanne borrowed the money from her mother to print the posters.

****

The Caribbean Expo

The Expo was a much bigger occasion than Suzanne had imagined; over the three day period thousands of people flocked to the venue in the Docklands. She made over three times as much money as she had invested in the stand and printing her posters. But it was the third day that was to change Suzanne's life forever...

She spotted him in the distance; he stood out like a neon light, seemingly head and shoulders above everyone else. As he approached her stand, Suzanne began to get a strange feeling in her stomach, like butterflies. Did she know this guy?

When he reached about two feet away, she could see that she didn't know him, and at over six feet tall he really *was* head and shoulders above everyone else! Then she realised that he wasn't even heading towards *her* stand, but the stand opposite! She *had* to get his attention; "EXCUSE ME!" she called out to him on impulse. He turned and began walking towards her. She suddenly started to feel nervous; she wasn't in the habit of pursuing men, plus, she was meant to be working!

As their eyes met, she flashed him a huge, inviting smile. He accepted the invitation.

She knew he thought she was attractive, and she thought he was attractive too.

"Hi! I wondered whether you'd be interested in my posters" she said cheerfully, flicking her hair as he reached her stand.

"Hmmm....they're nice, did *you* design them?" He asked, looking at them.

"Yes, I wrote the poetry too"
He stood silently, reading one.

"I can tell, you're deep" he commented when he had finished. Suzanne laughed. "Would you like one?"

"How much are they?" he enquired.

"Well you can buy one for £4.50, two for £8.00 or three for £10"

He chose three different designs, saying "My mum will appreciate these" and paid her the £10.

"What made you come here today?" Suzanne asked, trying to prolong his stay as she rolled the posters up slowly, putting an elastic band around them. Neat, heavy eyebrows adorned his sparkling dark brown eyes. He was dressed casually but neatly in a pair of jeans, shirt and shoes. As she handed him the posters he smiled with full, luscious lips revealing perfect teeth. But it wasn't his *looks* that had attracted her to him in the first instance. In fact, she couldn't quite place her finger on *what* it was.

"My friend invited me" he replied, pointing to another brother at the stand opposite.

"Oh, sorry, I didn't realise you were with someone!"

"It's alright. So how long have you been doing this?" he asked, indicating towards the posters with his tube.

"I've just started actually – I only had them printed this week!" she replied, smiling proudly.

"What were you doing before?" he asked.

"I used to work in admin, but I left my job two weeks ago so I could focus on starting my business"

"Wow, sounds pretty much like me..."

He proceeded to tell her how he had just left the job he'd been doing for over 7 years, as well as ending his long term relationship. It sounded as if they were both at a turning point in their lives. In a weird kind of way, during the time they were talking, it was as if time stood still; everything around them became like a blurred whirlwind, as if they were in some kind of time warp. Suzanne forgot she was meant to be selling; in that moment, nothing else existed in the world but the two of them. In the two minutes or so that they conversed, they both shared personal information about themselves, as if they had known each other forever.

"I have to go – do you have a card?" he asked.

Suzanne picked up one of her home-made business cards and handed it to him. He read it and smiled at her slogan; *'Touching the Heart...through Art'*.

"I'll call you" he said, looking at her with promise in his eyes.

"I'll look forward to it" she smiled encouragingly.

"My name's Charles, by the way" he added, extending his hand. His smile was as warm as a summer's day, making her feel all hot and sweaty. As their hands made contact, what felt like an electrical surge passed from his hand through Suzanne's whole body; she wondered if he had felt it too. They shook hands quite formally, but there was a lingering in the time they should have released contact.

"Suzanne"

As Charles walked away, Janice asked "Who was *THAT*?"

****

He Calls

Two days later, true to his word, Charles called. A number came up that wasn't stored in Suzanne's phone, and she knew instinctively that it was him. She hadn't mentioned her boys to him yet, and they were busy playing in the living room making quite a lot of noise.

"BE QUIET!" she called out to them as she picked up her mobile phone.

"Hello, Suzanne speaking" she answered, trying her best to sound business-like.

"Hi Suzanne, it's Charles; remember we met at the Expo on Sunday?"

"Oh, hi Charles, of course I remember, nice to hear from you!" Charles sensed the genuine appreciation in her voice and responded to it.

"How are you? I couldn't wait to call, but I thought I should give you a couple of days to rest after your busy weekend. How did it go?" He asked.

"It was great! The sales went really well, and I made so many great contacts – including you!" She answered excitedly.

"How many other 'contacts' did you make?" Charles asked, as if defending his territory.

Suzanne laughed. "Not like that, I mean *business* contacts!"

"Oh, well that's alright then – so I don't have any competition?" Charles asked again.

Suzanne could see where this was heading, so asked "Could you do me a favour and call me back a bit later please? I'm just with my boys at the moment, they go to bed at 8.30pm; if you call back after then, we'll be able to talk properly. Is that ok?"

"Oh! I didn't know you had children – how old are they?" he asked in a surprised tone. Judging by her slender figure, he'd figured she was still childless.

"Six and eight" she responded, almost defensively.

"Oh ok, I'll call back after eight-thirty then"

As Suzanne put down her mobile, she wondered whether he *would* call back. He obviously hadn't banked on her having children.

After dinner, spending 'Quality Time' with the boys and tucking them into bed, she sat down to relax. It was 9pm. Just as she was about to think "I knew he wouldn't call" her mobile started ringing. It was him!

"Hi Charles!" She answered "Thanks for calling back – and sorry about earlier"

"Nothing to be sorry about, I understand. Are you ok to talk now?"

"Oh, yes! What would you like to talk about?"

"Well I'm not one to beat around the bush – are you single?"

She could hardly believe he was still interested even though she had two boys!

"Yes I am *single* but I'm not *available*, if that's what you mean" she said though.

"Why not?" he asked inquisitively.

"Well, I'm just starting my business, and I have to focus on getting it off the ground"

"That's all well and good, but couldn't you do with some help?" he asked again.

Suzanne thought before replying "Maybe, but I just feel this is something I have to do on my own"

Out loud he said "Fair comment" but in his head, he was thinking "Another independent Black woman!"

He changed the topic by asking "So what do you do for fun?"

"Oh, I write! I *love* writing poetry, and occasionally, I go out and perform it as well"

"Hmmm....sounds interesting, maybe I'll join you next time you go"

Suzanne panicked at the thought – she wasn't *that* good! She was still building her confidence performing in front of a crowd.

"Ok...that would be nice" she lied. "What about you? What do *you* like to do?" she changed the subject.

Charles told her that he was an accountant by profession, but he also liked to study Numerology in his spare time. There was a lot more to numbers than meets the eye, he told her. Suzanne told him about *her* fascination with Astrology, and the way people's date of birth seemed to affect their personality. They already had something in common.

"Do you have any children?" she asked him.

"No, not yet"

She thought that was unusual for a Black man.

"How old are you?" she asked.

"36, why, how old are you?"

"Nearly 28...what Star Sign are you?" she asked.

"Pisces, why?"

"Oh, that's perfect!" she said delightfully.

According to Astrology, Pisces was supposed to be one of her two best matches.

"What Star Sign are *you*?" He asked.

"I'm a Scorpio!"

"Oh, ok."

His first girlfriend had been a Scorpio and she'd cheated on him, leaving him heartbroken. It had taken him years to get over her. 'But then, I shouldn't paint all Scorpios with the same brush, should I?' he considered again.

They spent over two hours getting to know each other over the phone that evening. Amongst other things, Suzanne told him she was a church-going Christian, and how much she loved God. Charles told her he loved God, but didn't go to church. He told her he was in the habit of going to the gym most mornings, and she told him she liked going to the sauna and steam. He asked about the boys, and she told him all about them.

Before ending the conversation Charles said, "It's been really nice talking to you Suzanne; I'd like to carry on this conversation over dinner, if that's alright with you; what are you doing on Saturday?" It was Suzanne's weekend to have the boys.

"I'm busy with the boys this weekend, but I'm free *next* Saturday" she replied.

"Ok, it's a date!" Charles responded confidently. "But don't think I won't be calling you every day up until then" he added. Suzanne laughed.

"Yes, it's been lovely talking with you too; I'll look forward to it!"

"Goodnight then"

"Goodnight Charles"

****

Self-Esteem Demon

Over the next two weeks, Suzanne and Charles spent every evening talking on the phone. They learnt so much about each other; their likes and dislikes, their hopes and dreams, their past and future plans. Despite not having any children of his own, Charles always asked about her boys, which she appreciated. They discussed any issues the boys were facing at school, and he always gave whatever advice he could.

Charles was a newly-made bachelor, owned his own home, had a good job, had no children, and to put the icing on the cake, he was tall, dark and handsome. Did I mention that he was *Black*?

But Suzanne wondered what he saw in *her*? She was a single mother, on a low income, had no car, lived in a rented property – she was hardly in his calibre, she thought.
During one of their conversations, Suzanne's low Self-esteem demon reared its ugly head;
"What do you see in *me*?" she asked him.
"What do you mean, what do I see in you?"
"Well, I'm hardly in your calibre, am I?"
"I'm...not sure what you mean"
"Well look at you, you own your own home, you have a nice car, you've got a good job, you have no children..."
"Suzanne, do you really think having a house, car and job make me happy? Those are just *things*, Suzanne. *Things* don't make you happy; having someone to *share* those things with does, though"
"I see what you mean, but I wouldn't feel right joining my Self to someone else until I've achieved something for my Self, especially someone like you"
"Why not?"
"I wouldn't feel good enough"
"Well how will you know when you're good enough for say, someone like me?"
"When I've achieved something"
"Like what; what is your goal?"
"Well...I'd like to run a successful business doing what I love"
"Which is?"

"Writing and performing poetry"

"So what steps are you taking towards your goal?" Charles asked.

"Well, I'm already working on my first poetry collection, and I also plan to record a poetry CD to go with the book"

"Good!" Charles commended her. "So how will you know when you've reached your goal?" he asked.

Suzanne closed her eyes and visualised herself holding her first collection of poems with its complimentary CD. She was on a stage winning some kind of award. She didn't tell him that though

"I'll be financially free" she said.

"Ok...what does 'financial freedom' mean to you; what will it allow you to *do*?" Charles probed.

"I'll be able to buy my own home, take my boys on holiday during school breaks, buy a decent car, buy the clothes I like..."

"Ok, so we're back to the *things* again. Never mind...so do you know anyone who's already achieved your goal?"

"I do actually! I have a friend who's *just* released her second poetry CD and book of lyrics"

"What resources do they have that you can use?"

Up to that point, Suzanne hadn't even *thought* about asking that friend if she could use their recording equipment to record *her* CD! She thanked Charles for helping her 'see the light'.

"So are you ready for me now?" he asked.

"What do you mean?" She asked, puzzled.

"Well, you just made the changes internally to attract the things you desire, so it's only a matter of time before they show up. Are you ready for *me* now?"

"You deserve the best that life has to offer, Charles."

"Don't you believe you *are* the best that life has to offer Suzanne? Don't put your Self down"

Suzanne found it hard to believe that she was the best, even though she *wanted* the best. She seemed to be in conflict with her Self.

Again, her low Self-esteem issues were creeping in, trying to sabotage her.

Charles concluded the conversation; "You ask me what I see in you, so let me tell you; I see a girl with great ideas who lacks the knowledge to take things further at this time. Still, you have the courage, strength and determination to pursue your dreams and care for your boys with limited resources. That's what I see"

The other things didn't matter to him: What mattered was the way he was beginning to feel about her.

****

First Date

The day of their date finally arrived. Charles had said he would pick her up at 6.30pm, and sure enough, his black BMW pulled up outside at almost six thirty on the dot. Suzanne looked excitedly in the mirror one last time to make sure her wig was in exactly the right place and that her make-up was perfect. It was a warm summer evening, so she was wearing a sleeveless red dress that hugged her slim figure, reaching just below her knees. High-heeled red sandals, red lipstick and nail varnish finished off the look, coupled with fake diamond earrings, and she carried a light cardigan in case it got cold later. Her clothes weren't expensive, but she looked and felt a million dollars.

As she stepped outside and pulled her front door shut, Charles was already standing by her side of the car with the door open. She kissed him lightly on the cheek before getting into the car. After making sure her clothing wouldn't get caught, he shut the door gently.

"A real gentleman" she thought.

All the way to the restaurant, they laughed and joked and listened to music. It was as if they had known each other for ages. When they discovered they had the same taste in music, they agreed to do a compilation CD for each other.

Charles pulled up outside a Thai restaurant in Muswell Hill. He had already booked a table, so they didn't have to wait to be seated. They followed the waitress to their table and sat down. Charles excused himself to use the men's. The restaurant was nice; not overly posh, but pleasant surroundings and a warm atmosphere with soft piano music playing in the background.

When Charles returned, the waitress brought the menu, and as Suzanne looked through, Charles made his recommendations.

"Would you like to try the mixed platter? I always have it when I come here, I like the variety"

"Ok, let's have that then!" Suzanne agreed. She liked a man who knew how to take control in a situation without dominating, if you know what I mean.

"What would you like to drink?"

"Water for now" she replied.

"Me too"

Charles called the waitress over and ordered the meal and a bottle of spring water.

As they began eating, it wasn't long before Suzanne had to ask the question;

"Why don't you go to church?"

"Well..." Charles thought carefully before responding;

"I think all religions were created to control the masses. If there were no religions, people would think and act for themselves, but the 'powers that be' can't have that. So they created *religion* and *politics*. If they don't get you with one, they'll get you with the other. I choose to take part in neither"

"That's an interesting concept" Suzanne reasoned, "But if there was no religion or politics, wouldn't this world be in a state of anarchy?"

"Not necessarily. I believe that if everyone learnt to live by Universal Laws, the world would live in peace and harmony"

"What are 'Universal Laws'?" she asked inquisitively. She'd never even heard of them before.

"Universal Laws are Laws of Nature which are indeed universal, that means they apply to *everybody* – not just Christians, or Jews, or any particular group of people. I believe that when God created the universe, certain Laws were put in place to keep everything in order. The universe isn't 'out there' somewhere; we are *in* the universe, and therefore subject to its Laws. Gravity is one of them. When you understand these Laws and live by them, you'll be able to live the life you were put here to live; an *abundant* life. If you look around at nature, abundance is everywhere. The only time you see lack, is where man has interfered with what nature does naturally."

"Hmmm...That's really interesting; can you name some of these Laws?" Suzanne's thirst for knowledge grew.

"'You Reap What You Sow' is one of them" he replied; "scientifically they would call it 'Cause and Effect'; for every *action* you take, there must be a re*action*. Every action you take must have an outcome, or produce a *harvest*. So if you sow good deeds (or seeds) you'll reap a good harvest. If you sow bad seeds, you'll reap the results of your actions."

Suzanne thought carefully about what he had just said before responding;

"Wow! No wonder Jesus said to 'love your neighbour as your Self'! If everybody treated others as they would like to be treated themselves, this world *would* be a better place! Now I can *see* how these Laws would work if everybody was to put them into practice!"

She could also now see why Charles always seemed to be calculating his movements.

"Where can I learn more about these Laws?" she asked him.

"Just go online and Google 'spiritual laws' or something" he responded "You'll be surprised at what comes up – but don't take everything you read as gospel, make sure you have at least two or three of the same answer before you take it as fact."

Again, this reminded her of a scripture in the bible, where it said something like 'in the mouth of two or three witnesses a matter would be established'. She felt as if God was speaking to her through Charles; his words nourished her soul.

"I can lend you some books as well", he added. "You're welcome to come over to my place sometime and pick a few if you like"

"I might just take you up on that!" she replied with a big smile.

Charles hadn't been brought up in church, but he had a strong sense of Self. He was half Barbadian and half Ghanaian. His father had been a strong influence on him, instilling good cultural morals and values into him as a child, and making sure he was connected to his African ancestry. His mother was Barbadian; she had brought him up to believe that he could achieve anything, as long as he worked hard and got a good education. Religion had not played a key role in their household.

Charles shared an African proverb with Suzanne that his father used to say:

> *"THEY had the bible and WE had the land,*
> *Now WE have the bible*
> *and THEY have the land!"*

He conveyed to Suzanne what his father had told him about the bible being used to gain control over the wealth of Africa, and to mentally enslave 'our people'. He told her about the slave trade, and how Africans had been sold into slavery to work on plantations in the West Indies for free, and how the economy of countries like England and the United States of America were built on the backs of slaves. He informed her that all West-Indians were in fact *displaced Africans*. They had been stripped of their African names and given their slave master's names (which they still have today), stripped of their language, their religious beliefs, their culture, their very *identity*. They weren't *people* to the white man, they were 'stock' to be bought and sold, and were treated worse than animals. At first she didn't believe him; she had seen the film '*Roots*' and knew about slavery but hadn't identified herself with any of those people as being her ancestors. Her parents had never mentioned anything to her about them coming from Africa either. They were proud 'West Indians'. When she explained this to Charles, he asked her where exactly is 'West India'?

They continued to discuss the concept of 'God', what it means to 'have faith', the bible, and why there were so many different religions. Suzanne had a tendency to be argumentative, especially since she had been indoctrinated by the church to think a certain way. But Charles had a way of diffusing her negative energy whenever it arose.

Even though they were talking about church and God, they were both aware of the underlying current. They were inches away from each other across the table and the heat they both seemed to be generating was beginning to set sparks flying.

Charles was very wise and knowledgeable, and had *standards*, Suzanne thought. He was a one-in-a-million kinda guy really; good-looking, well-mannered, well-spoken, loving, spiritual, respectful, intelligent, financially stable, and...Black! What more could she ask for?

"HE MUST BE BORN AGAIN!"

She could already hear the voice of her pastor booming from the pulpit.

If the man hadn't accepted Jesus Christ as Lord and Saviour of his life, she would be 'unequally yoked to an unbeliever'.

But Charles was *perfect*, she argued within herself; she was sure they had met by some kind of Divine Order – he was everything she had hoped and prayed for, God's best promise; Faith, Hope and Love all rolled into one.

There was only one problem...he wasn't a *Christian*. Did it matter? Her conscience wouldn't allow her to say 'no' – she was too indoctrinated.

'If we're going to carry on this relationship' she thought, 'he has to get *saved*, and we're going to have to get *married*.'

After their meal, Charles took her for a drive; they ended up on the Embankment, where they stood admiring the neon lights illuminating the buildings and shimmering on the water.

As they walked over the bridge, he put a protective arm around her shoulder and asked "Will you go out with me?"

"We *are* out!" Suzanne joked with him.

"You know what I mean"

"We'll see..." she replied. Suzanne would have loved to have said "Yes!" but she was still thinking about being 'unequally yoked to an unbeliever'.

The evening went even better than they had both anticipated; they had so much in common, and felt like they could talk to each other about anything. Because they had spent the past two weeks building up their relationship over the phone, they already felt like they knew each other intimately. They both had a good feeling about this.

It was getting late, and cold. Charles offered to drop her home, although neither of them wanted the evening to end. They had waited nearly two weeks to see each other again, and weren't in a hurry to leave each other's company.

Although Suzanne was a practising Christian, her weakness was strong black men. It had been over a year since she'd had sex, but she knew she didn't want to sleep with Charles, especially on the first date.

As they pulled up outside her house, she invited him in for a cup of tea. They spent the next few hours talking, drinking herbal tea, and listening to music in the living room.

As they sat on the sofa, Charles eventually had to say something about the gold symbol hanging around Suzanne's neck. "Why do you wear that cross?" he questioned her in a bemused tone, pointing at it with his eyes.

"What's wrong with it?" She asked, looking down at it and taking it protectively into her hand.

"Oh...let's just leave it for now; I'm not sure you'd be ready to hear what I have to say anyway..." He knew how much her beliefs were ingrained into her, and he didn't want to upset her, or what was turning out to be a perfectly good evening. But Suzanne's curiosity got the better of her.

"What do you mean?" she asked.

"Oh, nothing"

"Go on, tell me!" she insisted.

"Are you sure you want to hear this?" he asked again, just to be sure.

"Yes, go on!"

"Ok, then answer the question; why do you wear that cross?"

"To remind my Self of what Jesus did for me when he died and rose again"

"The cross is a symbol of death – why do you choose to focus on his death instead of his resurrection, which one is most important?"

Suzanne began to feel uncomfortable. No-one had ever questioned her faith like this, only her Self.

"The cross is a symbol of my salvation through Jesus Christ" she answered, faithfully.

"The cross is a symbol of death. The *Ankh* is a symbol of *life*" Charles replied as he pulled a silver symbol hanging on a chain from under his shirt. It looked very similar to the cross, except that it was joined in a loop at the top. Suzanne peered at it.

"Where did you get that from? Are you trying to make a mockery out of Christianity or something?" she asked, crossing her arms.

"The Ankh was created by our ancestors, long before Christianity even existed" Charles informed her calmly. He proceeded to tell her how the Ankh symbol was written indisputably in hieroglyphics by their ancestors all over Egypt as proof that it existed long before the cross.

"I won't to go into too much detail about it right now..." He could see this was enough for her to handle. "...but if you want to learn more, the truth is out there. It's not a secret. And if you're interested in learning about the history of Christianity, look into the story of Isis and Horus".

"Isis and who?"

"Horus. I'll email you some more information."

With that, he pulled her close to him in a warm embrace. He didn't want to fall out with her over religion. They continued to talk as they sat huddled on the sofa.

By 1.30am it became apparent than he didn't want to leave, and she didn't want him to go either. But she was determined not to sleep with him. Still, he managed to convince her that they could just lie on the bed together and cuddle; they didn't have to take their clothes off, they would just lie on the *top* of the bed – after all, they both had will-power, didn't they? So they moved to her bedroom. Lying on top of the bed, they talked and talked into the early hours of the morning, until finally falling asleep in each other's arms, fully clothed.

****

The Following Morning...

The following day was Sunday. No work for Charles, and the boys would be at their dad's until the evening, so Charles and Suzanne had the day to themselves. Suzanne had adopted the habit of getting up early from when the boys were babies, and it had stuck with her ever since. No matter what time she went to bed, she was normally up by 6am the latest. She liked to get up early to pray, read her bible, exercise and get washed and dressed before the boys got up at 7.30am. Sometimes she would just be inspired to write. Charles was an early riser too. He habitually went to the gym before going to work; he would get there by 7.00am, do an hour's workout, shower, and head straight to the office from there.

So even though it was Sunday and they'd had a late night, they were both awake by 7.00am. Suzanne woke up first, took off her clothes, and did some stretches in the bathroom before having her shower. While she was in the shower, Charles had woken up, stripped down to his boxer shorts, and gotten into the bed. When Suzanne came out of the bathroom wrapping her dressing gown around her, he was sitting up waiting for her.

The magnetic pull towards each other was irresistible.

As she walked towards him, she couldn't help eyeing up his natural muscle definition; his broad shoulders, well-defined pecs, and strong, muscular arms pulled at her heartstrings. He smiled at her boyishly.

"Good morning! Did you sleep ok?" she asked as she made her way over to the bed.

"Like a baby" he replied.

"Me too"

As soon as she sat on the bed, he pulled her towards him. Without resisting, she lay down beside him with her back to him. She could feel his hard-on through the sheets, but not wanting to get all turned on, she sat up. So he sat up too. She looked down at the covers; the size of his erection practically made the bed look like a tent.

"What's that?" She asked jokingly.

"A present for you" Charles joked back.

She couldn't resist touching it. As she caressed it through the sheets, she could feel it getting harder and harder. "There must be at least nine inches here" she thought, smiling to herself.

Charles closed his eyes, and resting his head back on the headboard he let out a soft groan. He too hadn't had sex for a while now. They were both aroused.

While Suzanne caressed his manhood, he slipped his hand inside her dressing gown and caressed her left breast. 'Mmmm...cherry nipples!' he thought.

Lifting the covers, he invited her to join him.

His dark chocolate skin against the white Egyptian cotton sheets and white boxers was enticing.

There was no doubt about it – she was in lust!

She stood up and let her dressing gown fall to the floor. Standing before him was a real life Nubian goddess – with a wig on. She could feel her nipples hardening under his gaze as he admired her slender figure and smooth, milk-chocolate skin. He swung his legs off the bed and placed one foot either side of her on the floor. With her breasts right in front of him, she offered a nipple to his hungry mouth. Taking both breasts in his hands, He sucked on the one he had met earlier, squeezing it as if trying to get milk. He then acquainted himself with her right breast.

When he'd had his fill, Suzanne knelt before him, pulled down his boxers and examined his throbbing penis. It was a piece of art; her fingers could hardly meet around its girth, and as it stood erect, all nine-and-a-half inches of it leaned to one side. A large vein ran down its underside, and he'd been circumcised, so his head stood out loud and proud. This was her smooth dark chocolate-coloured dream!

"Does it have a name?" she asked, knowing men liked to do this.

"Pride" Charles replied.

"Pride?" She thought this was a bit of an odd name for a dick, until Charles explained;

"You read the bible, don't you? Doesn't it say 'Pride *comes* before a fall'?"

It took a few seconds for Suzanne to get it, but when she did, she burst out laughing.

"No it doesn't, actually!" she replied, but still, she thought it was funny.

"It also *stands* for 'Black Pride'" Charles added, raising his hand in a fist.

"Hello Pride" Suzanne introduced herself, then looking up at Charles, slowly took Pride into her mouth. Charles let out a deep-throated groan. Suzanne lubricated his shaft with her tongue, as she slowly and rhythmically moved her head up and down over his organ, using her hand to massage the bottom end that wouldn't fit into her mouth.

"Oh...*damn!*" Charles gasped, as she continued to give Pride head, paying particular attention to his bare helmet. Charles grabbed Suzanne's head and pushed her unto him, but she moved her head away, giving him a look that let him know the only place out of bounds to him was her hair.

After Suzanne had finished introducing herself to Pride, Charles pulled her up by the hand and invited her to join him under the covers. Pressing against each other hungrily, they explored each other's bodies; kissing, touching, discovering, learning, bonding.

Straddling her on all fours like an animal that had just caught its prey, Charles branded his mark all over her skin with every hot kiss. Starting at her forehead, he lay kisses on her face, neck, chest, and when he reached her breasts, cupped each one in his hands, pushing them close together. He sucked on one erect nipple, then the other, paying each one individual attention. Suzanne's nipples were super-sensitive; she moaned and writhed underneath him as he continued to lick, suck and tease them gently with his teeth. When he had finished, he continued his journey of exploration around the map of her body, kissing every place he encountered. He left a burning trail as he kissed her arms, sucked on her fingers, kissed her abdomen, thighs, calves, ankles and feet. Then he traced a line with his hot tongue gently back up from her foot to her inner thigh, until he reached her garden.

Her flesh tingled in anticipation of what she knew was coming. Parting her labia, he revealed the juicy pink flesh underneath. He thought it resembled a flower. As the tip of his tongue made contact with her sweet spot, what felt like an electrical current ran through her body, making her jump. She let out a soft gasp. Tasting her sweet nectar, he began moving his tongue backwards and forwards, then in slow, circular motions; her back arched involuntarily with each cycle, as he increased the intensity and speed. Soon his tongue was darting up and down, back and forth, making her clitoris go as hard as a man's erect penis. He ate her like it was his favourite meal. Suzanne moaned with pleasure, holding his head between her hands, guiding him to make sure he was hitting the right spots.

She raised her head from the pillow to catch a glimpse of his face, to see if he was enjoying this as much as she was; his focus was totally on the job in hand (or should I say 'tongue'?)

"Oh Charles, that feels *soooooo gooooood!*" she whispered to him.

He raised his head briefly saying "I aim to please" before burying his head between her legs again. He loved the way she smelled; her fragrance reminded him of a garden in full bloom; it left him all heady.

As he continued working his magic, she could feel the waves of orgasm approaching; "Oh my god, I'm coming!" she gasped, as her eyes rolled to the back of her head. The thought of her coming in his mouth excited him; he pulled the whole of her mound deep into his mouth and concentrated his effort on her clitoris, licking it with increased pressure. "Charles, I'm coming!" she almost shouted again as the waves hit. Her body convulsed with one spasm after another; it felt like an electrical current travelling from her clitoris, up her torso, down her arms and legs to every other nerve in her body, ending in the tips of her fingers, toes, and the top of her head.

He drunk every last drop of her sweet juices.

After Suzanne had climaxed, Charles mounted her, ready to ride. He looked deep into her eyes as he entered her slowly inch by inch. She could feel every inch of him as he delved deeper and deeper into her hot tunnel. He was a perfect fit; it was as if they were made for each other, like Adam and Eve.

"I love the way you said my name when you climaxed" He murmured in her ear.

"And I love the way you made me come" she whispered back to him. As they kissed passionately, Suzanne could taste her come on his tongue. As he began to increase the intensity and speed, Suzanne moaned with each thrust.

"Oh my god, that feels so good" she whispered to him. Without warning, Charles drove deep into her. She cried out, as pleasure and pain mingled together in a bitter-sweet combination. He watched as her breasts rose and fell beneath him as she breathed deeply, holding on to his shoulders for support, her feet wrapped around his waist. He did it again; one hard, then one soft. Each time he drove in hard, she cried out, turning him on even more.

"Give it to me baby!" he called out to her.

"I'm giving it to you!" she cried back.

He grabbed hold of her ankles and placed them on his shoulders. She crossed her feet behind his head, her back rising up off the bed. As he entered her again, he kissed her ankles, running his hands up and down her long smooth legs. He continued kissing her feet and legs as he drove Pride in and out of her wet vagina, which made a soft slurping noise with each thrust as if saying 'thank you, thank you, thank you, thank you, thank you'.

"Tell me what it feels like, inside of me" Suzanne moaned to him.

"Oh damn, it feels like...it feels like... " he could hardly get the words out, he was so intoxicated.

"...It feels like I'm entering the centre of your yoniverse, the deeper I go, the hotter it gets!" he finally managed to get out, quite eloquently.

This was sheer, unadulterated happiness – it wasn't just sex; it felt more like a deep, spiritual connection.

"How could something so wrong feel so right?" Suzanne questioned her Self. Her religious beliefs were trying to creep in and spoil her fun. She'd save the guilty conscience for later.

Pulling her up off the bed while still inside her, Charles carried her around the room, trying to suck her nipples at the same time. *Now* she understood why he worked out so much! As he propped her up against the wall, she wrapped her legs around his back while he took her weight in his hands and lifted her up and down on his manhood. She felt as if she was stealing something from her wedding night; this is just how she would have liked it to be. He returned her to the bed, and as he lay her back down again, she squeezed her vaginal muscles around his great obelisk.

"Oh, shit! That feels great, do it again!" Charles groaned in his deep, sexy voice. She squeezed again, harder this time, muscle-massaging him as he slid slowly back and forth.

"Oh, F**K!" he cried out. She had never heard him swear before.

As he directed her into the doggy position, she placed her hands on the bed for support, with her feet on the floor. The versatility of her body drove him crazy. As he entered her front passage from behind, he let one hand dangle at his side as he admired her small waist and curvy backside. She buried her face in a pillow to muffle her cries of passion; she could feel the bend in his banana-like organ massaging her g-spot, sending small electrical currents rippling through her whole body with each thrust. Reaching round, Charles played with her breasts, squeezing her nipples in between his thumbs and forefingers. He then reached down and pleasured her clitoris while still pounding her from behind. With all her erogenous zones being catered for, she could feel herself coming again. Grabbing hold of her hips and riding her like a black stallion, Charles headed for the finish line...

When the ultimate moment 'came', they both froze for a moment within their own ecstasy before collapsing in a heap of skin and sweat. With Charles still inside her, Suzanne lay face-down on the bed, bearing the weight of his body. She could feel his heart beating rapidly against her back as their frantic breathing calmed down in unison with every passing second. His skin felt good against hers as he encapsulated her, making her feel like a captured prey.

She had no desire to be freed.

She could feel him still throbbing inside her, and if it wasn't for the condom he was wearing, their body fluids would have mingled together. In that moment it was as if time stood still as they savoured the feeling, drifting off slowly into sleep..............

...............Like a butterfly I flutter among the roses, then higher and higher until I can see the treetops below me. I soar even higher until I feel like one of the stars illuminating the night sky. It feels so free, to be able to fly limitlessly; the night air brushes against my face as I'm drawn to the light above me.....Suddenly I'm aware that I am not alone and looking down, I see a man with *wings of an eagle* flying just below me; his arms are outstretched as if waiting to catch me. The look on his face is like that of an angel and I know, I just know I would be safe in his arms, but no, it is not my intention to fall from this grace, so I beckon him to join me on *my* level.......even though the space between us is only the distance of a ladder, he struggles to attain to my height, as if some invisible force is holding him back. I wait patiently for him, fluttering my red wings to help him focus, eager to experience the warmth of his embrace.......Finally, as he reaches me I fold my arms across my chest, and when he catches me, he kisses me gently on my neck, the warmth of his breath.............

........Suzanne was awakened from her dream by Charles planting warm, gentle kisses on her neck as she lay cradled in his arm.

"Oh wow....what time is it?" she asked him, still in a daze.

"It's nearly 5 o'clock" he murmured into her ear.

"Oh my god, the boys will be back at six!"

"That's ok, I've got to go anyway, I have to prepare for work tomorrow"

It was at this point that Suzanne fully woke up to the realization of what had just happened; she realised she had lost it all; track of time, her dignity...and her favourite wig!

She suddenly felt bare and exposed; as Charles got up and started getting dressed, she searched around the bed, hoping he hadn't noticed. Finding it down the side of the bed, she picked her robe up off the floor, slipped it on, and tucking the wig inside it, excused herself quickly to use the bathroom. She hoped the closed curtains would have limited his ability to see what she was up to.

Five minutes later a calm Suzanne re-entered, wig now intact. Charles was just tying his shoelaces. He *had* noticed, and couldn't help commenting;

"You have a beautiful face Suzanne, why do you hide it behind that wig?"

Embarrassed, she replied "It's just easier for me to manage, that's all – my hair is so *thick*!"

"Oh...well you know I think you'd look good even if you were *bald*". Charles meant it, but the thought of walking around with a bald head did *not* appeal to Suzanne!

Walking him to the front door she caught a glimpse of herself in the hallway mirror. "Was he being serious about me looking better without the wig? Nah, he was just saying that to make me feel better" she thought.

As Charles left, he kissed her *long* and *slow*. As they engaged in one final embrace, she could feel her knees giving way beneath her.

"I'll call you later" he whispered into her ear as he left.

As she closed the door behind him and leant back against the door, she slowly slid down onto the floor, smiling to herself as she replayed the whole night and day in her head. No man had ever had this effect on her before.

"He is definitely 'The One!'" she thought.

As frantic as the sex was, there had been something deeply spiritual about their lovemaking. But it didn't take long for feelings of guilt to start creeping in.

"Oh no, I've sinned *again*!" she thought in despair. With her head in her hands she realised she was going to have to 'repent' again. Yet the experience had felt so natural, so beautiful, so right – how could it have been wrong?

As Suzanne knelt on her knees to ask for forgiveness, she questioned God;

"Why do You have so many expectations of me, when You have made me so *weak*?"

****

Lucid Dream # 1

Suzanne had been on the phone with Charles until nearly 1am. It was already 7.00am, and the boys would be up in half an hour. It didn't make any difference whether it was a weekday or weekend, they were always up by 7.30am. Suzanne never used an alarm clock either, preferring to let her body wake up naturally. So she woke up late, emerging from a lucid dream. In it, she had seen Charles walking towards her in a cream suit and tan-coloured shoes. The suit had a red rose in its lapel...they were getting married! She recalled the way his broad shoulders shifted from side to side as he walked, and the big smile on his face as he sauntered towards her. It didn't last long, but she remembered it as clear as day when she woke up. She called Charles and relayed the dream back to him.

"*Me* in a cream suit and brown shoes?" he laughed. Charles always wore dark colours; grey, black or blue.

"Well at least he wasn't laughing at the idea of us getting *married*", she thought, smiling to herself. She wrote the dream, and Charles' response, into her journal.

****

Love and Fear

They were on the phone again.
It was as if they couldn't get enough of each other, but due to their individual circumstances (Suzanne's boys and Charles's work schedule) they only really got to spend quality time with each other every other weekend; however Charles would sometimes go over

to Suzanne's after the boys had gone to bed, and leave before they got up in the morning.

This particular evening they were discussing how much power the devil has. Charles was trying to get Suzanne to focus on the greatness of God, rather than anything the devil could do. He told her he didn't even believe in any such thing as a devil.

"How can you *not* believe in the devil?" Suzanne asked in disbelief. "...Look at the state of the world! If it wasn't for the devil, I'd be living the life of my dreams – my life wouldn't *be* in this mess!"

"We are *all* responsible for the state of the world" Charles responded. "*We* are the ones creating this reality, not God. He's given us the same creative power that He has, through our collective thoughts, words and actions. Your life is the way it is because of your *thoughts* about it, Suzanne."

"*God* is in control of my life" she said with conviction.

"Sweetheart, think about it – if God is in control, why *aren't* you living the life of your dreams? Do you honestly believe God would withhold anything good from you?" he asked.

She didn't know what to say in reply to that.

"Hun, when you begin to realise that it's *your* thoughts, words and actions that are creating your reality – not God or the devil – then you will have taken responsibility for the 'mess' you say your life is in. Until you take responsibility for your own life, you're powerless to change it.

You said you want to learn more about the Natural Laws of the Universe, so let me explain one to you now: One of the Laws is 'You Attract What you Fear'. If you choose to focus on any such thing as the devil, all you're going to do is attract more 'devilish' experiences into your life. Fear – or what you call 'the devil' is the complete opposite to Love, which you call God. They're at opposite ends of the Polarity, which, by the way, is another Universal Law. It would be impossible for you to experience one without the other. How would you know God is Love, if there was no *opposite*? Fear is the opposite of Love. D'you see?"

Suzanne remained silent. This was a lot for her to comprehend, and totally different to anything she'd ever been taught. Was this true?

"Honey, when you begin to study these Laws for your Self, it'll all make sense" He concluded. Changing the subject, Charles asked what she would like to do on their next weekend together. They agreed to spend it at his place for a change.

****

Conversation with God

They pulled into the drive at Charles's three-bedroom end-of-terrace house.
It was a typical bachelor's pad; the living room was spacious with brown leather sofas, a large plasma screen on the wall, and a Playstation 2 plugged into the T.V.
It was fairly neat, with only a few newspapers and books scattered on the coffee table. She liked his taste in decor, it was similar to hers, she thought; wooden floors, plain walls, and minimal furniture. She looked over at one wall lined neatly with shelves of books from top to bottom. The saying...

'If you want to hide something from a Black man, put it in a book!'

...certainly didn't apply to him!
Remembering Charles's promise to lend her some books so she could learn more about Universal Laws, she walked over to his library and scanned the rows of Self-development, African History books and novels on his shelves. One particular book *'Conversations with God - Book One'* caught her attention. She picked it out and opened it at a random passage:
'...Words are merely utterances: noises that stand for feelings, thoughts, and experience.
They are symbols. Signs. Insignias. They are not Truth. They are not the real thing.
Words may help you to understand something. Experience allows you to know. Yet there are some things you cannot experience.

So I have given you other tools of knowing. And these are called FEELINGS...Now the supreme irony here is that you have all placed so much importance on the Word of God, and so little on experience. In fact, you place so little value on experience that when what you experience of God differs from what you've heard of God, you automatically discard the experience and own the words, when it should be the other way around...Many words have been uttered by others, in My name. Many thoughts and many feelings have been sponsored by causes not of my direct creation. Many experiences result from these.

The challenge is one of discernment. The difficulty is knowing the difference between messages from God and data from other sources. Discrimination is a simple matter with the application of a basic rule: Mine is always your Highest Thought, your Clearest Word, your Grandest Feeling. Anything less is from another source.'

Suzanne could feel the tears welling up in her eyes. It was as if God was standing there talking to her Himself. She recognised His words immediately.

"Can I borrow this book?" she turned and asked Charles. He walked over to see which one she had chosen.

"Mmmm, good choice...why that one in particular?"

"Well it reminds me of the letter *I* wrote to God – it's as if He's replying in this book!"

"Ok...well, feel free to choose another one"

"No, this will do for now, besides I can always come back and exchange it when I've finished this one, can't I?"

"Of course you can".

****

Right Time to Meet

It was Sunday, so Suzanne took the boys to church as they had missed last week because they had been at their dad's (and she had been at Charles's). She felt it was important for them to have some spiritual grounding, so apart from taking them to church every other Sunday, she prayed and read the bible with them every night before they went to bed. She also used this time to find out how their day at school was, and to talk with them about anything else they wanted to discuss. They called it 'Quality Time'.

Suzanne had been dating Charles for three months now, and felt it was a good time to introduce him to the boys. During Quality Time one evening that week she had told them all about him, and asked if they would like to meet him. They couldn't wait, so she'd invited him over for Sunday dinner.

He had passed on her invitation to accompany them to church in the morning, opting instead to pick them up outside and travelling back to her place together.

Praise and Worship was Suzanne's favourite part of the service. She really felt the presence of God come down as the choir sang and the whole congregation rejoiced, giving glory to God together.

"I have a message this morning for certain members of the church (pronounced 'choch')" the pastor informed his congregation as he began his sermon.

"As I relay this message that the Lord has given me I am sure that those for whom this message is intended will recognise themselves. Are you listening to me somebody? Is it ok if I pass on the message that the Lord has given me today?" the pastor asked in his strong West African accent.

"It's ok!" The congregation responded in anticipation.

"Do you promise not to shoot the messenger?" he asked.

"We promise!"

"Oh, you say you will not shoot the messenger, but Jesus had a message of Love from the Father for the whole of mankind, and they crucified him! Ladies, do you promise not to crucify your pastor this morning?"

"Yes!"

"The message the Lord wants me to tell you is this: *He sees you*! Somebody turn to your neighbour and say 'Your Father sees you'!"

The congregation obediently do as they are told.

"Somebody turn to your *other* neighbour and say 'My Father, He sees you'!"

There is murmuring and laughter in the congregation as they do his bidding. Still not satisfied, Pastor Olumawadere continued;

"Tap the person in front of you and say 'My Father, he sees you!'"

"Turn to the person behind you and say 'My Father, he sees you!" and then;

"Turn to the people hiding right at the back of the choch and tell them "My Father, he sees you'!"

When he was sure the congregation had got the message, he continued;

"Now, I want you to open your bible to Hebrews 4:13. Sister Sonia, will you read what the Lord has to say?"

Sister Sonia, a young, attractive woman in her early twenties stood up and read in a steady confident voice; *"Nothing in all creation is hidden from God. Everything is naked and exposed before His eyes, and He is the One to whom we are accountable."*

Pastor 'Olu' echoed the last line.

"To whom we are *accountable*? To whom we are *what*?" He asked the congregation. They respond as one:

"Accountable!"

"Now will you turn to Psalm 33 verse 13"

He picked out another young attractive woman in the church;

"Sister Letishia, will you read what King David had to say to the Lord? Beloved children of God, are you listening? The Lord is waiting on you to heed His word so that you might be saved – sister Letishia, read!"

Sister Letishia stood up: *"The Lord looks down from heaven and sees the whole human race."*

"And sister Suzanne, will you be so kind as to read for us Proverbs 15 verse 3"

Suzanne stood up and read; *"The eyes of the Lord are everywhere, keeping watch on both the evil and the good."*

"Ah-*HA*! Please read that again sister Suzanne, because some people weren't paying attention!"

Suzanne read the scripture again, this time slower, steadier and louder.

"So you see my dear people, this essential quality of our God as an *all-seeing God* is found throughout holy scripture! Do you know what this means, ladies? It means that the Lord is not merely telling you He has *good* vision, He does not need reading glasses like your pastor (peering over the glasses perched at the end of his nose) He has *more* than 20-20 vision – the Lord our Father has *X-ray vision*! ARE YOU LISTENING TO ME SOMEBODY?"

Suzanne wondered where he was going with this.

He continued;

"This means that there are NO SECRETS! This means that you cannot hide from Him...but the Lord has revealed to me that some of His children are attempting to keep secrets from Him! Some of you are not married, yet you are sitting in His holy house in unholy undergarments...*Vic-toria's Secrets*!

(The congregation gasped at this revelation, including Suzanne)

"Yes! You are not satisfied with Marks & Spencers anymore...now you are going to *Ann Summers*! Now you are going to *Victoria's Secrets*, but there are no secrets from the Lord! Now I ask you ladies, do you think it is *appropriate* to wear this kind of clothing to choch?"

Suzanne sighed with exasperation.

'Here we go again!' she thought as he continued admonishing the young women in the church about wearing underwear that accentuated their sexuality. She had come here to be 'edified', not bombarded with misquoted scripture. Pastor 'Olu' read from 1 Timothy 2:9; *"Likewise also that women should adorn themselves in respectable apparel with modesty and Self-control'*. In other words sistars, you are sending your brothars to HELL because it is written in Matthew 5 verse 28; *...'I say to you that everyone who looks at a woman with lustful intent has ALREADY committed adultery with her in his heart'*. Is this your intention sistars? Do you want to send your brothars to HELL?"

Suzanne began to lose interest; she couldn't even *afford* Victoria's Secret! Her mind wandered to the chicken she had left on a slow cook in the oven. The peas were already cooked, and when she got back in, she would add the rice and boil it down, and make the macaroni cheese. She didn't want to spend too long in the kitchen, as Charles would be meeting the boys for the first time today.

When Pastor 'Olu' quoted Lauren Hill's *'that was the sin that did Jezebel in'* Suzanne began to imagine herself wearing expensive sexy lingerie for Charles.

After the service, Suzanne and the boys left the church to find Charles double-parked outside waiting to pick them up.

Micah and Elijah took to Charles immediately. They supported the same football team, so that got them off to a good start. They already had something in common.
All the way back to Suzanne's, the four of them laughed and joked. Looking at them, anybody would have thought they were a regular happy family.

They weren't quite sure *when* their mum had started seeing Charles, because by the time she introduced him to them, it was obvious they had known each other for quite a while already.

As the boys got to know Charles, they looked up to him with respect because they could see that he loved their mum and treated *her* with respect.

As long as she was happy, they were happy.

****

Year Two: Who Am I?

'Conversations with God Book One' had become Suzanne's new bible; she felt *joy* when she read it, it resonated with *Truth*, and she felt God's *Love* through it. She laughed, cried and said "Thank You!" and "I love You!" to God countless times while reading it, with immense feelings of gratitude. She knew it was an answer to her prayers. Every question she had asked God in her letter was answered in this book. In it, she learned that God had *no expectations* of her; she was here to experience life as she chose. God simply wanted to experience Him/Herself *through her*, and wasn't going to judge her on the choices she made. All she had to do was be aware of the natural consequences of her actions, called Cause and Effect.

She invested in her own copy so she could give Charles back his one. She learnt much about the real meaning of life, and most importantly, how her *thoughts* were the *root cause* of everything happening to her. If she wanted to change anything in her life, she had to change the way she *thought* about it, just as Charles had told her.

She began putting into practice what she was learning, just as she had done with the bible. Her first lesson was that everything starts with a thought. Before anything could be created or invented in this physical world, someone first had to have had the *idea, vision,* or *desire* for it. *Thought* is the first level of creation. The words you speak are the second level of creation. And when you put ACTION to your thoughts and words, the creative process is complete, and whatever you are *thinking* about, *speaking* about and putting *action* to with *corresponding feelings* cannot fail to manifest.

Suzanne came to realise that the reason she had been experiencing so much negativity in her life was because of her negative *thinking*. Her thoughts were the *root cause* of all her problems, and unless she took control of them, she would be powerless to change her life. If she wanted to change her life for the better, she had to change the way she *thought*.

"I'm not just a human being, I'm a *thinking* being! From the time I wake up in the morning to the time I go to bed, I'm thinking *all the time*; why was I never told in church that my thoughts are creative?" Suzanne wondered incredulously.

She also learned that she had the power to create heaven or hell *right here on earth* through her thoughts, words and actions. She finally understood that by focusing on the negative, she was in fact attracting *more* negative things into her life. This is how she had been creating 'hell on earth'. She thought back to her 'rant at God'; instead of focusing on all the things she could be grateful for, she had been focusing on all the 'bad' things that were going on in the world, and in her own life.

****

Metaphorically Speaking...

Suzanne discovered that the Tree of Knowledge of Good and Evil mentioned in Genesis was only a *metaphor* for good and evil *thoughts*, and that if she allowed a thought to take root in her mind it would bear a harvest after its kind; *good* or *evil*.

Her mind was the metaphoric Garden of Eden, and her *thoughts* were the *seeds*.

She came to realize that the Tree of Knowledge of Good and Evil were simply two *choices* that Adam and Eve could have made; they could either have chosen to entertain *good thoughts* or *evil thoughts*. 'The devil' was simply a metaphor for temptation to think 'evil' or bad THOUGHTS. "Whoever heard of a real-life talking snake?" she thought, smiling to her Self.

If Adam and Eve had continued eating from the Tree of Life by entertaining *good thoughts only* (which according to the book of Revelation was located *right beside* the Tree of Knowledge of Good and Evil) they would have kept their thoughts pure. But they were tempted to think bad thoughts, and they did. The consequences of their actions were separation from God (Good), corruption, pain, disease, poverty, and ultimately, death. Suzanne thought long and hard about this. Now she could see how we, Adam and Eve's descendents, were still under 'The Curse' – because we still insist on entertaining 'bad thoughts'!

"All we have to do to 'break the curse' is to focus on thinking *good* thoughts!" She concluded.

'Good thoughts' are thoughts that make you feel good, put a smile on your face, a spring in your step, and that cause no stress in the body. When you think good (perfect) thoughts, it lifts your spirit, heals your body, and puts you on a positive vibration, which is the frequency you have to be on to attract good things.

Suzanne decided to do her best not to entertain the 'bad' thoughts that often came to her, and to do her best to only let *good* thoughts take root in her mind so that she could begin to create the life of her dreams – heaven on earth.

"So if the Garden of Eden is a *metaphor* for the mind, and our thoughts are the seeds, and the Tree of Knowledge of Good and Evil is a *metaphor* for knowing that you have the *choice* to think 'good' or 'bad' THOUGHTS, and the Tree of Life is a *metaphor* for good thoughts which produce a harvest of abundant life and the snake is a *metaphor* for temptation to think bad thoughts, then who, or what, are Adam and Eve?" She wondered.

****

Undoing the Indoctrination

Suzanne studied *'Conversations with God Book One'* as if her life depended on it.

She learnt that in order to change the indoctrination she had received around sex, she had to *reverse* the thought-word-deed process. That is, she had to DO the deed (have sex!) then have a new *thought* about it. So while she was making love with Charles, she thought about how wonderful the experience was, and that it was the best gift God gave. Instead of thinking that she was doing something 'wrong', she now thought about how 'right' it felt, and how much she loved having sex.

"I LOVE sex!" she spontaneously exclaimed once in the middle of their love-making.

"You don't have to tell *me* that!" Charles remarked.

In time, she began to feel better about having sex with the man she loved, and the feelings of guilt and condemnation passed away.

She did the same thing around money. Whereas she had been brought up to believe that *'it is easier for a camel to pass through the eye of a needle, than for a rich man to enter the kingdom of heaven'*, she now began to go by her *own experience* of having money; the more she had, the better she felt. When she didn't have much money, she felt bad. So she developed new thoughts around money, and 'made believe' that she had plenty of it so she could feel good about it. Every opportunity she got, she would give money, as she now understood the Law of Sowing and Reaping. Money is a seed; if you wish to *have* more money, *give* more. The more you give, the more you will receive. So she would look for opportunities to 'bless' people, and then have the thought "I LOVE having money!" – Even though the love of money is supposedly the root of all evil.

From her experience, it was the *lack* of money that was the root of all evil...

****

Visualise to Materialise

Suzanne lived in the heart of Camden, which had a rich cultural mix; never before had she lived anywhere where it was so apparent that the rich and poor lived side by side. Suzanne lived in the top half of a dilapidated council house, on a road where other houses also sold for millions. Not that long ago, a house four doors down had sold for over a million pounds. She went to view it, out of interest. She was amazed that a house like that could be just four doors away. It was perfect for her and the boys, she thought. Each bedroom had its own en-suite shower and toilet, and there was still space for her to set up her home-office. She tried to believe God for the money to buy it; she played the lottery religiously, hoping to win the jackpot so she could buy the house with cash. But nothing happened. Maybe she didn't really believe it was possible – or maybe God had a bigger and better plan for her.

At the top of her road, there was a pub. In the middle of the night she would often be awakened by people returning home 'in the spirit', talking to each other loudly, singing, whooping and laughing at the top of their voices, fuelled by the alcohol they had been drinking. In stark contrast, she would wake up in the morning to the sound of birds singing.

Despite living in a council property, her goal was to buy her own house with cash. *How* she was going to achieve it, she didn't know. She just believed that she could somehow. To support her goal, the universe would send her little gifts to fuel her desire. Every month, a Fabric magazine would be delivered to her house for free. In it were advertised the most exquisite houses, in areas like Primrose Hill, Hampstead Heath, Highgate and Muswell Hill. These houses sold for millions. They were of the highest standard, with swimming pools, in-house cinemas, gyms, Jacuzzis, everything a heart could desire. Suzanne would cut out pictures from these magazines and put them on her 'vision board'; this is where she stuck images of the things she wanted to attract into her life.

During her 'visualisation' time, Suzanne would imagine herself actually *living* in her dream house; watching films with the boys in their private cinema, relaxing in the steam room and Jacuzzi with her partner, writing poetry in their beautiful garden; she saw it all in detail.

Her dream was far from her current situation, but her current situation was not her reality; she was determined to reach her goals. Suzanne's plan was to set up a business, and it would be something that she could hand down to her sons – she didn't think she could rely on the 'system' to provide them with a decent job. How many well educated black men still couldn't attract high enough paying salaries to support a family? Although her sons were doing well in school and were headed for university, even a degree couldn't guarantee that they would get a well-paying job. So she was thinking ahead; "I'm going to build a business empire, something I can hand down to my children and my children's children".

****

Invitation

The house phone rang. It was Charles. Suzanne hadn't heard from him in a couple of days.

"Hi babes, how are you today?" He asked cheerfully.

"I'm fine, how are *you*?" She replied, trying her best to sound as cheerful as him.

"I'm good! I was just wondering, what are you doing tomorrow evening?"

"Tomorrow? Oh yes, I'm going to a networking event with a friend of mine" she remembered. Every now and again she would attend these evenings where she could meet other professionals and hand out her business cards. His ego couldn't help but ask; "Is that a *male* friend or *female* friend?"

"Female...why?" she half-laughed, but in her mind she was thinking; "What, do you expect me to be sitting around waiting for *you* to call?"

Masking his embarrassment for asking, he replied "Oh, I just thought you might be free that's all – what about Thursday?"

"Let me check my diary..." she paused, pretending to be checking the date, knowing full well that she had nothing planned. "Well it looks like I'll be free on Thursday. What did you have in mind?"

"Well I thought I might come over to yours and just chill and relax, you know?"

Suzanne did enjoy his company, but he seemed to be getting a bit too comfortable – and still no commitment from him. In her mind she still wasn't 100% sure if she was the only woman he was seeing.

She invited him over. She had the whole evening planned; dinner, a Tyler Perry DVD and then sex! Suzanne had all the Tyler Perry films in her Black film collection; she especially loved the way he portrayed images of successful black people. It gave her hope.

****

The Preparation

After she had showered and oiled her skin, Suzanne traced a line of one of her favourite inspired aromas *'Lovers Attraction'* in dots from her neck down to her groin area, hoping he would join them up.

Charles arrived with a bottle of Suzanne's favourite red wine tucked under his arm, and a bunch of flowers. He looked drained, but she could see he'd made an effort. He had previously taken note that she always liked to have freshly-cut flowers in her house.

"Something smells good" he said, kissing her on the lips.
"Well I hope you like it, I was experimenting!" she replied with a big smile as he handed her the bottle and flowers.
"Thank you! How was your day?"
"Oh, don't ask – terrible. I really don't want to bore you with it all, either. Right now I just want to forget about it all for a while. All I need right now is you..." he replied, moving in for an embrace as he sniffed in her fragrance deeply. As he hugged her, Suzanne could feel that despite being stressed from his day at work, he was still turned on. As she opened her mouth to answer him, words rolled off her tongue from nowhere;

"...You're not ready for me, see you're still carrying the negative energy you picked up along the way during your day..."

"That sounds like a line from one of your poems! Is it?" Charles asked warily.
"It could be!" she replied with a big smile, even though she'd only just thought of it.
"I'm beginning to think I'm just your guinea pig, that you're experimenting on me, never mind your cooking!" Charles said, backing away.
"Not my guinea pig, my inspiration!" she said as she helped him remove his coat.
"I'm starving!" he said, sniffing the air.
"I ate earlier with the boys, so do you want to eat now?" (Suzanne rarely ate after 8pm).

"Yes please! What did you cook?" he said, rubbing his hands together. Charles had been working late preparing Tax Returns, so had built up quite an appetite since lunchtime.

"I made a big pot of soup with yam, sweet potato, pumpkin, dumplings, green banana, plantain, carrots, kale..."

"Sounds good to me"

While she was serving his meal, she had the idea to give him a treat. Leaving him to eat alone, she went into the bathroom and ran a hot bath, adding the essential oils of Lavender and Jasmine, which she knew would help relax his muscles and ease his tension.

As she was preparing his bath, the sound of the running water started her inspiration flowing; she felt a poem coming on, so she ran for her notebook and pen and wrote;

'As you walk in, I can feel your passion...rising
But you're not ready for me,
See, you're still carrying the negative energy
you picked up along the way during your day,
So let me run you a bath
and help you wash all your troubles away.
Leave behind all the pressures of life,
The worries and strife
And enter, if you will, into my Queendom
A safe haven,
A place of mental freedom....   (Track 2 on the CD 'Seeds of Love')

The words flowed as easily unto the page as the water into the bath. By the time it was filled, Suzanne had finished writing her poem. She titled it *'The Preparation'*. She then lit some tea-lights and placed them around the bath, which created a warm, soft glow; she knew this would also help to relax his mind and body. Finally, she put on the CD she had compiled earlier, and with the soft music playing and the bath ready, she called Charles in. He had finished his soup and fallen asleep on the sofa. She allowed him to sleep for 15 minutes, then woke him gently, leading him by the hand into the bathroom. He smiled at the scene she had created.

"Get naked" she ordered in a soft-spoken voice. He only needed to be told once. Before you could say "Jack Robinson" he was starkers. Helping him into the bath, she left him to relax undisturbed.

"Aren't you going to join me?" he asked.

"No, I had a shower earlier. This is for you"

Charles closed his eyes and allowed the aromatherapy to do its work. Twenty minutes later, Suzanne returned with just a sarong wrapped around her body. She proceeded to wash him down with some handmade soap she had bought, and then showered him down quickly to get rid of any residual negative energy, dirt and soap. Finally, she rubbed his body down with a soft, clean towel. Letting his manhood lead the way like a divining rod, he followed her into her Queendom.

Suzanne laid a clean white towel on the bed and instructed Charles to lie on top of it. Lying on his front, he rested his head to one side on his folded arms with his eyes closed, in eager anticipation. Suzanne straddled his body, and kneeling on either side of him, poured some of Aziza's *Aphrodisiac Love Potion Massage Oil* into her hand, rubbing them both together. Then starting with his shoulders, she used her thumbs to get into the deep tissue muscle between his shoulders to get rid of all the knots. Charles encouraged her to go deeper. He could feel the tension being released as she applied pressure to the area between his shoulders, as if she was kneading dough to make bread. As she massaged his back, she admired the way his mahogany skin glistened from the oil she was administering, making his body look all the more appealing. He had a great physique; muscle definition without being too bulky. She could feel her juices starting to flow, but today wasn't about her.

To bring his energies into balance she gave him a Spinal Flush; first she loosened up his back by massaging down both sides of his spine, applying her body weight to get pressure. She then used her thumbs to work between the notches of his vertebrae from the bottom of his neck all the way down to his sacrum. Staying on each point for a few seconds, she moved the skin in a circular motion, deeply massaging each point with firm pressure. When she reached the bottom of his spine she went back to the top and repeated the process to ensure she had dispelled all the congestion that had stored up in his spine, blocking the flow of his vital energies. To complete the final flush, she brushed her open palms down the length of his back in a sweeping motion.

"Mmmm....you really know how to make a man feel like a king" he murmured.

"Well, you're *MY* king" she replied softly, bending down to kiss him on the cheek.

"Roll over" she said, helping him turn onto his back.

Opening his eyes, he saw that she was still wearing her sarong. He removed it saying he didn't want her to get oil on it. She straddled his torso, and while she massaged his arms and chest he played with her breasts, squeezing her nipples in between his thumbs and forefingers, which made her even more horny. But she was determined to finish the job in hand.

"Your turn" he offered.

"I haven't finished yet" she objected; she was enjoying giving the massage just as much as he was enjoying receiving it.

Rubbing some more oil into the palms of her hands, she gently massaged his temples, face, the top of his head, and neck. As she continued down to his chest, she ran her hands over his firm pecs. At this point, she was enjoying playing with his body as much giving a massage. He lay perfectly still, apart from his Pride which throbbed beneath her.

After massaging his shoulders, arms, and hands, she gave each finger a gentle pull to release any tension in them. Then continuing down his torso, she admired his washboard stomach and the defined lines in his groin as she continued down his legs, giving the muscles a good knead. She finished off by massaging his calves and feet, making sure to apply pressure to the points in his soles.

"You've missed something" Charles said.

She knew what he meant, but pretended she didn't.

"What?" she asked naïvely.

He took Pride in his hand and wiggled it at her.

"He's feeling left out"

She laughed, and talking to it cooed "Oh, are you feeling neglected? Let me see what I can do about that then..." Taking Pride in her hand, she began to massage it with some more of the oil. She could feel it pulsating as her fingers slipped up and down it, while she used a twisting action. Charles let out a grateful moan. He had long since taught her how to handle his family jewels; she gripped and pulled his balls back gently with one hand, stretching the skin which he'd told her created even greater sensitivity. She then continued to massage his tightened shaft using slow, then fast wrist-action, with the other hand.

"Oh my goddess, that feels so.....good" he groaned.

She quickened her pace, alternating between squeezing and stroking. His breathing became erratic.

"Sh....IT!" he cried out. By now, he was writhing as if in agony, unable to control himself. Suzanne could tell he was about to come, so she pressed a finger on the large vein on the underside of his penis near his scrotum, and squeezed his shaft at its base.

When he had calmed down, she poured some more oil unto his fully-grown phallus.

She was now in control, and she knew it. Now that 'Pride' was nicely oiled, she sat on 'him'.

"Oh, yeaaah!" Charles sighed in appreciation as she mounted him slowly. When his entire length was inside her completely, she paused. Charles looked up to see why she had stopped. Leaning forward with her hands on the bed at either side of his head, she looked into his eyes and asked "Are you enjoying this?" The look of satisfaction on his face told her she didn't even need to ask.

"You bet I am!"

"Good, because I aim to please" she purred, slowly rising.

He grabbed hold of her hips, begging her to go faster with his hands. He watched as her 36c breasts bounced up and down before his eyes like two gazelles as she rode him furiously, slipping up and down on his lubricated dick with ease. He cupped each breast in his hands, offering them support. The look on her face as she let herself go said it all; she was in complete ecstasy.

Suddenly he took control; in one quick movement, he flipped her over and proceeded to give it to her hot and cool, fast and slow, wicked and wild; one moment pushing and grinding urgently, the next more softly, slowly, tenderly and deeply, then in the next moment shallow and quick; between her soft sighs and his heavy breathing, the frenzy of their love-making matched the slow R 'n B tracks still filling the room. As she surrendered her body to him fully, the intoxicating elixir she radiated filled his nostrils, completely consuming him.

"F**KING HELL!" he cried out as he climaxed. (Charles only ever swore when he was at the height of passion).

"I'd rather f**k in heaven" Suzanne replied with a giggle.

He felt totally rejuvenated.

****

Another Level?

They awoke in a warm, sticky embrace.

"Good morning, my queen" Charles whispered in her ear as she stretched, opening her eyes.

She snuggled under his arm and replied "Good morning!"

He'd never called her 'his queen' before.

"Does this mean we've moved to the 'next level'?" she wondered.

"Man, last night was phenomenal!" Charles said "You blew my mind!"

Suzanne laughed. "Well it takes two, you know!"

They had been dating for just over a year now, but Suzanne still wasn't sure where she stood in the relationship.

"Where do we go from here?" she asked, trying to get some kind of commitment out of him.

"What do you mean?"

"Where do you see this relationship going?" she made herself clear.

"Let's just go with the flow and see where it takes us, shall we?" he responded calmly.

But Suzanne was beginning to feel impatient. When was he going to be ready to *commit*?

He kissed her gently on the forehead, gave her a tight squeeze, and got up to use the bathroom. She watched as he rose from the bed and made his way across the room. His body reminded her of carved mahogany, dark and shiny, muscles flexing with every move he made.

'Natural muscle definition under your skin, with rich tones of melanin!' she thought, and then thought 'I must put that in one of my poems!' He had no idea how much he inspired her. Suzanne reached for her notebook; she always had one to hand, for when those moments of inspiration struck, like lightening. If she didn't capture it right away, she couldn't guarantee she would remember it later. Sometimes they would come in the middle of the night. She had learnt by now that if she didn't write it down there and then, it could be forgotten and lost by the morning. So she kept a Dictaphone in her bedside table drawer, and carried a notebook with her wherever she went.

'I wonder if he'll have time for a quickie before he leaves?' she wondered. She could hear him in the shower, singing away to himself. In one quick movement, she instinctively jumped from the bed and quick-stepped towards the bathroom.

"Can I join you?" she asked, pulling back the shower curtain.

Squinting through the soap around his eyes, he gave a broad smile and replied "Be my guest!" Suzanne pulled a plastic cap over her weave and stepped into the bath, joining him under the shower. He welcomed her in, wrapping his arms around her from behind.

With her back against his front, he began soaping her body to match his. Using both hands, he started with his favourite part, her breasts, and worked his way down her torso to her flat stomach, round to her firm backside, up her back, down her arms, up her thighs, until reaching her smooth waxed vagina. Then moving in front of her, he unhooked the shower head and knelt on one knee.

As if about to perform an operation, he carefully parted her labia with his left hand and directed the flow of water at her clitoris with his right hand. Moving it backwards and forwards, he watched as it hardened. In between showering her flower, he licked it with the tip of his tongue.

"Oh my god, that feels *so good,* Charles!" Suzanne moaned, trying to hold on to the tiles to stop herself from slipping. Nevertheless, she could feel her knees giving way beneath her. Just as she was about to fall, Charles stood up and held her around the waist. She wrapped one leg around him as he put the shower head back in its holder. Lifting her unto his erect penis, he directed Pride into her wet opening. As Suzanne began gyrating around and up and down, he held on to her bum cheeks, while his muscular legs supported her weight. It wasn't long before he gave a deep-throated groan of gratitude as he came, while she gave a kind of sigh of relief.

****

Awakening His Inner Child

Charles was an accountant, but secretly he wished he'd followed his dream of being an artist. He had been very good at drawing and painting at school, but his parents had advised him to study for a 'proper job' if he wanted to be able to support a family in the future. Since he was also good at maths, Accounting was a safe bet, he'd decided, and would provide a good, steady income. Charles was excellent at his job and this was reflected in his pay-packet, but still, he felt unfulfilled. His inner child was crying out to be heard; he wanted to paint, he wanted to draw, but he just couldn't find the time. Or was it that he didn't *make* the time?

He admired Suzanne for not giving up on her dreams, and not giving in to 'the system'. She refused to go down the 9-5 route, and even though money was tight, she certainly seemed happier than him. She believed there was 'more to life' and was following her bliss at whatever cost. Something had to give, and Suzanne had decided to make whatever sacrifices necessary to achieve her goal of making a living from doing what she loved – writing and performing her poetry.

Charles could see that despite her limited resources, she was striving towards her goals. He was willing to do whatever he could to help, but she always refused, telling him this was something she had to do by herself. In her mind she was thinking that Charles wasn't the father of her sons, so why should she rely on him? But this wasn't *his* way of thinking.

"I just need a reason to get up and go to work in the morning" he would often tell her, to no avail. He hated his job, but having a family to provide for would have made it all worthwhile.

Suzanne couldn't see that her prayers had been answered; Charles was willing to provide the financial support she needed to pursue her dreams, but she was unwilling to unwrap the gift.

Still, she inspired him in more ways than one…

****

Lace Seduction

As they lay huddled on the sofa together with soft music playing in the background, Charles admired Suzanne's strong West-Indian/African features in the dim light.

"Can I paint you?" He asked, out of the blue. Suzanne was taken aback, since he had never shared his secret passion for art with her before.

"*Paint* me?" she asked curiously.

"Well, I could start by *drawing* you – just for fun" he replied.

She looked at him in surprise. "I didn't know you could draw!"

"Well I haven't done it in ages, but I'm thinking of getting back into it again, and what better way than to start by drawing my favourite lady!"

She paused, smiled, shrugged her shoulders and said "OK, when?"

"No time like the present!" he replied, reaching over for his briefcase.

"OK then! What are you going to draw on?"

Charles pulled out a drawing pad, pencil and rubber.

"Oh, so you had this all planned!" Suzanne remarked.

"Well I was hoping you'd say yes, and I just thought I'd be prepared"

"Well then let me change into something a bit more... *interesting*" she said, heading towards her Queendom.

"Before you go..." Charles requested "...Can you...lose the wig? I'd prefer to draw you in all your *natural* beauty".

"...Sure" she replied, not feeling sure at all. She couldn't believe that Charles wanted to draw her with her 'nappy' hair, whereas *he* couldn't understand why *she* insisted on wearing the wigs and the weaves when she had a perfectly good head of natural hair underneath.

Ten minutes later Suzanne re-appeared wearing a red and black lace number, with her own natural hair out. Because it had been in plaits under the wig, it was a mass of wild curls. Charles eyed her up from top to bottom; her 'fro was striking in all its natural, untamed glory. The lace and satin bodice she was wearing pushed up her breasts, enhancing her cleavage; the matching thong barely covered her smooth waxed vagina. The bodice and thong were coupled with black suspenders and stockings, and the look was finished off with a pair of high-heeled black patent shoes. The whole ensemble drove him crazy – he could feel his Pride rising, but now was not the right time, he thought – down boy!

"Damn!" Charles reacted "How am I supposed to concentrate with you in *that*?"

"Come on, be professional about this" Suzanne teased, strutting sexily over to the couch.

"How do you want me?" She continued to tease him as she perched herself provocatively on the edge of the sofa, crossing her legs.

"This woman!" Charles thought, smiling to himself.

"Ok..." He really wanted to catch her profile, the contours of her eyes, full lips, nose and forehead, and her slender figure. For a mother of two, she had a great body, he thought.

"...Why don't you kind of lie back, rest on your elbows, and drop your head back a bit?" he said in response to her question. She got into the position requested, bending one knee.

"How long do I have to stay like this?" she enquired.

"I'm not sure; do you think you can hold that position?" He asked back.

"I don't think so, not for long, anyway"

"Ok, you get yourself into a comfortable position, and I'll be happy with that"

Suzanne rolled unto her right side, propped her head up with her right hand, and looking at him seductively, rested her left knee in front on the couch.

"Perfect!" Charles called out, as if directing a film.

He suddenly began to feel nervous. He hadn't done this in over 20 years; what if he made a mess of it? What if she didn't like it, and thought he was insulting her looks? What if – He had to take control of his negative thoughts in case they crippled his creativity before he even got started; "I can do this. I am a brilliant artist. I am talented" he told him Self. With pencil in hand ready to begin, he thought he had better protect his interests for later that night:

"Babe, can I just say before I start that you are a beautiful work of art yourself, and no matter how this turns out, I think you're gorgeous"

"Oh, that's so sweet!" Suzanne got up from the sofa and started making her way towards him. He dropped his artist's pad and pencil on the floor, ready to receive her. Straddling his lap, she French-kissed him full on the lips, wrapping her arms around his neck and her tongue around his tongue. He grabbed each of her bum cheeks, pressing her against his hard-on. Suddenly she broke away saying "Ok, let's get back to business! You've got a drawing to do, remember?"

As she slowly meandered her way back to the sofa, she took a fresh red rose from the bouquet in the vase on the table, and getting back into the pose, positioned the rose strategically under her nose.

"Mmmm...nice touch!" Charles commented. But secretly he was beginning to wish he had never asked to draw her. 'Look at her! All ready for a good sex session and now I have to spend God knows how long *drawing* her instead! Mind you, she wouldn't *be* dressed up like that if I hadn't asked to draw her in the first place...' All these thoughts were going through his head as he sat there staring, pencil in hand, ready to begin. Then his imagination began to go wild as he pictured himself taking her from behind, massaging her smooth, supple ass as he drove Pride in and out of her wet vagina with the thong still on, pulling it to one side...

" – Have you started yet?" Suzanne burst his bubble.

"Uh? Oh...Yes, I'm just starting now..."

Charles put the pencil to the paper. Where do I begin, with her eyes? Her body? Her hair? Before feelings of defeat could set in, his inner child took over and began to play by putting bold strokes onto the paper. He allowed his inner child the freedom to create – this was fun! Charles began to feel something inside coming alive as he let him Self be free. He did his best to capture not only her outer beauty, but her *inner* beauty and femininity as well.

He emphasized the fullness of her lips, the sensual curve of her hips, and the ancient seductive look in her eyes. He enjoyed drawing her cleavage, accentuated by the tight bodice. He then took time to draw the lace detail on the top of her stockings, and the shine in the shoes she was wearing. He'd never seen them before – in fact, they looked new. He hoped she would wear them next time they went out together.

"Why has she given me all this extra work to do with the rose?" he thought as he copied each petal carefully. "It *does* add to the composition, though". As he was drawing the thorns on the stem, he thought about how much a rose is like a woman; beautiful to look at, but hurtful if not handled correctly.

Suzanne watched Charles as he focused entirely upon his work. It was as if he no longer saw her as his woman, but an object to be studied. She saw him go into his 'zone', and respected it, as she had often been there when engaged in her writing. She observed as he studied different parts of her body intently, drawing, rubbing out, and drawing again. She thought she may as well use this opportunity to think about the business empire she was planning on building...

Some forty-five minutes later, Charles announced that he had finished. Suzanne couldn't wait to see it. Jumping up from the sofa, she quickly wiggled over to where he was sitting. As he handed her the picture, she sat on his lap. Taking the picture from him, she looked at it and gasped "Oh Charles, it's... it's... *beautiful*! I had no idea you were *this* good at drawing!"

"I'm glad you like it" Charles breathed a sigh of relief.

"Can I keep it?" She asked.

He had poured his heart and soul into that drawing, and now she wanted to *keep* it!

"I...suppose so" he said reluctantly.

Suzanne noticed that he had entitled the drawing *'Lace Seduction'*.

"Mmmm...nice title" she smiled at him.

"...You have real talent here Charles, you should take it more seriously". Noticing he hadn't signed it yet, she asked for his paw print. He signed and dated it, and gave it back to her half-heartedly.

Placing the drawing on the table, Suzanne wrapped her arms around his neck again, and kissing him passionately, gave him what he'd been dreaming about all along...

****

Surprise

The following morning Suzanne got up early and started doing her yoga stretches, while Charles hit the floor and started doing press-ups. They spent about 20 minutes exercising together before Suzanne declared "I'm hungry. What would you like for breakfast?"

"A bowl of thrusties would be nice!" Charles joked, with a cheeky smirk on his face.

"Ha ha very funny – you want to spend the day in *bed*?"

"We can either go back to bed, or we can get ready and go out" He announced.

"Out where?" she asked in anticipation.

"Shopping!"

"Shopping? Really? To buy what?"

"Well, what do you need?"

Suzanne wasn't sure if he was being serious. No man she'd ever dated had taken her shopping before, so she thought she'd play along.

"That depends on what my budget is!"

"Would £250 be enough for you?"

"£250! Are you serious?" She still thought he was joking.

"Listen honey, today is all about you" he said. "Whatever you need, we'll go get it – as long as you stick within the budget!"

Suzanne finally realised he *was* being serious, and gave him a big hug and a kiss.

"I really appreciate that Charles – let's go shopping then!"

"And pack a bag" Charles added "We're going out tonight, you might as well stay over at my place"

Suzanne looked up at Charles, and looking deep into his eyes, said "I love you, you know"

"Yeah, I love you too...now let's get moving!" he said, slapping her playfully on the bum.

" – And pack those shoes you were wearing last night!"

****

They arrived at Charles' house laden with bags of shopping. Charles had bought Suzanne a new outfit to wear that night (which he had chosen) and he had even bought her some new underwear – Victoria's Secret. Since she still had money left over in her budget, she had bought something each for the boys. Suzanne knew how to buy clothes cheap, not buy cheap clothes!

"So where are we going tonight?" Suzanne asked.

"Well I've booked a table at this lovely West Indian restaurant I know you'll like, and then *you* can decide what we do after that"

"That sounds lovely! What time did you book the table for?"

"7 o'clock"

"Well we'd better get a move on, it's already nearly 5 o'clock!"

They enjoyed getting ready together; Suzanne had her shower first, then while Charles was having his, she brushed her weave and put on her make-up. Charles came out of the bathroom still wet, with just a small white towel wrapped around his waist. Admiring his physique, Suzanne thought; *'Look at you, standing tall and strong, brilliantly black, sun-kissed skin, with beautiful eyes for looking in...'* She ran for her bag to get her notebook so she could write it down before she forgot.

"What are you writing?" he asked.

"Oh, nothing, just an idea for a poem" she responded shadily, scribbling into her notepad.
He looked at her suspiciously;
"What are you up to?"
"Nothing!"
"Then let me see"
"No!" (She didn't like showing people her work until it was finished).
He made a dash at her notebook, trying to catch a glimpse of what she'd written.
"Get off!" she cried out playfully, as he tried to tackle it out of her hands.
"I know it's about me, I want to see it!"
"Ok ok, I'll show you!" she gave in; she didn't want her hair and make-up getting messed up. He read the line of poetry and smiled. She felt embarrassed.
"I wish I hadn't shown it to you now" she mumbled.
"Why? It's a great line; it shows how deep you think"
His answer put her at ease.
"Do you think I should use it in a poem?" she asked.
"It's not what *I* think that matters, it's what *you* think – follow your spirit" he replied.
"I'm just glad I could inspire you" he added, smiling at her broadly.
'You don't know how much!' she thought.
"Thanks Charles!" she said to him.
She loved the things he came out with sometimes. He had a way of helping her to believe in her Self and her abilities.

****

'Trust'

Suzanne loved spending time in Charles' company.
Their relationship was intense and passionate, and their arguments equally so. Sometimes they would have a disagreement and then wouldn't speak for weeks. Despite this, it was as if the Forces of Nature kept pulling them back together.

But was it love, obsession, or just a natural reaction to each other's chemistry?

On this occasion, they had just spent a lovely weekend together, and now Suzanne hadn't heard from him in *two days*. She called his landline. No answer. Should she call his mobile? No, he might be in a meeting. She wondered what he was doing when they weren't together. Did he have another girlfriend? Was he dating other women? Or was he just so busy with work that he forgot to call? Her low Self-esteem demon usually reared its ugly head whenever they weren't together, and while she tried to get visions of him with other women out of her head, 'the voices' would tell her that she wasn't good enough, pretty enough, or successful enough for him. The only way to combat them was by constantly telling her Self that she *was* worthy of him, and that she was 'enough'.

She was feeling tempted to call his mobile, but her inner voice was again telling her not to. She didn't want to come across as being 'jealous and possessive', so she always tried her best not to ask those sort of questions when he *did* finally call. To get rid of the tension she was feeling, she decided to put pen to paper:

When we come together
We're like a river flowing effortlessly,
Safe in your arms
Your embrace is the only protection I need.

But we both need time to grow, baby
To develop ourselves individually
So I'm giving you the space that you need
With no expectations from me

(And I want you to know)

I trust you baby,
I know you've got your things to do
And I've got mine too

But we know our love is true
And I know I can depend on you...
(Track 3 on the CD 'Seeds of Love')

    She felt much better when she had finished. Her inner voice was always telling her to have no expectations of Charles, that 'expectations inhibit the flow of love' and that 'The least expectations you have of someone, the more likely they are to surpass them'. But having no expectations of him was proving to be difficult. How could she *not* expect more of the relationship, when everything was going so good? Why *shouldn't* she expect him to want to take it to the 'next level'? Commitment! That's what she wanted. Was that asking too much?

    'Stuff that – next time he calls, I'm gonna give him a piece of my mind!' she thought.

Later that evening, Charles called.
    "Hi babes, how are you?" he asked cheerfully.
    "Could be better" she replied, off-key.
    "Why, what's wrong?" he asked in a concerned tone.
    "I don't think you appreciate me!" she started.
    "What makes you say that?" he asked, surprised.
    "Well look, we spent a lovely weekend together, and then you don't even call for *two days*!"
    "Babe, I've been busy, you know my work schedule"
    "What, too busy to even pick up the phone?"
Silence.
Charles was tired. He didn't need this headache right now. He'd only called to hear her voice, and now she was *attacking* him with it!
    "Charles? Are you still there?"
    Silence.
    "I know you're listening! Don't ignore me when I'm talking to you!"
    "What do you want me to say?" he asked wearily.
    "Well you could at least have the decency to answer me when I'm talking to you!"
    Silence. He knew where this was going.

If Suzanne had taken the time to listen to what her inner voice was saying, she would have known to stop right there. Maybe if it hadn't been her time of the month, she might have handled the situation differently, but no, she kept on going;

"How do I even know you're not sleeping with other women? For all I know you could have a dozen other women out there besides me!"

He felt offended. "Babe, you know I'm a one-woman man"

"So where are you when you're not with me then?" she demanded to know.

He wanted to remind her that apart from working full time, he was also on his own personal development programme; he studied Numerology some evenings, and was also learning how to apply Universal Laws him Self. He had set Suzanne on *her* Path of Truth, but he still had his *own* journey to make as well. So when he got home from work in the evenings, after having a shower and making himself something to eat, he would study for two or three hours before retiring to bed. If he called Suzanne, he knew they would be on the phone for ages. Even texting her didn't work – after receiving a text from him, she would then try to hold a whole conversation by text! So he rather waited until he had the time to talk to her properly. But he didn't tell her that.

"Suzanne, I really have to go, I have another busy day ahead of me tomorrow"

"Charles, if you hang up on me, we're through!"

"We'll talk about this tomorrow, I promise"

"I'm serious Charles, if you hang up on me, it's over!"

Charles hangs up.

In a fit of rage, Suzanne deleted his number from her phone.

But out of the chaos and confusion something beautiful was growing, like a rose growing out of the crack in a concrete pavement.

****

Who Am I?

Suzanne joined a Black History course and began learning about the great civilisations that had been built by her ancestors. If she had carried on only reading European literature and watching their 'programmes' about Africa, she would have continued to believe that all indigenous Africans were uncivilised and lived in mud huts.

But now she learnt the Truth; that they were highly advanced in their knowledge of the sciences including Astrology, Chemistry, Mathematics, Philosophy, Music and the Arts. She became fascinated with Ancient Kemet (or Egypt, as it had been renamed by the Greeks). Up to this day no-one knew exactly *how* the Pyramids had been built, since they were not only colossal, but had been constructed to exact mathematical precision. They had held ancient secrets too. She learnt about the Nubian kings and queens who had ruled the 11 dynasties *before* Ancient Kemet was invaded by the Greeks, Arabs and Europeans.

Ancient Africans shared their knowledge freely with these people, including their philosophy and knowledge of Universal Laws. But the Europeans took the information and suppressed it, keeping it within the 'select few'. The same religion they had taught to the Europeans was twisted around and re-packaged to form new religions, which were used to control the masses, and handed back to their descendants in a form of mental slavery. The amount of wars and killing of innocent men, women and children 'in the name of God', disharmony between different tribes in Africa, division based on colour of skin, and the oppression of women were all brought on by their new religions.

Now that she was learning Universal Laws her Self, Suzanne could still catch glimpses of them in the bible, but from what she could make out, most of them had been removed or watered-down so they were not effective.

Then there were the many black scientists and inventors that she hadn't learnt about in school. Suzanne was beginning to realise that if it was left to the Europeans, the only history she would know about was slavery.

But she was now slowly discovering that she had a rich history! Ancient Africans had built cities and even invented things like sewage systems long before the Western world had been developed. In fact, in Victorian England, Caucasians used to throw their toilet waste out of the window and didn't wash for months, which is how they developed diseases like the bubonic plague.

She learnt about the Moors, who taught Europeans everything they know, including the importance of cleanliness. Without the Moors on board the ships, Napoleon would have been lost at sea!

Unfortunately, the information that was shared freely with these Europeans was taken and turned against the very people who taught it to them.

Suzanne noticed that some Europeans appear to have a natural destructive nature which causes them to want to conquer every land and person they come into contact with. What they had put her ancestors through was nothing short of barbaric. But why are they this way? She didn't have time to learn *their* history, she was too busy learning her own.

What she *was* interested in though, was how Victorian England had been glamorised as a high society through stories like *Jane Eyre* and *Pride and Prejudice*. However the Truth was far from glamorous; apart from the rats, plagues and various diseases, white men used to treat their women like property, not allowing them to work or have any independence. Those poor ignorant wives had no idea what their husbands were getting up to when they went away on voyages for months on end, or how they gained their massive wealth. These were the men who ran the plantations and invested heavily in the slave trade. Not only were their wives oblivious to how their husbands made their money, they were also ignorant of the amount of Mulatto children their husbands fathered. 'Mulattos' were products of the rapings that occurred frequently on the plantations between the slave masters and the black female slaves.

When the white man arrived in Africa and saw the high status African women had within their communities, he sought to destroy that. They figured if they could break down the Black Woman (the nucleus of the Black Family), they could break down the whole

Black Community – then the wealth of natural resources in Africa could be *theirs*, which was their ultimate goal.

They even tried to erase African history and re-write it to make it look as if it was their own. But as hard as they tried, African history, being the oldest and richest, could not be erased. There was too much of it, made obvious by the many works of art, architecture, and ancient manuscripts left behind.

Learning about her rich history gave Suzanne a new sense of pride and identity.

She realised she was so far away from home, from her roots: Africa, the Motherland. The womb of civilisation. This was her roots. This was her history. *This* was her heritage! All nations were birthed out of Africa; her mother, father, grandparents, great-grandparents, ancestors. She wondered how she could have strayed so far as to have lost sight of her own Self.

When it finally dawned on Suzanne that her roots were actually in Africa and *not* the West Indies, it came as a big shock to her. Both of Suzanne's parents were from Jamaica, and none of them had ever talked about Africa being their Motherland. They were proud 'West Indians'. In fact, to even *imply* that they were African seemed offensive to them. Even today, Suzanne could still see a divide between Africans and West Indians. Recalling her school days, Suzanne remembered she and her friends calling Africans 'boo-boos' – Recently she'd heard that some Africans refer to West Indians as 'slave babies'.

Her mother, who was separated from her father, never talked about her African ancestry, or of her ancestors being brought to the West Indies to work on the plantations as slaves, nor did she have any recollection of their cultural traditions, spirituality and history *before* they were made slaves. All she had ever talked about was Christianity, and how if she didn't accept Jesus Christ as Lord and Saviour of her life she would spend an eternity in hell.

They had been completely brainwashed.

Now here she was in her mid-thirties, suddenly discovering that her ancestors were actually *African*! What Charles had told her was *true*! As she learned more about her-story, she began to understand why she was instinctively an 'independent Black woman', and why she and so many of her sister-friends were single parents. She read the Willie Lynch letters; she didn't know if they were authentic but they seemed to get to the root cause of why the Black community was the way it was today; she now understood *why* she felt she had to be so independent: During slavery, the slave masters would take the strongest male from the tribe, tar him up, whip him in front of the whole community, tie each of his legs to a horse, then whip the horses, ripping him in two. This sent the Black Woman into an emotional state of shock – the Black Man who she had looked up to was no longer able to protect her. She had to fend for herself. The women were raped in front of their men, who were powerless to do anything to stop it, otherwise they were likely to lose their *own* lives, or a hand, or foot, or be whipped until the skin on their backs was raw. Certain Black men were used as 'studs' to 'breed' their women to provide more 'stock', like animals. They never knew when their children were going to be taken away and sold, so they formed no emotional bonds with them. They beat their children mercilessly as *they* were beaten, to teach them how to behave – if *they* didn't do it, the slave master would. The Mulatto children, products of the raping which occurred frequently, were treated better than the black children, because they had 'better quality blood'. The slaves were taught to believe that 'the lighter, or *whiter* you are, the more superior you are'. Black women were then given priority over the men; *they* had to represent the slaves when speaking to the slave master. Their whole system, way of life, culture, religious beliefs, names, language and heritage was broken down and stripped from them.

When a friend gave her the film 'Sankofa' to watch, it traumatised her.

"No wonder the Black community is in the state that it's in today! Now I can see why black men – especially *West Indian* men – find it difficult to stay with their partners after 'breeding' them! No wonder black women have this air of independence about them! No wonder our children are lost – they don't know who they are! No wonder the Black Family and Community lack unity – we're still suffering from Post Traumatic Slave Syndrome –

we've been programmed to *think* and *act* in a certain way!" she lamented.

According to the Willie Lynch letters, the way to *reverse* the programming lay with the Black Woman. But she could see how the media were brainwashing her and her sisters to believe that unless you looked, talked and dressed European, you were not beautiful. It was hard to find a Black Woman in all her natural beauty on the front cover of a glossy magazine or on the tell-lie-vision. There were so many images of Black women with long, straight weaves and wigs, that it was bound to affect their subconscious minds. The subliminal message being sent out was that unless they were either light skinned with long hair, or had Western features (or all three!) they were not beautiful or that they didn't 'fit in' to society.

"No wonder so many of us Black women don't feel pretty unless we're wearing a long straight wig or a weave , or relaxing our hair, or bleaching our skin– even if it doesn't actually make us *look* any better! Our blood has been so mixed, we don't even know who we *are* anymore" she lamented.

Self Love had been replaced by Self hate – a result of Colonialism.

She was soon able to recognise the descendants of slaves (those who still had the 'slave mentality') and the descendents of slave masters (those who still had the 'slave *trader*' mentality). She felt it was important to note that not all black people had a slave mentality, and not all white people had a slave trader mentality.

After watching the film '*Goodbye Uncle Tom*' she was also able to recognise yet another 'breed' of black people; the black man and woman who thought that because they had well-paying jobs they were in a better 'class' than their brothers and sisters. They were even prepared to sell-out their own in order to keep their status, and could not relate with anything to do with their ancestors or what had happened during the Black Holocaust.
They couldn't see that they were still slaves to the white man's system.

Greatly impacted by everything she was learning, Suzanne was moved to write a poem:

Who am I?

I am a remnant of my ancestors,
Torn from my Motherland
By the rape of slave traders.

Who am I?

I am a watered-down version of an African Queen;
My blood is diluted, so mixed, that it's now in-between;
My skin is no longer its original colour;
Rich, dark, like black gold;
The colour of…tar.

Yet still,
I have Royal Blood flowing through my veins,
For my ancestors were kings, queens, rulers,
Inventors, scientists, leaders…
(Track 4 on the CD 'Seeds of Love')

She made a commitment that day to use her gift of writing poetry to help free her people from mental slavery.

****

Year Three: Mind...the Gap!

For eight months, Suzanne had no contact with Charles. She missed him enormously, but being the stubborn Scorpio woman that she was, she refused to be the one to make contact first. The first few weeks were like being on an emotional roller-coaster; she didn't know if she could take much more of it...she felt sick.

Instead of wallowing in Self-pity, she decided to focus her energy on developing her business, as well as her personal and spiritual development. She threw her Self into her writing, recording her poetry, studying the Laws of Nature and her African Ancestry. There was so much to learn.

She was still selling her Christian posters at various events, but never making as much money as she had on that first occasion. Sometimes, by the time she paid for the stand, took into account her travelling expenses and getting something to eat, she might just about break even. But at least her work was getting out there, and she was receiving good feedback on how much they inspired, motivated and encouraged people to 'keep the faith'. They were really touching people's hearts, which is what kept her going.

She had tried getting them into the larger churches Christian bookshops which would have made life a lot easier, but the first question they would always ask was "Are you a member?"

There was no way the pastors of all these churches would agree to her being a 'part time' member, but how else could she get her posters into them all? If the church is the 'body of Christ', Suzanne saw her Self as a blood cell; this *should* give her the freedom to travel throughout the whole 'body' with no limitations. But no, each pastor wanted to know if she was a 'member', and 'how long had she been attending'. How was she supposed to get her prophetic poetry 'ministry' off the ground if she had to be a member of every church?

So she focused on selling her posters at various events.

Just by chance (or was it 'synchronicity'?) while Suzanne was selling her posters at an event, someone handed her a leaflet offering free meditation classes in Covent Garden. She began attending. There, she learnt about her 'inner space', and how to go into 'the Silence'.

First she learnt how to *observe* her thoughts and not try to do anything about them, but to just *watch* them to see how they were. Her thoughts reminded her of naughty children, running around the playground of her mind, screaming, shouting, and behaving unruly.

Then she had to learn how to take control of her thoughts, by *choosing* the ones she wanted to entertain. It was important to learn which thoughts to hold on to, and which ones to release back into the universe. She had the *choice* to decide whether or not she wanted to hold on to a thought, or let it go. If she decided to keep it, another thought like it would follow, then another, and soon a whole train of similar thoughts would follow. If these were *good* thoughts, she could remain in a state of bliss. But if they were '*bad*' thoughts, it could lead to sadness, stress, or even depression.

Now she understood why she often suffered from bouts of depression - Wrong thinking! She learnt that 'depression' was just a fancy name for 'negative thinking patterns', and that if she didn't learn how to 'nip her negative thoughts in the bud' they would grow and spread fast, like weeds. She also learnt how to 'create a space between her thoughts' in order to keep her mind from getting cluttered, like an overgrown garden.

Suzanne liked the metaphor of the garden; not being too green-fingered herself, she had discovered first-hand how difficult it was to grow a beautiful garden. She had found that the flower seeds she planted seemed to take ages to grow, while the weeds sprung up quickly! If she didn't constantly weed the garden, the weeds would choke her flowers and stunt their growth, or even kill them. It was the same with her thoughts; if she allowed a negative thought to take root in her mind, more similar thoughts would spring up. Her job was to keep the garden of her mind well cultivated, so that it remained filled with beautiful flower-like thoughts, instead of choking weeds. When a negative thought-seed sprung up, instead of dwelling on it (watering it) and letting it grow into *more* negative thoughts, her job was to uproot it and replace it with a positive thought-seed. So she began to put what she learnt into practice by replacing thoughts like "I don't feel well" with "I feel good" and "I can't afford it" with "I am abundant".

Since she had already learnt that all thoughts are either rooted in *Love* or *fear*, she made a conscious decision to focus on planting seeds of Love in the garden of her mind. A positive thought was rooted in Love, and a negative thought was rooted in fear – there was no other place for them to come from. Mother Nature had shown the way through the Universal Law of *Sowing and Reaping.*

Learning how to meditate helped her to control her negative thinking patterns, and in turn she learned how to control her *feelings*.

'Self Love' by Cezanne

She learnt that her *solar plexus*, or 'sun centre', which was located at the back of her stomach, would let her know if she was on a *good* vibration. If she was thinking positively, she would radiate *positive* energy, helping her to attract the things she desired. If she was thinking *negatively*, she would radiate *negative* energy, attracting people, situations and events on that same vibration.

So whenever she got that horrible churning feeling in the back of her stomach, she knew she was on the wrong track. If she was feeling *good* feelings, like butterflies, she knew she was on the right vibration.

Suzanne learnt that she was in fact a *human magnet*, attracting things that were on the same frequency as her Self. The reason 'bad things' kept happening to her was because of her own negative thinking, and that thinking negatively sent out a 'bad vibe' into the universe. If she was on a *good* vibration, she would attract *good* things, if she was on a *bad* vibration, she would attract *bad* things. Her job was to keep her Self feeling happy all the time so she could remain on a good vibe. The way to keep her Self feeling happy was to think good thoughts, since her *thoughts* were creating her *feelings*.

Now she innerstood why the bible said:

'Whatever things are true, whatever things are honest, whatever things are just, whatever things are pure, whatever things are lovely, whatever things are of good report; if there be any virtue, and if there is anything praiseworthy, MEDITATE ON THESE THINGS' (Philippians 4:8)

If she was feeling good, she knew it was because she was *thinking* something good, and if she felt bad, she knew it was because she was *thinking* something bad at that time. She began to learn how to be guided by her feelings instead of being *controlled* by them. If she felt bad, the way to make her Self feel good again was to change her thoughts to happy thoughts. So she looked for ways to help keep her Self feeling good all the time.

She stopped watching the tell-lie-vision, since she realised that watching the news *especially* made her feel depressed. She invested the time she saved watching 'programs' into learning how to meditate and developing her Self.

It was the job of her conscious mind to protect her subconscious mind from negative influences. If negative suggestions through the media reached her subconscious mind, they could become her reality. For instance, if the news announced a new flu virus and she chose to believe it, she would be more likely to catch that disease than if she didn't know anything about it, or if she heard about it, but chose to reject the idea. Or if it was reported that the economy of the country was in recession and she believed it, it was more likely to affect her finances.

Suzanne also created music playlists that would uplift her spirit. If she was feeling low, she would put on a CD with positive, inspirational lyrics that would make her feel good again. She deleted all the music from her playlist that were not influencing her in a positive way, or that made her feel down when she listened to them, especially the doomy gloomy love songs that spoke of broken hearts and unrequited love. She used to enjoy wallowing in Self-pity listening to them, but now, they were no longer conducive with her new way of thinking. As much as she loved them, they had to go.

She also began attracting books, CD's, DVD's and free seminars that gave her a more in-depth understanding of how her mind worked, and how she could learn to control it, instead of *it* controlling *her*. None of them were Christian literature, but they often referred to the bible, which confirmed to her that the scriptures still contained some Truths.

What bothered Suzanne was the fact that none of the literature was written by Black people; this proved that the ancient manuscripts where the original knowledge had come from were no longer in the hands of their rightful owners, or their descendants.

As a result of everything she was learning, Suzanne started to become insensitive to *other people's* feelings; her job was to keep her *Self* in a constant state of bliss – it was other people's jobs to do the same. Why should *she* be responsible for how other people felt? "If *your* thoughts create *your* feelings, surely it's everybody's responsibility to keep *themselves* feeling happy, and not expect someone else to do it for them?" she reasoned with herself. It was hard enough work trying to manage her *own* emotions, without having to worry about other people's as well! She decided that no matter what anyone said or did to her, she wouldn't take it to heart – that way, she couldn't be offended, and could remain feeling happy. Feeling happy was the ultimate goal, because to attract the 'good things' that she wanted in life, she had to be on the same 'vibration' as them.

Was she becoming Self-ish and heart-less?

She then remembered the first Law that Charles had told her; "Treat others as you would like to be treated your Self", or as the bible put it *'Do unto others as you would have them do unto you'*.

"If everybody on this planet would just learn to root all their thoughts in *Love*, this world would be a better place...but it starts with my *Self*." she thought.

> *"Be the change you want to see!"*
> (Mahatma Ghandi)

****

Meditate to Create

Suzanne sat upright in a comfortable armchair with her eyes closed.

Whenever her boys were away at their dad's for the weekend, she looked forward to spending time alone. She was never lonely; *loneliness* and *being alone* were two different things to her. Being alone gave her time to connect with her inner Self.

As she sat poised in the chair, she allowed her mind to be free from the thoughts that were always coming at her from different directions. Breathing slowly and deeply, she slowed her thoughts right down, and focused on creating a space between each thought, and then making that gap larger and larger. She kept absolutely still as she did this. Entering into the Silence, she found peace, Love, and joy, and a kind of contentment she never experienced anywhere else before. She was learning how to take control of her physical being, instead of *it* ruling *her*.

Some thirty minutes later, Suzanne opened her eyes. She felt refreshed and uplifted, as if she had just returned from a great holiday. She enjoyed sitting in 'the Silence'. It seemed to rejuvenate her somehow.

On occasions, Suzanne would spend an evening watching DVD's that she had chosen her Self, preferably a comedy or something light-hearted. This way, she was able to maintain her happy state. But this evening, she decided to spend time alone, without the noise of anything external to interrupt her thoughts.

She ran a bath, adding some sea salt and lavender essential oil. As she relaxed her body and mind in the water, words came floating to her. She reached for her notebook and pen lying on the floor by the side of the bath. By now, she knew to be always ready for when those bolts of inspiration struck;

I am fertile soil!
I am fertile soil!
When I plant the seeds of Love in the garden of my mind
They're gonna blossom...

*Think of every **thought** you have as a **seed**,*
The thoughts you sow, you will reap;
Thoughts rooted in Love will grow into beautiful flowers
While thoughts rooted in fear will grow into fast-growing weeds!

All thoughts are either rooted in Love or fear
(Fear is the opposite of Love)
Thoughts rooted in Love will produce a harvest after their own kind

And thoughts rooted in fear will produce a harvest after <u>their</u> own kind
So plant the seeds of Love in the garden of your mind!

Thoughts rooted in fear produce a harvest of sickness, lack, poverty and disease.
While thoughts rooted in Love produce a harvest of health, wealth, happiness and peace!

"Every day is a SEED to your future happiness, success and well-being, so plant the seeds today for the future you want to see BLOSSOM!"

Just remember, you reap what you sow...
(Track 5 on the CD 'Seeds of Love')

As Suzanne lay in the bath she could see how Mother Nature really *had* shown the way to learning the true nature of our thoughts!

She was by now aware that not all thoughts were produced from her own mind; that some came from 'other sources'. In church, they called it 'the devil'. She had often imagined this ugly little red figure sitting on her shoulder with horns, a pointed tail, and a dagger in its claws, trying to entice her to do things she knew was 'bad'. But all the 'devil' could really do was make suggestions to her; it was her choice to decide what thoughts she wanted to entertain. Again, this reminded her of Adam and Eve in the Garden of Eden, being tempted to eat of the Tree of Knowledge of Good and Evil.

When she thought about it, if she added a 'd' unto the word 'evil' she got 'devil', and if she took the 'o' out of the word 'good', it became 'God'. Was this just a coincidence, or a play on words? *God* and the *devil*. *Good* and *evil*. Good thoughts, bad thoughts. Right and wrong.... a pattern seemed to be emerging: What if they really were just opposite *forces*? She remembered what she had learnt about the Universal *Law of Polarity;* 'everything must have its opposite'; and according to the *Law of Relativity*, if there was no bad, you wouldn't be able to experience *good*; if there was no wrong, you wouldn't know what is right, and that one was only created in order to be able to experience the other.

```
devil (evil)                              God (good)
  (fear)      <——————————>       (Love)
                  (Polarity)
```

"So maybe *evil* (the devil) was only created in order for us to be able to experience *good* (God)! If there was no opposite, how would we *know* God is good?" Suzanne reasoned with her Self. The more she thought about it, the more it made sense.

"If this is the case, then we're not meant to focus on the *bad*, we're supposed to focus on the *good* things in life!" This reminded her of another one of the Universal Laws: *You Attract What You Fear*. If you focus on the negative force, or the devil, you'll only attract more negativity into your life. If you focus on the goodness of God, the wonders of nature, and all the things you can be grateful for, you will attract more things to BE grateful for: '*Like attracts like*'. Suzanne realised that up until then, she had almost *enjoyed* giving attention to the things the 'devil' was 'doing to her', more than giving God the glory for the things *He* was doing in her life! She suddenly remembered the words in the 'poem' "Look to Me!" that God had given to her when she asked Him for 'the Truth'. It was reminding her to focus on His Love. She made a decision; from that moment on, she wasn't going to focus on the devil anymore. She would focus on the goodness of God and all the things she could be grateful for.

She decided to spend some time right there, in the bath, in prayer and thanksgiving, singing and giving glory to God.

Togetherness

Suzanne spent a lovely weekend with her boys; after they had worked as a team to clean the house, they went food shopping together. They boys spent the rest of the afternoon doing their homework and playing video games, and in the evening they all watched a DVD. At ages eight and ten, Micah and Elijah were really into Sci-Fi movies, so as they watched '*Transformers*' Suzanne explained the symbolism used in the film, and how things like 'the cube', and the characters in the film were taken from real life scientific facts. On the Sunday they went to church, had dinner, and prepared for school the next day. After they had spent 'Quality Time' together and the boys went to bed, Suzanne sat with her feet up in the sofa, drinking a cup of peppermint tea. As she sat there, her mind ran across Charles. She wondered what he was doing right now. She questioned her Self whether it was possible to love someone without being emotionally attached to them. She knew she still had strong *feelings* for Charles, but is that what love is? Just a *feeling*? What happens when those feelings fade, do you just move on to the next person? But her feelings for him *hadn't* faded. She knew she still loved him, but didn't feel as if she *needed* him as much as before. She felt less anxious, more calm, less desperate perhaps.

As she sat there thinking about him, she wondered if *he* ever thought about *her*.

"Why did I delete his number?" she questioned herself, staring at her mobile phone, wishing she could call him. But no doubt, even if she *did* still have his number, her inner voice would probably say "wait for him to call you". She hated it when that happened. Just then the phone rang. It was Charles!

"I don't believe it! I was just thinking about you!" she answered excitedly.

"Well, I must have sensed it" Charles replied calmly.

"You've been on my mind, too. It's been a while...how are you?" he continued.

"I'm ok" she wanted to tell him how much she'd been missing him, but the words just wouldn't come out.

"Just ok?"

"Well no, I'm *great*, actually. What about you, what have you been doing with your Self?"

"Well you're not going to believe this – I've been painting!"

He explained that the drawing *'Lace Seduction'* that he'd done of her had got his creative juices flowing, and he had dedicated nearly every weekend to painting since they broke up.

"Can I come and see them?" she asked.

"I would love you to"

"When can I come?"

"Why not now?" Charles had always been one to live in the present.

Suzanne looked at the time. It was nearly 9pm. She knew the boys wouldn't wake up until at least 7am, and if they did, they would only go to the toilet and go back to bed. If she left now, she could be back long before they awoke.

"...OK, are you coming to pick me up?"

"Why don't you jump in a cab and I'll pay for it when you get here" he suggested.

That would give him time to tidy up a bit, and put clean sheets on the bed.

"Great! See you in about an hour then!"

****

Suzanne arrived at Charles' wearing a skirt, high heels and a tight top. Nothing else. As the cab pulled up outside his house, he opened his front door and watched as she walked confidently towards him. He greeted her formally giving her a hug and kiss on the cheek, but as soon as he had closed the front door, he kissed her passionately. He didn't tell her how much he'd missed her, but his actions spoke louder than any words ever could. Then taking her by the hand, he led her into his spacious living room. On every wall hung a new painting, signed and dated by him Self. Suzanne walked around slowly taking in the detail of each painting. She could see where all his sexual energy had gone these past eight months. Just looking at them, she could tell something deep had been going on in his subconscious mind.

"They're *beautiful*...though I wouldn't expect anything less, coming from you" she complimented him.

"Thank you. Choose one"

She thought she heard him wrong; "Did you say *choose* one?"

"Yes, as my way of apologising for not calling you sooner"

Suzanne knew straight away which one she wanted.

"Can I have that one?" she pointed to the woman emerging from a red tulip.

"Self Love? Sure, it reminds me of you anyway."

"Well maybe I should let you keep it then!"

"No it's ok, I'm putting them into print, so I'll just do one for my Self and frame it"

"Well I'm glad to see you're finally taking your art seriously!"

"Thanks to you" he pulled her close to him in a small gesture of appreciation. As they stood hugging and kissing, Charles could smell the essence coming from between her legs. He turned her around away from him and started kissing her neck from behind, while reaching up under her top and fondling a breast with one hand, reaching slowly to lift her skirt with the other. To his delight, she wasn't wearing any panties. He reached between her smooth thighs to feel her moist, soft opening. Suzanne let out a sigh as his warm fingers began massaging her clitoris. Suzanne could feel the urgency of his passion, which intensified her own carnal desire for him. She turned around and began tearing at his clothes, which gave him permission to do the same to her. Kissing passionately, they stripped each other down, leaving a trail of clothes across the living room floor leading to the sofa, all the while keeping their lips locked and their tongues sensually wrestling. As they passed the dimmer switch, Charles masterfully reached up and turned the lights down. As he sat on the leather sofa, Suzanne straddled him. That was when he noticed that she wasn't wearing a wig or a weave.

"At last!" he commented.

"At last what?" (She thought he meant at last they were together again).

"You're in all your natural beauty!" he complimented.

"Oh, you noticed" she said, laughing. She had taken off her wig, taken her hair out of the cornrows, and combed it back into one just before she left home, knowing he preferred the natural look.

"Can I take it out of the bun?" he asked, already helping himself. She didn't stop him. As soon as he had released her hair, it turned into a mass of wild curls. Suzanne tried to smooth it down, thinking it looked too messy.

"Leave it, it looks fine" he reassured her.

She looked erotic, wild, and exciting in the dim light, while his 4'x5' painting *'Black Butterfly'* formed a calming backdrop on the wall behind her.

He couldn't wait any longer.

"I want to feel me inside of you" he murmured into her ear, searching for her opening with Pride. Suzanne raised herself unto her knees to make it easier for him. As she sat on him slowly, they both let out a sigh of relief.

Holding on as if for dear life, they began moving together rhythmically, slowly at first, then getting faster and faster until they reached a frenzy.

Suzanne rode Pride as if she was at the races; she liked to think of it as her 'rod of correction', it sure as hell whipped *her* into shape, anyway!

Talking to each other and laughing, they changed into all their favourite positions.

"This is *real* Poetry in Motion!" Charles joked as he pushed her gently towards the side of the sofa, forcing her unto her elbows. As he took her hips in his hands he slowly kissed one warm bum-cheek, then the other. She parted her legs slightly to make it easier for him to enter her secret garden.

As he inserted Pride, he began gyrating his hips and waist as he moved back and forth. Suzanne could feel the bend in his cock massaging her g-spot; the sensation drove him wild too......As he galloped towards the finish line, he could feel the heat as he reached the centre of her yoni-verse;

"WHO AM I?" she demanded to know passionately as he drove deep inside her.

He didn't hesitate in reminding her who she was;

"You're my Queeeeeeeeeeeeeeen..." he groaned as he came.

****

Two hours later, his cock was still hard as a rock, and leaking.

But Suzanne couldn't take any more. As they lay in his bed locked around each other's bodies, they talked about what they had both been doing while they were apart. Suzanne told Charles about the progress she had made 're-programming her mind', and learning Universal Laws. She also told him about some of the things she'd learnt in her African History class, and how it had helped to develop her *Self* and *racial* esteem. She informed him that as soon as she had the opportunity, she was going to visit her Motherland.

Charles told her he had visited his father's home country, Ghana, when he was in his late teens and it had changed his life. He was well overdue for another visit, and suggested they think about doing a trip together.

Suzanne had to get back home before the boys got up.

He offered her a spare toothbrush. She brushed her teeth to freshen her breath, but decided against a shower, preferring to keep the lingering scent of their passion clinging to her body like a secret subtle reminder for as long as possible. She found her now crinkled skirt and top amongst the clothes strewn across the floor. After zipping up her skirt, with arms up, she squeezed back into her top. Charles watched her breasts disappear like a curtain at the end of an award-winning play.

He called a cab to take her back home. When the cab came, she left, kissing him on the lips. Even after she had gone, he could still smell her essence lingering in the air, on the sheets, and on his skin.

"This is going to be a long day" he thought, as he got ready to go to the gym. He then decided against the gym as he was already knackered, opting to go straight to work instead.

****

That evening, Charles called as soon as he got in from work. He wasn't going to make the mistake of not calling her again.

"Can I come over?" he asked.

"I would have loved you to, but I've got some work I have to do" Suzanne responded warmly. It was winter, and her body clock seemed to change around that time of the year; she would normally go to bed around 8.30pm, not long after the boys, then wake up at about 4am, and write until about 6am. There seemed to be a different type of energy at that time; inspiration flowed more easily, and she seemed to be able get more done. If Charles was to come over they would go to bed late, and then she would wake up too late to write. Plus, she was still a bit sore from the night before. Charles understood reluctantly. He'd tasted her sweet nectar again, and now he wanted more.

"What about tomorrow evening?" he asked.

She paused before replying; "...Ok".

As much as she enjoyed his company, Suzanne felt as if she was on some kind of a mission; as if she was being driven to accomplish something.

They spoke for over an hour before he began telling her about all the things he was going to do to her next time he saw her – in detail. He told her how he could still smell her scent on his sheets, and how it was driving him crazy. He continued with his detailed explanation of what he was going to do to her when he came over the following night, and all the different positions he was going to put her in; they both pleasured themselves, talking each other into a heated frenzy, until they both climaxed loudly down the phone.

****

Be Still...

Suzanne spent a two-hour long session sitting in 'the Silence'. As she did so, she used the painting Charles had given her as a focal point.

Out of the blue, she received revelation of a scripture that she had heard so many times before in church, but *never* in this way;

'Be still...and KNOW that...I...AM...GOD!'

The thought scared her at first.

How could she go around telling people she got the revelation "I am God"?

But then, didn't the bible itself say that God made man in His image and likeness?

In church, Suzanne had always heard the scripture interpreted to mean 'Be still and know that I am God' – in other words, don't do anything, just 'wait on God' to sort out your problems.

With this new revelation, Suzanne realised that *she* was God – in the flesh! It wasn't her *flesh* that was made in God's image and likeness it was her *spirit*, which resided in her body!

Now that she had the revelation, what did it actually *mean*? She continued to sit in the Silence for the answer. Suzanne realised that she had the same creative powers as The Great Creator, just in a lesser amount: 'God' had made it very clear in *'Conversations with God Book One'* that thoughts, words and actions, with corresponding *feelings* produce RESULTS – which is the Creative Process.

This is how we have the power to create, just like God. This is what makes us *little gods and goddesses*.

Suzanne finally began to feel in control of her life. She was no longer a *victim* of her circumstances, but the *creator* of them. By taking control of her thoughts, she could take control of her *life*.

She realised she was now living in the residual of her *past* thoughts, words and actions. If she didn't like anything she had created, she had the power to change it. All she had to do was focus on what she *wanted* to happen, instead of what she *didn't* want to happen. Her mistake in the past had been to conjure up all sorts of worst-case scenarios in her mind, then wondering why they happened, not realising that *she* was the one creating them.

She began using her meditation time to picture all her heart's desires in detail, feeling the feelings of already having it *now*, and expressing deep feelings of gratitude for what she already had.

She also used this time to focus on loving her Self from *within*.

****

Conversations Within

If prayer is time for talking *to* God, then meditation is time for *listening* to God.

As Suzanne sat in 'the Silence' her still, small voice began to speak to her. In the Silence, it seemed much louder than usual.

"Who is *this*?" she asked in her mind, surprised.

And the voice replied "It is I, me, YOU!"

"But...Who am I?" she asked incredulously.

"You are a soul, living in this body.

You are pure, creative spirit.

*You are the Source; everything comes from YOU (Your **O**wn Universe)*

And everything returns to You.

You are a triune being; Mind, Spirit and Body,

And you have the power to think creatively"

Suddenly it was as if Suzanne remembered Who she really was, and the voice inside was no longer a stranger to her. She realized that she had been looking in all the wrong places for the answers to her questions, when all she really had to do was look *within*.

(Track 6 on the CD 'Seeds of Love')

****

All Night Spa

For their next weekend together, Suzanne suggested they do something different and go to an all-night spa in Kentish Town, which she'd heard was supposed to be really good.

"Mmmm...sounds like fun..." Charles said, smiling broadly. He was already imagining her butt naked in the steam room.

They arrived at the spa at midnight. It was a Saturday, and very busy. People were walking around in the nude as if it was second nature to them. Charles whispered to Suzanne "I'm not walking around naked in here!"

She laughed. "Don't panic; you can wrap your towel around your waist if you're not comfortable going nude"

Charles checked out the place; there was a swimming pool, Jacuzzi, and a lounge area where you could lie and relax, as well as the sauna, steam rooms and showers. "This should be fun!" he thought.

Suzanne headed for the women's changing rooms, while pointing at the men's changing rooms; "I'll meet you back out here in 10 minutes, ok?"

"Sure".

They met up as agreed in the lounge area. Charles was wearing a white towel wrapped around his waist, and flip flops. Suzanne had a white towel wrapped around her chest, with a bikini underneath. She had taken her hair out of twists and wrapped her head with a small white towel.

"What do you want to do first?" she asked.

"Do you fancy a swim?" Charles asked.

"My hair will get ruined!" Suzanne complained.

"Ok, what about the Jacuzzi?" Charles suggested.

"Alright then" she agreed.

They made their way over to the Jacuzzi, leaving their towels on the side. Suzanne got in first, lowering herself into the warm bubbling water, while Charles watched her cleavage disappear into the bubbles. They relaxed in the Jacuzzi for about 20 minutes, hardly talking to each other, just enjoying being in each other's company. Although there were other women walking around naked, Charles didn't even seem to notice.

Leaving the Jacuzzi, they headed for the showers.

After showering down together they entered the steam room. Once their pores had opened up, they left and showered down again. This time Suzanne unwrapped the towel from around her head and wet her thick, natural hair. Charles offered to shampoo it; he loved being able to play with her real hair. Pouring the shampoo into the palm of his hand, he rubbed them together and massaged it into her hair. She closed her eyes and enjoyed the head massage he gave her as he washed her hair with care. Directing her under the shower, He then helped her rinse it out, then repeated the process. When he had finished, she loaded it with conditioner and oil, and placed a plastic cap over it.

They returned to the steam room so Suzanne could give her hair a good steam.

There was only one other couple in the steam room, and they were too busy giving each other massages to take notice of Suzanne and Charles. Suzanne opened the sea-salt, olive oil and essential oil mixture she had made up. Sitting on the warm tiles, she began scrubbing her arms and legs, feet, hands, chest and buttocks. She offered some to Charles, who followed suit. She scooped a small amount into her hands and began scrubbing his back. Then he did hers. By the time they finished, both their bodies were silky-smooth. Suzanne then spread her towel on the tiles and laying down, allowed the mixture to penetrate her skin. Charles sat on the tiles opposite, watching her. Her skin glistened from the heat and oil; eyeing up her perfectly toned body, he was unable to control his penis from rising.

Suzanne was unaware of the attention she was receiving, since she was lying on her front with her head on her folded arms facing away from him, and her eyes shut. She only became consciously aware when he got up and sat beside her, and began caressing the small of her back, then her buttocks, as if he was massaging them. She tensed the muscles to make them even firmer. His hand slid effortlessly over her smooth, polished skin. He slipped his hand down into her bikini bottom, and following the crack, down to her secret garden.

"Not here, Charles!" she admonished him. But she couldn't help letting out a slight moan as his fingers began to caress her clitoris. "I was almost sleeping you know" she said gently, so as not to put him off. "Do you want me to stop?" He murmured. "Mmmm.....you can't stop now" she purred, turning over unto her back. He slid his free hand up her torso and grasped hold of her right breast. Her nipples were erect despite the heat. Still massaging her clitoris, he leaned forward and began to suck her right nipple. It tasted salty from the scrub.

"I'm feeling dizzy" Suzanne said in a faint voice. By now, they had exceeded their time in the steam room, and coupled with their own body temperatures rising, the heat was getting too much.

They left the steam room, and with Charles offering her support, they headed for the showers.

Charles pushed the knob to start the shower running, and seeing that she was still a little off-balance, helped Suzanne in and stood behind her. Holding her around the waist with both arms, he became her wall so that she didn't fall.

"Are you ok? We did stay in there a bit too long this time" he asked in a concerned tone.

"I'm fine, thanks" she replied, holding her head. "I just need some water".

He immediately reached for the bottle of water in his bag outside the shower, and unscrewed the lid.

"Here sweetie, drink this". She took a long swig at the bottle before handing it back to him. He had a few gulps, put the lid back on and placed the bottle back in his bag.
"Feeling better now?" he asked.
"Much better, thanks" she smiled up at him. Now she felt better, she took the plastic cap off her hair. It was almost shoulder length and very thick.

Although she loved her natural hair, she still had the mentality that it was too much work to maintain. So she would plait it all down and put a wig on top. Sometimes she would get it hot-combed at the front and wear a weave at the back, so the weave blended in with her own hair. It always looked great to start with, but after a few days her hair would start to revert back to its nappy state, and then everyone could tell that she had a weave. But she wasn't going to relax it; she knew better than to put those chemicals on her head. She had done the 'big chop' and cut the relaxer out of her hair when she was pregnant with Micah, after doing some research on the dangers of the chemicals used in them. Since then, she had slowly and painfully gone through the transition of growing natural, but not being brave enough to wear her hair short, she had been wearing the wigs and weaves ever since.

After washing out the conditioner, she towel-dried her hair;
"What am I going to do with it now?" She thought out loud as she looked in the mirror. It looked ok in a big 'fro, but if she didn't

take the time to comb, grease and twist it, by tomorrow it would be all dry and frizzy.

Charles couldn't stand the wigs and weaves; he thought they looked like mops – especially when they got wet. He'd occasionally hint and drop comments but he'd never told her outright how he really felt, until now.

"Well you know where I stand on that – I don't care what you do with it, as long as you keep it natural..." he replied " – with one exception"

"Oh? What's that then?"

"The only thing I'm not too keen on is locs"

"Why not?"

"I just think they look...untidy. And they can't be hygienic either"

For a long while, Suzanne had been considering growing locs, but hadn't quite made up her mind about them. She loved seeing them on other people, but wasn't sure if they would suit *her*. At the moment, all she knew was that she wanted to keep her hair natural – underneath her wigs.

Putting him to the test, she asked "Can you help me comb it through please, so I can twist it?"

"I'd be happy to!" he obliged.

Moving to the lounge area, Suzanne sat on a chair and handed Charles her large plastic wide-tooth comb. He parted her hair into four sections, and then combed out each section individually, greasing it as he went along, as he remembered seeing his mother do with his sisters. When he had finished, he stood back to admire his own work. Suzanne looked in the mirror.

"Good job!" she said, smiling at his reflection. Normally this is where she would plait her hair into small cornrows, cover them with a hair net, and put one of her wigs on top. But Charles seemed to enjoy playing in her thick, natural hair, so she decided to leave it out.

"I think I'll just leave it to dry naturally" she said to him.

"Good – at least I'll be able to touch your hair!"

She paused to look at him; it finally hit home to her how much this really meant to Charles. Realising that he was being sincere, she felt a sense of relief, happy to know that he was actually *supporting* her in keeping her hair natural.

When she thought about it; "How much money would I save if I didn't have to buy those wigs and weaves on a yearly basis? Probably enough to take a holiday!" She laughed at herself.

They left the spa at 7am, arriving back at Charles's place around 8am; he couldn't wait to get her naked and explore her silky-smooth body. As he threw her down unto his sofa and spread her legs, he joked "There's nothing I like better than freshly-steamed fish!"

Today he was having *salt*-fish...

****

Life Path Number

Later that morning, Charles made Suzanne her favourite breakfast; porridge with banana and Manuka honey. He made himself porridge too, but without the honey. They spent the rest of the day indoors, just chilling and relaxing, sleeping and listening to music. It was Sunday. Suzanne could have gone to church, but she was having such a great time with Charles. She no longer felt guilty about it. It was the natural thing to do.

As they sat relaxing on the sofa, Charles suddenly started looking for a notebook and pen, and announced "Right, let's work out your Life Path number, shall we?"

"What's a Life Path number?" Suzanne questioned, intrigued.

"According to Numerology, your Life Path number is the most important number relating to your birth. It reveals the road you're travelling, and gives a broad outline of the opportunities, challenges, and lessons you'll encounter in this lifetime. It's simple to work out, so let's start with your exact date of birth; what is it again?"

"5th November 1974"

"Ok, so what we do is take the number 5 from the *day* you were born, the number 11 from the *month* you were born, and the year, and add them all together. See?"

Charles wrote down all the numbers and added them up:

5 + 11 + 1 + 9 + 7 + 4 = 19

"Why have you kept the month as 11, but added the year as separate digits?" Suzanne queried.

"Good question Suzanne, you're on ball!" Charles commended her for spotting it.

"The number 11 is a 'Master Number'. Master Numbers are the only numbers you don't add together. However, even if we did, in your case we'd *still* end up with the same Life Path number".

"How do you mean?" she quizzed.

"Well, as it stands, your Life Path number adds up to 19, but if we added the two 1's individually, we'd end up with 28. See?" Charles added them up again:

5 + 1 + 1 + 1 + 9 + 7 + 4 = 28

"So is my Life Path number 19 or 28?" Suzanne asked.

"Neither. We still have to reduce the two digits to one single digit by adding them up again. In your case, both the 19 and 28 add up to '10'. See?" He showed her on paper what he meant:

1 + 9 = 10
2 + 8 = 10

"Suzanne, your Life Path number is '1'. Do you know what that means?"

"I have no idea" she responded in anticipation, knowing he would enlighten her. Charles reached for his Numerology book and flipped to the right section:

"Being a number 1 makes you... *'A natural born leader; you insist on the right to make up your own mind; you demand freedom of thought and action. You have drive and determination. You don't let anything or anyone stand in your way once you are committed to your goal. You are exceptionally creative and original and possess a touch of the unusual. Your approach to problems is unique and you have the courage to wander from the beaten path.*

You perform best when you are left to your own devices. Ideally you should own your own business and be your own boss. Hold fast to your life's dream and work with the determination you possess to realize it'". He paused looking up at her before adding "It also says *'Don't let pride and over-confidence be your masters. Remember, your talents and abilities are a gift from a Higher Source, which should promote gratitude and humility, rather than pride and conceit. More often than not a person with a '1' Life Path will achieve much in life as long as the drive, creativity, originality and pioneering spirit are fully employed'"*

"Wow, that's amazing!" Suzanne said in a surprised tone. "That sounds so much like me – how does that work?"

"Pretty much along the same lines as Astrology…it's the same science" Charles informed her. "Astrology deals with the way the planets were aligned on the day you were born, while Numerology deals with the numbers in your birth date. Both can give accurate descriptions about the potential your life holds, and what you came here to do – but you still have ultimate freedom to do with your life as you choose; to fulfill its potential completely, or to make some smaller version of your Self. It all depends on the effort and commitment you put in; however, the possible 'you' is contained within you from the moment you were born".

"Gosh… *everybody* should know about their Life Path number! So what's *yours*?" Suzanne asked him.

"9"

"Read yours then!"

Charles proceeded to read about his Life Path, which made him more humanitarian, Self-sacrificing, idealistic and generous.

"Hmmm….so are 1 and 9 compatible?" she asked.

"They could be!" Charles replied, smiling smugly.

He then proceeded to work out the rest of her Core Numbers and explained them to her as he went along. He explained that the *day* she was born also held significant meaning, and reading from his book, explained to her what being born on the 5th meant:

"Five is the first number to combine odd and even. 5 represents change, non-conformity, individualism, travel and adventure"

"I like the sound of that!" she pitched in "I've always wanted to travel!"

"Well it's written in your stars" Charles affirmed, looking at her intently. Going back to his book he continued;

"Five signifies opportunity, resourcefulness, and risk. 5 is extremely multi-talented and versatile, persuasive, sensual, magnetic, entertaining, scientific and analytical. 5 carries the magical mystique of quintessence that helps us experience the wonders of life. This vibration is the innate healer and teaches us to be flexible and adaptable."

Looking up at her he smiled as he added "I can vouch for that".

****

A Great Idea

In committing to be more attentive to Suzanne, Charles decided to spend more time doing things with her *and* her boys. So he started going over to her house straight from work a couple of times a week so that they could all have dinner together. He would also sit in and take part in 'Quality Time' before the boys went to bed.

Whenever Suzanne had the boys at the weekend, Charles would spend it with them at her house. Whenever she didn't have the boys, Suzanne would spend the weekend at Charles's.

They enjoyed being in each other's company, but still liked to pursue their own interests; Charles continued with his painting, and Suzanne continued with her writing. While he was painting, she would be sitting with her notepad, writing away. Sometimes she would just sit staring into space.

They would be together, but in their own zones. They would normally break from their individual worlds for lunch and dinner, and this is when they would engage in deep conversation.

"You must have so much stuff you've written by now" Charles questioned "What do you plan to do with it all?"

"I'm working on my first poetry collection, remember?" Suzanne reminded him.

"Oh yes....interesting" Charles mused, and then as if a light had suddenly come on in his head, he blurted out "I've got an idea!"

"What?" she asked in an interested tone.

"Why don't we go into *business* together – *my* artwork and *your* poetry – we could start a new range of inspirational Black greeting cards and prints!"

"Mmmm... that sounds great – the only problem is, most of my poems are far too long to fit inside a greeting card!" Suzanne laughed.

"Well I'm sure you can edit some to fit" he suggested.

"That's not a bad idea..." Suzanne looked around at Charles's paintings, and all of a sudden she began to see how some of her poems *would* fit in with the themes of his artwork.

"YES!" she shouted excitedly.

They linked hands and started jumping around the living room together laughing as if they had just won the lottery, at the thought of how much money they were going to make.

****

Think 'Kink'

When Suzanne learnt that a person's DNA can be traced through their hair even thousands of years after they had died, she started thinking more seriously about what she was doing, placing another person's hair on her head. Not only was she suppressing her *own* DNA, but she was taking on the DNA of someone she didn't even know.

Whose hair was it? Did she even know if the person was *alive* or *dead*? Apparently, it had been said that they were cutting the hair from corpses to fill the demand for the huge wig and weave industry. They were even getting hair from the temples in Asia, where people shaved off their hair to offer sacrifices. Before, she had taken pride in saying the hair she bought was '100% human', but now she wondered what would possess a naturally beautiful Black woman to stick or sew long straight hair belonging to someone else on her head and think that it's 'normal'? The worst case of 'Self-identity crisis' had to be seeing her sisters wearing long, blonde hair.

She also learnt that all energy travels in spirals, not in a straight line. Therefore kinky hair acts as a *natural* antenna to pick up frequencies from the ether.
The more curly the hair, the better able the person was to pick up the messages constantly being transmitted from Mother Nature and the Universe. When the hair is straightened, it cannot pick up on the frequencies, making the person less in tune with nature, and the messages Mother Nature sends out frequently.

Knowing this, why would she want to remove the natural kink from her hair?

Suzanne began experimenting more with natural hair styles. It took a while for her to get used to the inconvenience of having to actually comb and style her hair every day, instead of just putting a wig or weave over it. Before, she had used the excuse that it was quicker and easier to manage, and that it was just a fashion accessory, like wearing jewellery. But now, she took pride in wearing her hair natural; it gave her a new sense of pride and Self-identity. She wasn't trying to be something she was not any more. Her hair was naturally kinky, and she was going to love it and care for it as it was. She would just have to factor in an extra half hour in the morning to style it. The more she got used to it, the more she came to love it.
Walking down the street, she noticed that the brothers would give her approving looks, and one even commented that there needed to be more sisters like her.
She found a hairdresser that could do various styles with natural hair, and whenever she wanted to treat her Self or had somewhere special to go, she would go to the gym, use the steam room to wash and steam her hair, then go to the hairdresser to get it styled. It could last a couple of weeks if she wore a head tie to bed.
She realised that she looked just as good, if not better, with her own natural hair, rather than wearing somebody else's hair.

Year Three: Mind...the Gap!

She began to embrace herself in all her natural beauty.

****

Year Four: Finding Her Self

"Do you ever get the feeling that there's more to this world than we are led to believe?" Suzanne asked Charles as they lay in bed entwined around each other's bodies.

"Definitely!" Charles responded.

"...My advice to anybody would be 'when contemplating life, remember that *nothing is at it seems*'. I often wonder how this whole world would change if everybody knew their thoughts were creative".

"Yes!" Suzanne agreed "I mean, I only discovered that in the last year, and I'm *already* beginning to feel more in control of my life. Learning to take control of my thoughts has *really* helped me to begin to create the life of my dreams".

"And what *are* your dreams?" Charles questioned, hugging her close to his chest.

"Well, my main goal is to buy my house without a mortgage. I'd also *love* to set up a business empire, something that I can hand down to my children and my children's children. And I'd like my husband to help run it, you know, like a family business".

"Wow, those *are* big ambitions! What's *wrong* with getting a mortgage like everyone else?" Charles questioned her.

"Well, the idea has never really agreed with my spirit; I did some research on the word 'mortgage' and I bet you can't guess what it means?"

"Go on then, tell me"

"Well when you translate it from its Latin roots, the word 'mort' literally means *death* and 'gage' means *pledge*."

"Death...Pledge?"

"Exactly!" continued Suzanne excitedly "*Death Pledge!* The idea of committing my Self to paying this large amount of money every month for the next 25 years or until I'm *dead*, just doesn't appeal to me. I mean, who knows what's going to happen down the road? I want owning my own home to be a pleasure rather than a noose around my neck. I see myself buying my house outright".

"Oh, ok" he replied. Silently he wondered how she planned to do that though – maybe she was hoping to win the lottery, he thought.

"So what about this 'husband' of yours, what does *he* have to be like?"

"Well, he definitely has to be business-minded, trustworthy, reliable, and know how to handle money, because I plan to make a lot of it!"

"She's living in a dream-world" Charles thought, but thought he'd play along anyway.

"What else does this 'dream-man' of yours have to have?"

"Well he has to be tall, handsome, have a good sense of humour, be spiritually grounded, and love children. Oh, and he needs to be financially stable, so that he doesn't feel intimidated by *my* financial success" she finally ended her list.

"A bit like you, really" she added, looking up at him.

He smiled wryly. "Well at least you know what you want out of life"

"And what about you – what do *you* want out of life?" she asked him.

Charles sighed deeply.

"Just to be happy" he replied wistfully, looking past her out of the window at the grey sky.

"What does 'being happy' mean to you?" Suzanne pushed for something more specific.

Charles sighed again. Closing his eyes, he began;

"Being happy to me is a *state of mind*. You can be happy doing things you *want* to do, and you can also be happy doing things you *don't* enjoy doing, but which you know will lead to your ultimate goal.

"Give me an example" Suzanne pressed.

"Well for instance, I may not like my job, but I know that the money I earn doing it will lead to my *ultimate goal* which is *financial freedom* – knowing that makes me happy doing it. But there's been times when I've felt pressured to do something, and even though there's something niggling away inside of me telling me I shouldn't do it, I do it anyway, just to keep other people happy. That's when I know I'm not being true to my Self. I feel at my happiest when I am being congruent with my inner Self."

"What do you mean, 'being *congruent* with your inner Self'?" Suzanne asked. She had never come across that word before.

"Oh you know, I just mean being in *harmony* with my Self – when my *conscious* and *unconscious* minds are working together."

"Wow, that's deep" Suzanne commented. "So how do you feel about *us*?" (She thought she'd throw that in since he was in the deep-talking mood)

Charles took another deep breath before replying;

"Well, I love being in your company; you make me feel special, I feel at ease when I'm with you, like I can tell you anything. I get a warm feeling whenever I think about you, and whenever I'm away from you, what keeps me going is the thought of being back with you again."

Suzanne felt choked as she kissed him gently on the lips.

He continued;

"I'm happy when I'm with you; I *always* enjoy spending time with you, Suzanne. I want us to be together forever – why don't we have a baby? I'd love you to be the mother of my child" He murmured, looking her deep in the eyes.

That was a bolt out of the blue!

'Hasn't he *missed* something?' she thought; 'he's jumped straight over the *marriage* part to having a baby!'

"A *baby*?" she ridiculed him. "What, you think a baby will make sure we 'stay together forever'?"

Suzanne had never imagined herself as a single mum. She thought her relationship with her sons' father was going to last 'forever', but here she was now, a single mum aged 31 with two young boys to raise, and here was Charles asking her to have a third! There was no way she was having any more kids without proper commitment this time – marriage.

"It's a nice thought, but not one I can consider right now" she replied tactfully. Stroking his face lovingly she added;

"What about this business we're supposed to be setting up? *That* can be our baby!"

"Fair comment – but don't you want any more?" he asked "You're a great mother, you know".

"I wouldn't mind having another one, but the time has to be right. Besides, I don't want to end up a single mother to *three* children!"

"Babe, you know that no matter what happens between us, I'll always be here for you"

His words echoed that of her sons' father. Suzanne's mind flashed back to the time when the father of her two boys had said that to her. He too had promised that he would 'always be there for her and the boys'. But where was he now?

Suzanne tried her best not to project her disappointment with her ex unto Charles, but it was difficult.

"I just want to make you happy" he said, kissing her gently on the forehead.

"I *AM* happy!" She said, smiling up at him.

'She's always saying that', he thought.

In a way, she had taught him what it meant to be truly happy in life; it seemed to be something emulating from deep within her, not down to the things she owned (as she didn't have much), or how much money she had in the bank, or what people thought of her.

"I came into this world with nothing, I will leave with nothing, so why do I need to accumulate all these 'things' in between?" she often said.

But really, Suzanne *did* want things: She wanted the big house. She wanted the nice car. She wanted the best clothes. She wanted the best of everything. What she *meant* was, she didn't want more than what she needed; she didn't *need* 100 pairs of shoes lined up in the cupboard, or more than one house to live in, or more money than she could physically spend. However she *did* want to make a big difference in the world, and that would take money – lots of it.

Charles was different; he loved money, which is why he had chosen a career in accounts. In fact he loved studying figures in *all* their forms, including women's (which he thought resembled the figure '8'). The number 8 was his favourite number. According to Numerology, not only was it the *vibration* of money, but it also stood for infinity – no beginning and no end.

Charles was busy building his property portfolio. The more houses he had, the better, he thought. He believed that the sign of a successful man was in the car he drives, so he bought himself a second car. Having two cars was like having two coats to Charles; one for everyday and one for going out. His second car was a flash, black shiny convertible. He also upgraded his wardrobe to the best designer clothes he could afford, splashing out on colourful shirts, ties and sharp suits.

****

Her Own Universe

Charles noticed that since they had got back together, Suzanne seemed to enjoy spending more and more time on her own. She had explained to him that unless she spent time in what she called 'The Silence', she was not able to draw from her 'inner well'.

So she would seize every opportunity to be alone. On the weekends that the boys were with them, Charles would often take them out to football matches, or to the cinema, or just back to his place where they would spend hours on the play-station together, leaving Suzanne at home to spend time with her Self. She knew she could trust Charles with her sons; he was a good role model for them and completely dependable. She suspected that he enjoyed *their* company as much as they did his. She was in no doubt that he was great father material.

Whenever they returned, Suzanne would often look refreshed, and would have cooked a nice meal for them all to enjoy.

But Suzanne seemed to be becoming more and more of a recluse; she developed her own 'Self development' library, and seemed happy just spending hours reading, writing and 'meditating'. It was as if she was on some kind of a mission – her sole purpose (or should we call it her *soul* purpose?) became her writing. Her boys often commented that she had 'no friends', that she was 'no fun', and that she was 'boring'.

Charles began to notice this too. It was as if she was cutting her Self off from the outside world. She didn't even seem to need *him* anymore. She would rather spend time alone in her 'inner world' – he'd never met a woman who enjoyed her own company as much as Suzanne.

Charles preferred to paint in the natural daylight, so come evening time, he was free to spend time with Suzanne, but that was when *she* seemed to want to retreat into her own little world. Not even *he* could follow her there.

Suzanne had a habit of going to bed early during the winter months, almost as if she was hibernating. But then she would get up in the middle of the night to write. As soon as they had finished spending Quality Time with the boys, she would get ready for bed. So just when Charles was ready to 'get his freak on', Suzanne was only interested in going to sleep.

On this occasion, Charles decided to have an early night too. It was only 8.45pm, but Suzanne was already dozing off. He snuggled next to her under the thick duvet, pulling her close to him. Too late, she was already sleeping. As his Pride rose, he slipped it gently between her thighs from behind, searching for her opening. Suzanne moaned as if not wanting to be disturbed, but positioned her body to make it easier for him to access her. As he slowly and gratefully began moving back and forth, he could feel her juices beginning to flow. She still appeared to be asleep though. As he built up a rhythm, he reached round and played with her breasts, while kissing her gently on the back. She again let out a slight moan, as if not wanting her sleep interrupted. He paused for a moment, waiting to see if she would wake up and become responsive to his needs. No chance. Slowly, carefully, he carried on taking her from behind, until he finally let out a deep, soft groan as he came, falling asleep still inside her.

****

The Signs

It was ten o'clock on a Friday evening. Charles would normally come over in the late evening for the weekend, but Suzanne hadn't heard from him yet, so she gave him a call.

"Hi darling, what time are you coming over?"

"Oh, I'm not...you don't really have time for me – plus I have some work I have to catch up on" he answered in a hushed tone.

"Shall I come over to yours then?" she volunteered.

"No! He replied. "...I think I'd just like to spend this weekend on my own, you know, get in touch with my inner Self and all that."

There was a touch of sarcasm in his voice which Suzanne didn't pick up on.

"Oh, lovely!" she commended him. "Well have a great weekend, I'll speak to you soon!"

"I will" he said.

****

Two days went by and Suzanne still hadn't heard from Charles, so she called his landline. The phone rang and rang before going to the answering machine. So she called his mobile.

"Hi, this is Charles, sorry I can't take your call right now, but if you'd like to leave a message..." She hung up.

'Why isn't he answering any of his phones?' she wondered.
She tried his landline again. It rang and rang. This time she left a message asking him to call her as soon as he received it. She sat wondering where he could be. Maybe he was at the gym? No, he always went early in the morning. What if he's ill? Maybe she should go round there. She decided to try calling one more time. It rang and rang.
Just as she was about to hang up, Charles answered.

"Oh! Hi babe, how are you?"

"I'm...ok – can't talk right now, I'm kinda busy at the moment"

"Busy doing what?" she asked.
Suzanne heard what sounded like a woman sneeze in the background.

"What was that? Who's there?" she questioned him, trying not to sound panicked.

"It's just a friend...listen, I have to go, we'll speak soon, ok?" he said hurriedly as he hung up the phone.

Suzanne sat in shock. 'He has another *woman* there? I thought he said he wanted to spend time *alone*? When did *this* happen?'

She had been so focused on her Self that she hadn't even noticed Charles was feeling neglected.

"Bastard! He's gone and done exactly what I *thought* he would do! How could he?"

Should she go round there and speak to the woman, and explain that *she* was his girlfriend? 'No', her inner voice advised. So she sent him a text asking him to call her as soon as he got her message.

****

Is this...Love?

The next few weeks were like a living hell. Suzanne couldn't focus on anything. She couldn't eat, she couldn't sleep properly, she could hardly *think* straight. Charles still hadn't called. 'Probably too busy having fun with his new girlfriend', she thought.

Suzanne tried her best not to imagine him with this new woman. But she couldn't help picturing him walking down the street holding hands with her, driving in his car with her, relaxing on his sofa with her, making love to her, just as he had done with *her*. The pain she felt was unbearable; as if someone had got a knife and stuck it straight into her heart.

Feeling melancholic, she reached for her notepad and wrote a poem:

Is this Love:
A yearning, burning feeling in my heart?

Is this Love:
The pain of knowing we're breaking apart?

Is this Love:
Feeling helpless, knowing we're dying,
But not knowing what to do?

Is this Love:
Not eating, not sleeping,
Not wanting anything, but you.

All I ever wanted, I found in you.
But now I'm feeling blue,
Missing you, so much
Wanting you, so near
Wanting you to appear from nowhere...

Is this Love? Is this how Love's supposed to feel?
Oh, I wish I could heal my broken heart!

Is this Love:
The wrenching, tearing feeling at my heart?
The crying, crying, crying
As we slip further and further apart?
Oh the pain, it's too much for me to bear!

I'M CALLING OUT TO YOU
WITH ALL OF MY SENSES,
WHY CAN'T YOU HEAR?

But I need to move on,
Make a fresh start.
But it's so hard without you:
Is this...Love?

****

Be Happy NOW!

Once again, Suzanne threw her Self into her Self-development programme. She wasn't going to let the situation send her spiralling into depression, as it might have done in the past. Instead, she focused on her future, and what she wanted to achieve for her Self and her sons.

In her new bible, *'Conversations with God: Book One'* Suzanne learnt that happiness is a state of BEING, not *doing* or *having*. 'God' was explaining that most people think they can be happy by accumulating lots of *things;* by what they HAVE. But the trick is to just BE HAPPY. To reach that state of happiness, all you have to do is *do* the things that *make* you happy. Then doing the things that make you happy will eventually lead to you *having* the things you desire.

She made up her mind that she was *only* going to do the things that made her *feel* happy – she was going to continue 'following her bliss'.

She didn't particularly like doing housework, but she did it because having a clean, tidy house made her *feel* good, as she remembered Charles explaining to her. She loved being creative, so she decided she would continue to write to occupy her free time, with a view to it eventually leading her to being able to *do* and *have* the things she desired, like the nice house, clothes and holidays.

When she thought about it, being with *Charles* had made her happy, talking to *Charles* had made her happy, making love with *Charles*, had made her happy. But now she had to look for happiness elsewhere...but the more she looked, the more she kept seeing bits of him everywhere; guys with his eyes, lips, nose, smile...

"Man, I've got it bad", she thought to herself.

She had to find a way to get him out of her system, but since she wasn't ready for another relationship, she threw her Self into her work instead. She spent every bit of her free time and money writing and recording her poetry. She had 11 tracks recorded so far; only 2 left to go. Although it left no time for her to socialise, it was very fulfilling. Some of the people she met on the poetry circuit also got involved in the project; she collaborated with an acoustic guitarist by writing some poetry to his beautiful music. Another brother added some vocals and djembe drumming, while another played the sax on a track; it was all coming together very nicely!

She decided to stop doing stands at events for a while so she could focus on getting her poetry CD and book of lyrics finished.

Plus, her Christian posters no longer reflected where she was in life anymore.

****

The Purpose of Relationships

As Suzanne carried on studying *'Conversations with God: Book One'*, she learnt a new way of looking at relationships. She was to see all her relationships as *opportunities* for her to decide Who and What she chose to be, and to use them to create, express and experience greater and greater versions of her Self!

She decided to view all her relationships as *constructive*, regardless of how they turned out, since without them she couldn't grow. She thought back to her relationship with her two son's father, and remembered how broken she had been when the relationship had come to an end. She had made up her mind at that point, that she would never allow another man to affect her emotionally like that *ever again*. For two years, she had remained bitter and resentful, hating him and not allowing any other men close to her. Eventually, she had to forgive him because *she* was the one ending up all bitter and twisted, while he was happily getting on with his life. Her negative thoughts towards him only returned to haunt *her*.

So she had learnt the importance of forgiveness out of her suffering. This had helped her to become a more forgiving person – for her sake, not the other person's. She had also learnt that having un-forgiveness in her heart blocked the flow of blessings from coming her way. She was reminded of a scripture which said *'...and when you stand praying, if you have anything against anyone, forgive, so that your Father in heaven may also forgive you'*

It is impossible to receive God's blessings when you are holding on to bitterness and resentment for someone else. Suzanne learnt to just 'let it go'.

****

Honouring Her Feelings

Suzanne also learnt that when using relationships as a *tool* to re-create her Self, she first had to admit honestly to her Self and to others how she was *feeling*. This was going to be difficult; she felt emotions deeply, but rarely expressed her feelings openly. She had grown up in a love-less home, where the words "I love you" were never spoken, and where kisses and cuddles didn't exist. So she was out of touch with her feelings. She could count on one hand how many times she'd told Charles she loved him, believing her actions spoke for her. Now she was being challenged to honour her Self, by honouring her feelings.

How did she really *feel* about her break-up with Charles? She had tried to push her feelings to the side by focusing on her work, but no doubt about it, she had been heartbroken – again!

She had fallen in love with him deeply, but because she had not been able to express her feelings to him, she had lost him. Maybe if she had told him how much she loved him, he might have stayed. Maybe if she had been more sensitive to *his* feelings, he might not be with another woman now.

But before she could understand and honour *his* feelings, she had to first innerstand and honour her own. How did she feel NOW?

She was still healing; the deeper the love, the deeper the hurt. Even though a few months had passed, the wound still felt fresh.

Before Charles, she had *thought* she'd been in love, but the feelings had been based on *needing* to be loved, not giving love unconditionally, regardless of whether it was reciprocated.

Prior to him, the only other people she knew how to give and receive unconditional Love with, were her children and God.

She realised that Charles had been the only man she had really, truly been in love with. But she had lost him, because she was out of touch with her feelings.

She had not had the opportunity to let him know how she felt about the break-up, nor did she believe she would have done a good job of it. But that's why she wrote poetry.

Maybe she should write him a poem. Or a letter? She'd only just thought of it and it was a bit late now.

She decided to write him a letter, but just not post it to him.

In it, she told him that she had been very disappointed with the way things had turned out, and that she was glad she hadn't been stupid enough to have his baby. She asked him how he could have betrayed her trust after all they'd been through, and why he had bothered getting close to her boys if he had no intention of sticking around. She went on and on questioning him, crying tears onto the pages as she released all her pent-up anger and frustration. She wrote at least 16 pages before coming to a conclusion; that the relationship had been good, and had helped her to grow. All while she was writing, she continued to ask her Self "Who am I, and who do I wish to be in relation to this?" She forgave him for the hurt and pain he had caused her, and thanked him for the time they had shared, wishing him a great life (without her).

Suzanne remembered that it was not in another person's *action*, but in her RE-action that she would triumph, and that before reacting to any situation she should first re-mind her Self that she was patient, loving, kind and forgiving.

Suzanne decided that in future, she would enter her relationships not with a view of seeing what part of another she could capture and hold, but what parts of her *Self* she would like to see show up.

Her intention was to become the master of all her thoughts and feelings, so that no matter what happened in her relationships, all possibilities of hurt, damage and loss would be eliminated. She no longer chose to experience feelings of rejection, failure, or the pain associated with them.

As she lit the letter and watched it go up in flames, she felt a sense of relief.

****

Love-Sponsored Actions

Regardless of how other people treated her, Suzanne determined to keep in mind: "What am *I being*, in relationship to that? Am I being loving, joyful, peaceful, forgiving, or am I being angry, argumentative, resentful, or bitter?

By choosing to make all her actions Love-sponsored (instead of fear-based), Suzanne knew it would always produce the highest good for her Self, and in doing so, would produce the highest good for others.

Even where her children were concerned, she knew it wasn't her job to try and mould them into what *she* wanted them to be, but to teach them the basic fundamentals about life and allow them to experience life for themselves. They too were sacred souls on a sacred journey. She didn't know what they had come here to do, or to experience. Her job was to allow them the freedom to develop into what *they* chose to be, with her guidance.

Even though both boys had the same mother and father, and had come from the same womb, ate the same foods, watched the same 'programmes' on telly etc. they were so different. Micah was strong-willed from birth, with a mind of his own. You could tell him the same thing over and over again to no avail, if it wasn't what *he* chose to do. Should she try and beat this 'stubborn streak' out of him, or should she see this as a positive attribute to his character?

Despite his strong will, Micah had been a clingy baby, refusing to go to anyone but his mother and father. It was because of his clingy nature that Suzanne had been unable to return to her job.

Elijah, the older brother on the other hand, was very independent from birth. Being the first child, Suzanne had expected *him* to be the clingy one, but no, he was a very confident child who went to people easily. He started nursery just after his first birthday, when Suzanne had returned to work briefly before falling pregnant with Micah. Micah had cried incessantly from the moment he was born, and refused to take a bottle for the first nine months of his life, whereas Elijah had happily taken both the bottle and breastfed at night.

Elijah was of a more refined character, whereas Micah was rough and ready. Elijah liked doing things by himself, whereas Micah always wanted to be around people, especially his mother.

Even though they both had the same head-start in life, they were already two completely different characters and personalities, walking different paths. What worked with one, wouldn't necessarily work with the other.

"That's why children don't come with a handbook" Suzanne mused.

Even the subject of teaching a child 'right from wrong' appeared hazy to Suzanne. What is 'right', and what is 'wrong'? Right and wrong, as she had learnt, were only relative terms, depending on what part of the world you lived in, what religion you were indoctrinated into, what culture you were brought up in, etc. There was no such thing as right and wrong intrinsically.

Suzanne had worked hard to instil good moral values into her boys from a very young age. It is wrong to lie. It is wrong to steal. It is right to be on your best behaviour as much as you can be. It is right to pray and think of all the things you can be grateful for before you go to sleep. It is wrong to be cheeky to an adult – this one was hazy, as she had always encouraged her boys to 'answer her back' – to let her know their opinions on any given topic. She had always wanted to know what was going on inside their heads, instead of them just going along with anything she told them to do, but secretly rebelling inside. She didn't believe that children should just 'do as they are told' without having a chance to have their say. So her mother (their grandmother) thought her boys were 'back-chatting' whenever they spoke back to her when she asked them to do something. She didn't agree with the rule that children should just do as they are told. She had learnt so much from her boys just from listening to their point of view. Sometimes it was as if *they* were teaching *her*. To think you cannot learn from a child is an adult's biggest 'wrong', she believed.

At ages ten and twelve, they were just beginning to come into their own. Not quite teenagers, but 'young men' all the same,

Suzanne admired and respected them, just as much as she expected them to look up to and respect her.

They had been the ones to comfort her and assure her that everything was going to be alright, when Charles had disappeared out of their lives, being strong for her when they were obviously upset themselves.

****

The Goddess Theory

Suzanne was developing a deep love for her Self, and a realisation of Who She Really Was. Based on what she was learning in *Conversations with God Book One*, she wrote in her journal:

- ♥ It is not true that I am nothing without a man in my life. The purpose of our relationship would not be for him to complete me, but for *me* to share my completeness with *him*!
- ♥ I love my Self: I do not seek love for my Self through another.
- ♥ My goal in life is to know the highest part of my Self, and to stay centred in that. (Blessed are the Self-centred, for they shall know God).
- ♥ My most important relationship therefore, must be with my *Self*. I must first learn to honour and cherish and love my Self. I must first see my *Self* as worthy, before I see another as worthy. I must first see my *Self* as blessed, before I see another as blessed. I must first know my *Self* as holy before I acknowledge holiness in another.
- ♥ I am becoming consciously aware of Who I Am (God in the flesh). My personal relationships are the most important element in this process. Therefore they are *holy ground*.
- ♥ I see all those I am in relationship with as sacred souls on a sacred journey. I will always strive to see the god/goddess in every body, even when they are showing me less.
- ♥ In relationship, I will only ever be concerned about my *Self*, not about the other. It doesn't matter what the other is being, doing, having, saying, wanting or demanding. It doesn't matter

what the other is thinking or planning. It only matters what I AM BEING IN RELATIONSHIP TO THAT.
- ♥ What am I being? What am I doing? What am I having?
- ♥ My grandest dream, my highest idea, and my fondest hope should have nothing to do with my beloved *other*, but my beloved SELF.
- ♥ It's not how well my beloved other lives up to my ideas, or how well I live up to their ideas, but *how well I live up to my OWN ideas*.
- ♥ I will not lose my Self in my relationship. I will not give up Who I Am in order to be, or stay in a relationship.
- ♥ I am being the most loving person, because I am Self-centred.
- ♥ I am now and forever centred upon my SELF!

This was such a radical teaching! 'Put my *Self* first? Won't I be accused of being Self-ish and Self-centred?' She remembered Charles accusing her on more than one occasion of thinking that the world evolved around her Self.

"Everything is always about me, me, *me!*" he would say.

But doesn't the bible say to 'put God first'?

If she thought of her Self as 'God in the flesh', then surely it was 'right' to put God first? Suzanne understood that this Self-ish attitude would ultimately serve not only her Self, but others.

Even though it hadn't served her where *Charles* was concerned, she was sure she was on the right track. There was a much bigger picture emerging; this wasn't just about her and Charles anymore.

She now understood 'putting her Self first' to mean that anything she did for her Self, she did for another, and anything she did for another, she did for her Self.

Charles had no idea; not only did the whole *world* revolve around her, but the whole *universe*! Yes, the whole *universe* was at her command!

> *God said "Let there be light!"*
> *and there was light.*

...A random bible verse popped up while she was contemplating this; it took on a whole new meaning though; being made in the image and likeness of the Great Creator, she too had the power to *speak things into being*...

****

"I Am..."

One of the things Suzanne had earnestly sought God about was learning how to pray *effectively*. She was tired of praying, believing God that her prayer would be answered, and then nothing happening. But why would God withhold anything good from her?

Indeed, why.

So the issue had to be with the *way* she was praying, or what she was *thinking, saying* and *doing* while she was waiting for her prayer to be answered. The bible made it sound so easy;

'Whatever things you ask for in prayer believing, you will receive' (Matthew 21:22)

'Whatever things you ask for when you pray, believe that you receive them, and you will have them' (Mark 11:24)

But this 'ask, believe, receive' process didn't seem to be so easy when she actually put it into *practice*. How many times had she asked believing, but hadn't received what she'd been praying for? She'd asked for money, a husband, her own home, healing, the list could go on and on. And even though she thought of God as her spiritual Father, He certainly wasn't treating her like a spoilt brat; she *didn't* get everything she asked for. Why not? How did God decide who He was going to bless from who would have to go without, or wait? Did God even *make* such decisions? If not, what was the deciding factor for getting her prayers answered?

It was at this point in her spiritual journey that Suzanne came across the book: *'The Master Key System'*. In it, she learnt that 'I' is the Creative Principle; that is, anything following 'I' is creative, so whenever she started a sentence with "I..." she had started the Creative Process.

She also learnt that the word 'AM' is Present Tense which brings things into the NOW. *Every sentence beginning with "I am..." is an activated prayer* - whether it is a *positive* or *negative* statement.

So if she used Self-defeating statements like "I can't afford it" "I don't know" "I can't remember", "I'm stressed out", "I feel sick", or "I'm so depressed" she was just going to bring more of that to her.

Whereas if she used Self-empowering statements like "I am a channel for God's wealth to flow through", "I am a great creator", "I am experiencing abundance in every area of my life!", "I am whole, perfect, strong, powerful, loving, harmonious and happy!" she would attract the situations, circumstances, people, and opportunities to bring her wishes to her.

She learnt that praying is simply 'asking', and you ask through your thoughts, words and actions.

In Truth it is not necessary to 'ask' for anything, since everything is already available in the unseen realm. Just claim it! To bring it into the *physical*, Suzanne learnt all that she had to do was keep her *thoughts*, *words* and *actions* in alignment with her desires.

Her *thoughts* were creating her *feelings*, and her feelings were the *fuel* to whatever she was thinking, saying and doing. In other words, whenever she *emotionalised* her thoughts, words and actions they would become *super-charged*, and she was able to attract whatever she was *thinking about*, *speaking about* and *putting action to* even faster!

What had she been 'asking' for? Looking at where she was in life right now, she could see the results of her past 'prayers'. She had decided that she wished to be a world-renowned poet, and had taken the necessary actions towards her goal by writing and recording her poetry. But she hadn't been *thinking* or *saying* that she already *IS* a well-known poet – NOW.

'Speak those things that be not as though they ARE!'

...The way to make things happen was to *speak them into being,* with *EMOTION!*

Suzanne began visualising her Self as an award-winning poet, and speaking it out into the universe.

She suddenly remembered the poem God had given her the year she asked Him for 'The Truth'. Part of it had said;

> *"...I Am the Way that makes crooked paths straight,*
> *I Am the Key that unlocks the doors*
> *I AM the Great I AM!"*

God was actually revealing to her that *she* had the power to change her life, through the power of her "I am..." statements! Being made in the image and likeness of the 'Great I Am', Suzanne realised that she had the same creative power as God, and her "I am..." statements were the *keys* to creating the life of her dreams!

She felt powerful!

****

Believing in the Unseen

When Suzanne discovered that she could *be, do* and *have* whatever she could *imagine,* and that her *thoughts, words* and *actions* were powerfully creating her future, she decided to really push the boat out and not put any limits on her imagination.

She sat down and spent some time focusing on where she was in life right now, and what she wanted for her future. If her current situation was the effect of her *past* thoughts, words and actions, then all she had to do to create her perfect future was to keep all her thoughts, words and actions in line with her *desires* from now on.

She began to plan her future; she didn't *just* want to be recognised for doing what she loved, she wanted to make enough money from her poetry to live the life of her dreams. Her ultimate goal was to buy her house without a mortgage, so she would spend time each day visualising the kind of house that she wanted to live in, and imagining her Self *already* living in it with her sons – and husband – in detail. She had learned that when going through the 'visualisation process', everything must always be done in the NOW, as if it is *already achieved*.

She visualised her dream life with feelings of deep gratitude, and then her job was to think, speak and act as if she had already *achieved* her goals. Giving thanks *before* seeing her desires manifested in the physical not only showed her unwavering faith in the process, but helped her get on the right vibration to *attract* those things.

This is where her FAITH had to come in. She was to believe *without a doubt*, that she had *already received* what she was asking for, *before* she could see it in the physical.

'Faith without works is dead'

Then she had to 'act as if'. This was the most difficult part. In real life, she wasn't really that great at performing her poetry; sometimes nerves would grip her and ruin her performance. Left to her, she would have been happy just recording her poetry and selling the CD's with their book of lyrics online. But how would they sell unless she actively went out and performed them? She would have to sell a *lot* of CD's to buy her house with cash! But she believed in the process, and trusted that every time she went out to perform, she would get better and better. Every time she went out to perform, she would tell her Self "I am a first-class performer!"

The better she got, the more CD's she would sell. The more CD's she sold, the nearer she would be to her goal. In the meantime, her job was to visualise herself doing a flawless performance, and selling enough CD's with their book of lyrics to buy her home.

How would she *feel* if she had already achieved her goals? Once she was able to feel the feelings of having it *now*, she gave thanks to her Source, sometimes with tears streaming down her face.

****

Every time a 'vain imagination' came along (one that was not in line with her desires) her job was to 'cast it down', and not allow her mind to conjure up images of things she *didn't* want to see happen.

On one occasion, she received a letter through the door from the bailiffs. They were threatening to come and take away all her possessions if she didn't pay the bill within the next 7 days. As feelings of fear and anxiety overwhelmed her, Suzanne's mind started to conjure up images of men banging on her door and forcefully removing her goods. She knew that she had to take control of these negative thoughts before they got out of hand. If she continued with these vain imaginations, she would certainly *create* the event.

Suzanne sat in a chair and quietened her mind.

She focused on her breathing; nothing else, just her breathing. In the past her mind would have wandered all over the place but now she was able to catch it as soon as it started running away, bringing her full attention back to her breath. As it entered her body and exited her body she noticed how her outgoing breath was just slightly warmer than her incoming breath. She observed how her incoming breath didn't just expand her chest but seemed to go right down into her pelvic area, and rise up to expand her abdomen and continue right up into her armpits. She imagined that her actual *brain* could breathe as she inhaled slowly, fully and consciously, then held her breath. And then in a long slow controlled movement she exhaled totally. After a few minutes she hit a zone where she no longer needed to focus so intently on her breathing; her mind had become a peaceful void free of thoughts. Suddenly she opened her eyes, as she received a flash of inspiration. Grabbing her notepad and pen, intuition kicked in as she penned a poem:

Equilibrium

When the pressures of life get me down,

And the stresses of life make me frown
I've got to find a way to get my peace of mind
And create equilibrium.
In order for me to keep my sanity
I must find the balance between my mind, spirit and body
Let go of all the things causing strain on my brain
So I can keep my mental and emotional stability.

So I rise early with the morning sun
To give thanks for all the Lord has done
Take time out to meditate and pray before I start my day
When I focus on all the positive things in my life
I realise I'm too blessed to be stressed
There are so many things for me to be grateful for!
So by taking a few minutes to switch focus away from
I put my Self in a positive vibration...

'Blue Lotus' by Cezanne

Floating on a sea of consciousness

I realise that I am a Triune being;
"I am Love!" "I am peace!" "I am joy!"
These are my natural states of being
My inner world is creating my outer world,
My outer world is simply reflecting!

The Garden of Eden is a state of mind
The Kingdom of Heaven is within.

I let all burdens fall from my shoulders,
I let anxiety drop from my mind
I let all fear slip away from my heart
I release all feelings of guilt and condemnation
I am free from all burdens; mental, physical and financial.
I am now light.
Thank You! (Track 7 on the CD 'Seeds of Love')

Suzanne had finally found peace within her Self. Everything she desired, she learnt to first find it within. If she wasn't happy with anything she was experiencing, the way to change it was to go *within*. If she desired to be loved more, she had to first find love within, and learn to love her *Self* more. If she desired more peace and harmony in her life, she had to first create it *within*. If she desired to know God more, she had to first find God *within*.

****

"I Am What I WILL to Be!"

Suzanne learnt that there is a scientific formula behind praying, and that 'prayers' and 'affirmations' were in fact the same thing.

Affirmations are powerful "I..." statements spoken in the *Present Tense*, that when repeated often enough, reach the Subconscious Mind. The job of the Subconscious Mind (among other things) is to *make those things happen*. She learnt that the subconscious mind *only* deals with 'NOW', and that she could programme anything she desired for her future *into* her subconscious mind as long as she did it in Present Tense. Her subconscious mind was connected to The Source, and its job was to make those things happen by bringing along the right people, circumstances, events and opportunities.

Suzanne discovered that the good thing about the Subconscious Mind is that it can't tell the difference between what is *real* and what is *vividly imagined*. Nor can it tell the difference between what's happening *now*, what is *past*, or what is *future;* it only deals with NOW, which is why Affirmations have to be spoken in Present Tense. In order to stop the critical Conscious Mind from analyzing the statements and saying "No you're not!" she had to put her Self in a state of *total relaxation*. She was good at that by now.

So she made long lists of Positive Affirmations beginning with "I am...", "I can...", "I have...", "I love...", "I feel..." etc. For example;

"I am in perfect health; mind, spirit and body"
"I can do whatever I put my mind to"
"I have an abundance mentality" (There is enough/I am enough)
"I feel great all the time!"
"I love my Self"

Now she innerstood why the bible advised;

Let the weak say "I am strong"
(Joel 3:10)

Let the poor say "I am rich"

She realised that by constantly repeating 'Positive Affirmations' to her Self despite what the circumstances looked like, she could transform her life. She became more consciously aware of the "I am..." statements that she thought and said about her Self, and when a Self-defeating thought came to mind, she would uproot it and replace it with a positive, affirmative thought.

So she would replace "I can't...." with "I can....", "I haven't..." with "I have...", "I'm not good at..." with "I'm great at...", "I don't feel well" with "I feel fine" and so on.

She categorised her lists of Positive Affirmations into 'health', 'finances', 'business', 'relationships' etc, and began repeating them to her Self daily. She also wrote long lists of all the things she intended to BE, DO and HAVE, and compiled them into one long poem which she entitled *"I Am What I WILL to Be!"*

<small>(Track 8 on the CD "I Am...Cezanne!")</small>

'...Tell Us what the future holds, so that We may know you are gods!'

(Isaiah 41:23)

****

Year Five: Be Careful What You Wish For!

With her first collection of poems now completed, Suzanne wondered how she was going to get the CD pressed, marketed and distributed. She planned to duplicate 1,000 copies since it would work out cheaper to do it in bulk. This would be on top of the money she would have to find to print the book of poems. She thought it would be a good idea to give her customers the option of being able to read and listen at the same time, since some of her poems were quite lengthy.

All she had to do was to find someone to publish it, or she could *Self*-publish – but then she would have to raise the money. She decided to just *visualise* the book and CD as a finished product, and not to worry about where the money was going to come from.

She imagined her Self going out performing to large crowds, then long queues of people lining up waiting to purchase her CD's and get their books signed.

She also began attending open mic nights at least twice a week. This gave her the opportunity to perform her poetry in front of a non-judgemental crowd, which helped build her confidence. She always returned home with a buzz, which fuelled her desire to perform on stage even more.

Most weekends when the boys were at their dads, she would meet up with a friend or two and go to an open mic night. She wasn't interested in clubbing. On the weekends that the boys were with her she would take them too, if children were allowed.

Suzanne was following her bliss, and it seemed to be carrying her in the right direction.

****

"I Wish…"

Suzanne had learnt from *'The Secret'* that she could 'order' things from the Universe, much like ordering from a catalogue, and as long as she believed in the 'ask-believe-receive' process, the things would be delivered.

The first stage was to put her desires 'out there', while being grateful for what she already had. The second stage was to 'act as if' she was already receiving the things she had requested. The third stage was to be open to the abundance of the universe, and wait patiently, never doubting the process.

So she had ordered a beautiful five bedroom house, bought and paid for with cash. She also ordered enough money to be able to take her boys on holiday during school breaks, and to be able to shop 'til she dropped without having to worry about going overdrawn. She ordered enough customers to make her first poetry collection a great success, and she also ordered all the people and resources necessary to help make her business successful.

She spoke 'Divine Order' into her finances, business, relationships, health and prayed for health, wealth and happiness for all her family, friends and customers too.

Since Suzanne had always had a weakness for dark men with locks, she decided to 'order' one – but she wanted a Pisces, since according to Astrology (and judging by her experience with Charles) she believed Piscean men were her best match.

"Dark, with locs, and a Pisces, please" she put it 'out there'.

****

R U 'The One'?

Whilst out performing one night, one of the organisers of the event told Suzanne about a competition that was in progress. They were looking for poets of African descent to include in an Anthology, and the overall winner would get their poetry collection published for free. Suzanne eagerly took down the website details, and the following day, went online to get more information about the competition. This was it! This was just what she needed to get her book published; she was sure her collection would win – she could just feel it in her guts!

She called the number. A baritone voice answered. "Hello, Black Independent Publishers, Solomon speaking, how can I help you?"

"Oh hi Solomon, my name's Suzanne; I was just calling to get some more information about the competition you're running"

"Ok...what would you like to know?"

"Well, I've been on the website and viewed the criteria, and I just wanted to get an idea of the type of response you've had so far really"

"The response has been great – are you trying to weigh up your chances of winning?" he asked in an amused tone.

"Well, yes" Suzanne confessed.

"Well you have just as good a chance of winning as anybody else – but you've got to be in it to win it, so the sooner you get your poems in the better! What type of poetry do you write?" he asked.

"Love poetry mainly, anything to do with relationships"

"That always goes down well – go for it! Would you recite one for me now? I *love* poetry" Solomon requested.

"Really? Well most of my poems are really long, so I'll just give you a snippet of one, ok?"

"Ok, go ahead"

"This one's called *'Ode to My King Part 1'* and it's written in the style of ancient Egyptian poetry, ok?"

"Ok..."

Suzanne began; *"Beloved, what shall I compare you to? Spiritually, you are like a tree standing tall and strong, with roots that go much deeper than our wrong; see you remember the richness of our history, <u>before</u> slavery, when we ruled as Kings and Queens, scientists and inventors, building empires! And now, you bear the mark of our ancestors; you are strong both physically <u>and</u> mentally. You have the Genius Gene; man, you don't know how much you inspire me! ...Shall I stop there?"*

"No, no, keep going"

"Ok... Let me study YOU and get my degree from Mother Nature's university, for there is nothing more I'd like to achieve: Your eyes are like two pools, sparkling and watery, and in them I

see the perfect reflection of...me. Your nose resembles the ones cut off the great statues in Egypt; too defined for the white man's mind, but I like it!" (Solomon laughs)
*"Your lips are like two juicy mangoes, and your kisses, sweeter than honey. Your voice is like a deep, dark river, carrying me away to ecstasy...*I think I should stop there"

"Why, is it ex-rated?" Solomon asked "I was just getting into that!" *(Track 9 on the CD 'Seeds of Love')*

"No, it's not ex-rated – that comes in 'Ode to My King Part 2!"

"Well go on then, give me some more!" Solomon urged.

Suzanne sighed. "Ok...*Your neck is like a tower, strong and sturdy, and around it you wear a reminder of our history...*" Solomon interrupted her; "*I'M* wearing a reminder of our history!"

"Are you? What is it?"

"Some cowrie shells!"

"Oh! Well, you'll like the next line then; *"Your teeth are like a string of cowrie shells, and when you smile, you light up my world!"* (Solomon laughs again)

"Sorry, but this poem is six pages long - I couldn't *possibly* recite it all to you over the phone!" Suzanne concluded.

"Well I'd like to hear the rest of it – why don't we meet up, then you can give me a personal performance?"

Suzanne huffed.

"When my first collection is published, *then* you'll be able to read it all" she responded matter-of-factly.

"Oh don't be like that, you sound like just the type of sister I'd like to get to know. In fact there's an event going on this Saturday you might be interested in coming to – the African Market, we have books for sale, garments, jewellery, carvings, all sorts – they even do live performances, maybe I can even get you a slot to perform one of your poems"

"Mmmm...Sounds interesting, what time?"

"It starts at 11am. Give me your email address and I'll forward you the details"

"Ok..." Suzanne gave Solomon her email address and he ended the conversation;

"Try and make it if you can, I'd really like to meet you"

"I'll do my best" Suzanne promised.

He sent her the email straight away with the added message "I'll look out for you!"

****

The African Market

That Saturday, Suzanne attended the African Market with Micah and Elijah.

It was a beautiful event; Suzanne got there just in time for the opening Drum Call, and to witness libation for the first time; this is where they poured water and made an offering to their ancestors. It moved her spirit.

It was an indoor market, filled with stalls of African-inspired goods; books, garments, hand-made shea-butter skin care products and soaps, hand-painted ceramics, wood carvings, soft furnishings, jewellery, greeting cards and prints by Black artists, spiritual oils... "Our community is *so* talented" she thought.

She felt at home.

She enjoyed walking around looking at all the different stalls with the boys, who soon found other children to go and play with. There was a real community spirit in the place.

Suzanne got talking to some of the stall-holders; she was thinking that when her poetry CD and book of lyrics came out, this is just the type of place she'd like to promote it. She bought her Self some cowrie shell drop-earrings, and bought the boys each a leather bracelet with cowrie shells on them.

All of a sudden, she heard her name being called out; "Is Suzanne the Poetess here?" the compere asked. That *had* to be her – that's what she'd told Solomon when he asked for her surname. "Just put 'poetess'" she'd said. Fear gripped her all of a sudden, but she raised her hand anyway.

"Ah, good to see you here! Make your way to the stage, please. And next up we have..." he called the next performer on while Suzanne made her way to the stage, looking for her boys as she went. Spotting them, she called them over.

"Stay in this room, don't go anywhere, ok? I'm just going up to perform."

They said ok and ran off again.

When she reached the stage, the host asked a little about her, and she handed him her backing track CD. She hadn't been 100% sure Solomon was going to get her a slot, but she had prepared anyway.

"What's the title of the track you're performing today?" he asked.

"R U The One" Suzanne told him.

"Mmmm...sounds interesting!" he said with a wicked smile.

Suzanne retreated behind the stage and took a minute to go into her Self. She closed her eyes and took some deep breaths as she re-affirmed to her Self who she was. "I am bold as a lioness, I am a first-class performer, I can do this..." she repeated her affirmations to her Self, and just as she was opening her eyes, she heard her Self being introduced to the crowd.

As the backing track began to play, Suzanne asked "How many single sisters do we have here today?" Quite a lot of hands went up. So she asked "How many single *brothers* do we have?" A fair number of hands went up, but not half as much as the sisters. She dedicated the poem *from* all the single sisters *to* all the single brothers, and told the single sisters to keep their eyes peeled towards the end of the poem;

R U 'The One'?

Can you make my heart <u>beat</u> like an African drum? (du-dum, du-dum, du-dum)
Are you the star I've been hoping, wishing and praying upon?
Is it YOU sending ME positive vibrations, letting me know that I'M the one?
Do you love me, the Black Woman, and will you put me on a pedestal where I belong?
Will you hold me in high esteem and treat me like a Queen?

Can I look up to YOU, and give you the respect you want from me?
Do you conduct your Self with honesty, dignity, and integrity?
R U 'The One'?...

Suzanne worked the stage and put her all into her performance;
"...You are my brother and a King, so don't deny me my rightful position as your Queen,
I'M 'The One' you need; no other race can take my place,
I am your spiritual and intellectual equal!"

Engaging with the crowd, she singled out a few of the brothers who had raised their hands earlier;
"...Do you know your history? Are you mentally free? Do you know where you're coming from? Are you like a tree, standing strong? You must know these things for you to be 'The One'!"

She could see the crowd was really enjoying her performance. The sisters had big smiles on their faces as if she was speaking for them, while the brothers seemed unsure of how to react. Only a few looked like they were confident enough to respond;
"...I know this is a tall order, but brothers, if you think you fit the position, show me by the raising of your hand – that is, ONLY if you're 'The One'!" (Track 10 on the CD 'Seeds of Love')

Sure enough, only a few hands went up at the end. But one hand was raised sky-high and the brother was even approaching the stage! He helped Suzanne down the steps by the hand, and introduced himself.

"Hi Suzanne, I'm Solomon, I'm so glad you came!"

"Oh, hi Solomon – I should have guessed it was you!"

"Were you expecting someone else?"

"No – and thanks for giving me the opportunity to perform, by the way"

"Don't even mention it – it was blessed – I had no idea you were *that* good, and that poem – Yes, I AM 'The One'!" he asserted, smiling confidently.

His teeth were crooked, but he had a personality like dynamite; he was full of positive energy. He wasn't much taller than Suzanne, maybe a few inches, but he was dark with locs.

"Don't tell me – you're a Pisces" Suzanne said to him.

"How did you guess?" Solomon asked, looking surprised.

"Oh, I just had a feeling..."

"Let me get you a drink – that was a long poem!" he offered.

"I did warn you!" Suzanne laughed.

"But it was well worth listening to. I'd like to hear it again"

"Well as soon as my CD comes out, you can be my first customer!"

"Sounds great – when's it due out?" he asked.

"Not sure exactly when, but soon" she said vaguely.

"Well I wish you all the best with it – *and* with the competition! Have you submitted your poems yet?" Solomon asked as they made their way over to the vegan cafe.

"Not yet, I'm still deciding which ones to submit"

"Well you should definitely submit *that* one, *and* the one you recited to me over the phone the other day – I think they'll both go down really well"

"Thanks, I will" Suzanne smiled back at him.

Suzanne didn't know that the organisers of the poetry competition were also the organisers of the African Market. They had been bowled over by her poem, *and* her performance of it.

****

Flashback

I woke up thinking 'Damn, I wish I had a woman here right now to relieve me of this stiffie!'

A text came through from Sharon. "Do you fancy meeting up today?" it said. I like Sharon, but she's not the one for me, and I'd rather not build her hopes up; I know how emotional women can be. And besides, there are so many other options that I haven't even experienced yet. I don't know what I *want*, but I know what I *don't* want.

"Sorry, but I'm busy today" I rep-lied.

Then my mate David called to tell me about this Caribbean Expo going on in the Docklands. Said there was going to be loads of sisters there, so we should go. I didn't want to; I wasn't looking for anyone right now, I was quite happy being on my own after the break-up of my long-term relationship. But Dave, he was *always* on the look-out! He insisted he'd pick me up at 11am, so reluctantly I agreed to get ready and go with him.

He was right; when we got there I'd never seen so many black women all in one place, except in a nightclub.

"She's nice" Dave commented as this beautiful Black sister passed us, smiling at me. But I wasn't interested. Nothing really caught my eye.

So here was me and Dave having an in-depth conversation as we headed towards the 100 Black Men of London stand, when all of a sudden I heard someone call out "EXCUSE ME!"

When I looked in the direction of the voice, all I could see were colours; that's what caught my eye at first, the colours of the posters she was selling. Then, I noticed her eyes; amazing, large, deep, intense, dark eyes, beckoning me to come. "Come to bed" eyes, some might have called them, but honestly, I wasn't thinking along those lines at the time. All I was focused on was the deepness and intensity with which they drew me in. They were magnetic, and I was powerless to resist. I veered off to the right involuntarily, leaving Dave to carry on heading towards the 100 BMOL stand. I didn't even hear him call out to ask me where I was going.

As I reached her stand, I couldn't understand the strange feeling that came over me. Her eyes were still fixed on me and I began to feel all weak, light-headed, hot, warm inside, all at the same time. "What's going on?" I asked my Self.

I may be 6' 3", but in that moment I felt 3' 6".

She asked me if I'd be interested in buying one of her posters. I pretended to read one, but I couldn't really focus on the words properly. It was as if my mind and body was somewhere else, but my consciousness was locked into this person. Exhilaration, fear, anticipation, and confusion all mixed as I tried to hold it together. I could see her lips moving, but all I could hear were muffled words. It felt as if everything around us became a blur, and it was just me and her in the room.

...Once the noise came back, all I was interested in was how I was going to speak to her again. I just *knew* I was going to have to see her again, that's all that was on my mind. I chose three random posters and asked if she had a business card. After she handed it to me, I introduced my Self and began walking back to meet Dave. As I crossed over to the stand opposite I was thinking "I've got to look back – but I'm a guy, I *never* look back!"

I could feel her eyes piercing into me, and sure enough, when I turned around she was looking. She smiled and waved, and in that instance, we both knew something special had just happened.

I spent the rest of the Expo walking around in a daze. I kept looking at her card and smiling to my Self, thinking "I can't *wait* to call her!" I wasn't interested in anything else anymore. I found what I'd been looking for.

****

Newborn

Charles held his newborn baby for the first time.

"She's beautiful, just like you" he said as he kissed his fiancée on her forehead, rewarding her for all the hard labour she'd just done. "Well done"

They had decided to get married when she found out she was pregnant, but hadn't got around to it yet. It had all happened so quickly; from the time she announced she was pregnant, to him moving in with her, and now, the birth of their child. He felt proud; a father at last! At forty-one years old, this was something he'd dreamed about, but never thought would actually happen. Ok, so it wasn't with the woman he would have *liked* it to have been with, but still, "I have a family!" he thought.

Charles had been the only boy in his family. His two sisters were older than him, and although they were very close to each other, they weren't so close to him. Growing up, they thought he had been spoilt, being the only boy and the youngest, *they* had to do all the chores in the house, while Charles was treated like royalty. As a result, jealousy and resentment had built up towards him. So when his nieces and nephews were born, he hadn't had much to do with them. The only person he was still close to was his mother.

He didn't really know what to expect now that he was a father, since he hadn't had any experience with babies. But he would do his best – that much he did know. No-one and nothing would harm his baby girl.

"Charlie, can you call my family and give them the news please?" Maria asked.

"No problem".

He carefully handed his beautiful bundle back to her mother and reached for his phone inside his jacket.

"And can you get me something to eat?" she added.

"No problem, I'll do that right now" Charles responded, making the calls as he made his way down to the canteen.

****

The Ones

Suzanne chose 3 poems to submit to the competition, which was the maximum allowed; *'Who Am I?'*, *'R U The One?'*, and *'Ode to My King Pt. 1'*, all of which reflected her African ancestry.

As she collated the poems and application form, she again visualised her book of poetry as a finished product, along with the CD. She had every intention of winning. She imagined seeing her poetry book and CD on shelves in bookshops and libraries, being bought whenever she performed, being ordered from the internet, and she even imagined herself doing book signings with long queues of people waiting to get their books signed. She could see, feel, taste, touch and hear the sounds of sweet success.

She gave thanks with tears streaming down her face.

****

No Chemistry

Suzanne began dating Solomon.

To look at, he was the weakest-looking man she had ever been out with, but mentally, he was the strongest. It was as if the universe was playing some kind of cruel joke on her.

After all, he was dark, had locks, and was a Pisces. That's what she'd *asked* for. She had been sure with that combination the relationship was bound to work. He was also the most positive man Suzanne had ever met. He was always starting his sentences with things like "The beautiful thing about it is..." or saying "I'm so happy!", and he always *was* happy!

Solomon was the most loving, caring man she had ever met. He had three daughters, all slightly older than her sons, but in the same age group. He was a family man; although he was no longer with either of the two mothers of his daughters, he had his daughters *every* weekend, and *every* school holiday. They came first, as far as he was concerned. Suzanne had met them briefly at the African Market; they had been in the group of children her boys were playing with, so they were already familiar with each other.

She loved the way he interacted with his daughters as well as with her sons, and he was hard-working; not only did he work at the Publisher's during the week, he also taught Black History classes to the youth on a Saturday morning. His daughters already attended, and so Suzanne started taking her sons.

Every weekend, Solomon planned to do something different with his girls; swimming, shopping, cinema, eating out, he always had a schedule. Suzanne and her boys became part of their weekly planning. It was fun going out together, and it also gave them time to get to know each other properly.

For the first few weeks, they only met up with the children. Solomon had his girls every weekend, so the only time they could spend alone was during the week when the boys were in bed, or on the weekends when Suzanne didn't have her boys and the girls were in bed.

Suzanne liked and admired Solomon; he was a great guy. He was always telling her he loved her, and was constantly showering her with praise, and encouraging her with her poetry. He wasn't always able to accompany her when she went out to perform, but he was like the wind beneath her wings; you couldn't see him, but he was there, supporting her invisibly.

Suzanne and Solomon got along really well; they laughed a lot together, they liked doing the same things, their children got along together, they made a great team, as he kept telling her.

"I am 'The One'!" he would often say confidently.

She'd never met anyone quite like him before. He didn't do 'negativity'. He knew nothing about Universal Laws, yet seemed to operate them all effortlessly. He was the type of person who could attract anything he desired, because he was on the right vibration. One of those 'natural' Law of Attraction 'magnets'.

But still, something was missing.

Suzanne couldn't quite place her finger on what it was; she had gotten over the height restriction; he made up for it in so many other ways. And even though he wasn't that tall with only size 9 shoes, when she finally *met it*, she was surprised at how someone so puny could be so well endowed – but she wasn't complaining.

Their first night together left a lot to be desired. Solomon had been celibate for a lot longer than Suzanne could have been herself – six years. When he had split up with the mother of his youngest daughter, he had decided to focus all his energy on raising his daughters and working to provide for them. He was a great father but not so great a lover. What was Suzanne to do? Throw it all away because of that, or hope that things would improve?

She decided there was more to a relationship than good sex.

****

Locs?

Solomon combed her thick hair with his fingers. "Why don't you grow locs?" he asked.
"I've been thinking about it" Suzanne responded, running a hand through her thick hair to tame it as she looked in the mirror. She loved the way locs looked on other people, but wasn't sure if they would suit *her*.
Right now she was just happy that she was finally able to wear her hair natural and feel good about it.
"I think you'd look *great* with locs" Solomon tempted her.
"Do you?" she asked, looking at her reflection, trying to imagine herself with a head of locs...

'My King' by Cezanne

"Yeah, what are you waiting for? – you've got a good head-start there!"

7-8 inches of hair *was* a good start.

"I'm not sure..."

She was remembering what Charles had said about them looking untidy and hard to keep clean.
Solomon's ones always looked clean and tidy though. If she *was* going to grow locs, the rebellious streak in her probably wouldn't allow her to keep them looking neat and tidy though.

"Mmmm...maybe I will" she said.

"Then you'll *really* be my Queen" Solomon urged, hugging her from behind as he looked at her in the mirror over her shoulder, imagining them *both* with locs.

"Well, you're my King" Suzanne said, turning around and kissing him on the lips.

Lucid Dream # 2

Suzanne woke from another lucid dream. She was getting married (again). But as they were saying their wedding vows, it was as if the 'camera' zoomed into the groom's mouth. His smile wasn't Charles's. His teeth weren't Charles's. It wasn't Charles. Suzanne woke with a tear running down each side of her face.

"I *am* marrying my soulmate – whoever it is!" she re-affirmed to her Self.

****

You Won!

A letter came for Suzanne. She turned it over. It had a 'Black Independent Publishers' stamp on it. She closed her eyes and took a deep breath before opening it:
'Dear Suzanne,
Thank you for submitting your poems into our competition. We are pleased to tell you that you are the overall winner of our competition, and that your poem 'Ode to My King Pt. 1' has been selected to be included in our Anthology...'
Suzanne could hardly believe her eyes. She'd won! Not only were they going to include her poem in their anthology, they were also going to publish her whole collection as well! She hurriedly read the rest of the letter then excitedly phoned Solomon and her sisters to tell them the good news...

****

Year Six: Trust the Process!

The Anthology book sales were going really well, partly due to Suzanne's efforts. She was one of the few contributors who actively went out and performed their poetry as well. The publishing company had also published her own poetry collection, and both books were selling very well; Suzanne's idea to include a complimentary book of lyrics with her poetry CD was paying off; people seemed to like the idea of being able to read the words as they listened to her poetry.

Whenever she went out to perform, she always took a batch of both books with her, and her performances helped to sell them both.

Suzanne was making quite a name for her Self. She would wake up every morning thinking *"I love my life!"*

She was finally doing what she loved, loving what she did, and making a good living from it too.

As Suzanne began her rise to stardom, her relationship with Solomon began to decline.

He wasn't the type to want to hold her back, but he complained that she was out practically every weekend that she didn't have her boys. Yet he knew that writing and performing her poetry was her passion, just as much as the girls were his.

****

NOT 'The One'

It was Thursday. Solomon called...again.

"Is it ok if I come over?" he asked.

Suzanne hesitated before answering. "...OK"

She really wanted to carry on with her writing, but she couldn't put him off any longer. This was the third time this week he'd asked if he could come over, and it would be weekend starting tomorrow. She couldn't even think up another excuse.

So she reluctantly cleared her bed of all her papers, books and pens, and made way for the King.

They watched a DVD, talked for a while, and then it was obvious Solomon now wanted what he'd come for.

As he rode her in the missionary position with his face buried in the pillow, she thought about how the title 'My King' just didn't seem to fit him anymore, much like an ill-fitting crown.

After he had come, his penis slithered between her legs, leaving a slimy trail like that old serpent, the devil, trying to tempt her with his lies.

"No, you are *not* the One!" a random thought escaped from her mouth.

"What was that?" Solomon jerked his head up, looking at her, surprised.

She couldn't lie to her Self anymore. As she got off the bed, he watched his life-force trickle down her inner thigh, then he watched her wipe it away with a tissue as if trying to erase his memory.

"I need some time alone" Suzanne stated bluntly.

"Are you asking me to leave?"

"Don't put it like that, I just need to be alone" she replied without looking at him.

Without another word, Solomon picked up his clothes, got dressed, and left.

Suzanne ran a bath, scooping a handful of Aziza's *Lavender, Rose and Orange Body Scrub* into it. The Dead Sea Salt and essential oils softened the water, while the rose petals floated on top, adding a touch of luxury.

As she immersed herself neck-deep into the water, she let out a sigh-prayer;

"Please let him finish with me!"

He hadn't given her a reason to finish with *him*, so she felt she had to wait for *him* to make the decision.

Twenty minutes later, her mobile phone rang.

"Hi Suzanne, it's Solomon"

"Hi Solomon"

"Listen, I think it's best if we call it a day; I can see your heart's not in it anymore, and I don't want you staying with me out of obligation. I want all of you, not part of you"

Suzanne remained silent. She knew she couldn't give him what he wanted.

"You know I love you, and I always will..." she could hear his voice breaking –

"...But I know it's for the best"

"Thank you for understanding" was all that Suzanne could say without sounding too heartless.

As she pressed the 'end call' button on her mobile, she breathed a sigh of relief.

****

Second Time Lucky?

Suzanne decided to try again. Maybe she should focus more on his *physical* attributes this time. So she ordered a tall, handsome dark brother with locs, and a Pisces.

Believe it or not, a few months later Suzanne *did* meet another Piscean brother, this time tall, dark and handsome, with locs.

They met quite by chance, while they were both shopping in Suzanne's local supermarket. She had spotted him (dark with locs always caught her attention), and smiled. That's all she'd done, and carried on with her shopping, not giving him a second thought. But the next thing she knew, he was walking beside her, asking if she needed help with her shopping. He was carrying a basket while she was pushing a trolley so if anything, *she* should be helping *him,* she'd said. But it broke the ice anyway, and they got talking. He introduced himself as Malachi. Nice name, Suzanne liked it, but she wasn't sure about his yardie accent. They continued talking while doing the rest of their shopping. Malachi finished way before her, as he'd only come in for a few things, but he accompanied her while she finished hers, taking note of what she bought. At the checkout, they paid for their things separately and Malachi offered to help pack Suzanne's bags.

"Yu have cyar?" he asked.

"No, I only live around the corner"

"Mi wi gi yu ah lif'" he announced.

Suzanne thought carefully before replying "OK then"

He seemed like a nice enough brother; good looking, had a nice smile, and polite enough in his Jamaican way. As they took the short ride to her house, conversation flowed easily; it was as if they knew each other for much longer than an hour. When they reached her house, they sat in the car talking for another hour before Suzanne remembered the ice-lollies she had bought for the boys.

"I have to go, but thanks for the lift" she said gratefully.

"But wait! Ah so yu ah gwaan?? How yu mean, tank yu fe de lif'? Yu naah gimme yuh numbah? he said with a smirk on his face. Suzanne was attracted to his cheeky charm, but wasn't ready for another relationship yet.

"Me ah play out dis Sat'day y'noh, you wan' come?" he added.

"Playing out? What you mean, like in a group?" she asked interestedly.

He kissed his teeth.

"Cha! Which group? A sound system me deal wid" he replied, pulling a flyer from his car door and handing it to her.

"Oh…"

His sound system was called 'Jah's Blessings'. The gig was in South London. Suzanne wasn't sure she wanted to go all that way just for a night out.

Sensing her hesitation he offered "nuh worry yu'Self, if you wan' come, jus' gimme a call, mi will come pick yu up. Mi numbah de pon de flyer, seen?"

"Ok" she said, getting ready to head towards her door.

"So yu naah gimme yours?" Malachi asked again.

Suzanne paused to think before replying 'ok' and gave him her mobile number. He smiled happily and said he would call her.

"Is who you ah cook fah wid all dat shopping in a de bag dem? You need help fe carry dem in?" he asked.

"No, no, it's alright, I'll call my boys to come and help me". She called the house phone and the boys came out.

"Boys, this is Malachi" she introduced them.

They said 'hi' without even looking at him and headed back indoors with the shopping.

"Ok, thanks again for the lift" she said and waved him goodbye.

A couple of hours later, she received a text from Malachi saying how blessed he felt that they had met, and how he really hoped she would come on Saturday.

The boys would be away at their dad's that weekend, so she would be free, but did she really want to start anything with Malachi?

No.

She sent a text back saying "We'll see".

He sent a text back saying "If you come, I'll make it worth your while".

She sent a text back saying "I'll let you know by Thursday".

He replied "Ok, but can I call you tomorrow?"

She replied "Ok"

His last text said "I look forward to it princess"

Suzanne couldn't stand it when men called her 'princess'. That title suited someone a lot younger than her, she thought. If she had a daughter she would call her 'princess', but a grown woman?

Still, she couldn't help smiling at the fact that his texts didn't sound like how he spoke.

Sure enough, Malachi called the next day. He asked if she had made up her mind about Saturday yet.

"No" she replied.

"Oh, ok...I was thinking, have you ever recited any of your poetry to music before?" he asked.

"Yes, I've recorded quite a few of my poems to music" she informed him.

"Well I would love to create a track for one of your poems" he offered.

"Really? What, a reggae track? I haven't done a reggae track yet!"

"It could be reggae, could be jazz, could be soul, whatever you want" he practically sung.

"Really?" Now Suzanne was getting excited.

"Yeah man, you name it, I can do it!"

He told her that he had a studio set up in his house, and invited her over to see it.

"Sounds great!" she said enthusiastically.

It was only *after* the telephone conversation that she realised he seemed to have lost his Yardie accent.

****

Malachi's Date

Suzanne decided to go and see Malachi and his sound system play out that Saturday. He seemed like a good person to keep in touch with.

Malachi turned up almost an hour late, by which time Suzanne had almost changed her mind about going. He made no apologies for his bad time-keeping either. He looked fine, in a neatly ironed khaki-coloured shirt, army trousers with a red, green and black belt, and Dr Martin boots. His waist-length locks were neatly tied back away from his face, showing off his fine features. His dark chocolate coloured skin was smooth, and he had a small goatie beard and moustache.

Although Suzanne was attracted to him, she had her reservations.

She felt over-dressed in a tight knee-length black dress and heels.

She already knew before he confirmed it, that he was a Pisces.

All the way across London, Malachi played music his sound system had created and talked and talked about all the different places they had performed at, informing her that they had travelled throughout Europe, the West Indies and parts of Africa. They eventually arrived at the venue.

It wasn't really her scene; loud reggae music pumped forcefully against her chest, while the MC's took it in turns to 'toast' on the mic. Malachi was good; his charismatic presence and animated performance captivated the audience. He 'toasted' about the injustices of 'the system', how Babylon was going to 'bun', and how Black people needed to unite. It was good. But after two hours, Suzanne couldn't take anymore, and left the dark basement to head upstairs for some light refreshment. She bought herself a drink and found a comfortable sofa to sit on. It was only 11.30pm, and she'd already had enough.

Malachi came upstairs to look for her. "But wait, you need a res' a'ready?" he asked.

"Yeah, I just thought I'd rest my feet for a while" she said wearily.

She noticed his Yardie accent had returned.

He sat down beside her admiring her smooth brown legs; her dress had ridden up, revealing quite a lot of thigh. Suzanne tried to pull it down, wishing she'd worn something longer.

"Come mek we go back downstairs fe ah dance nuh? Is a long time I man no get fe rub up an' love up an' wine up an' grin' up and bump up fe mek me trousers lump up!" Malachi suggested.

Suzanne looked at him incredulously. She wondered if he had been smoking weed, because this didn't seem like the same person who had come to pick her up. Besides, she didn't know how to dance to reggae, especially the slow dub tracks, and had never been interested in 'rubbing up' Lover's Rock style. It just wasn't her thing.

"I'll be down shortly, I just want to finish my drink" she said, encouraging him to leave without her.

As he headed back downstairs, a beautiful sister with locs down to her waist came in. She was wearing a long flowing dress that reached down to her ankles, and flat shoes. They both began engaging in conversation as they headed downstairs together.

Suzanne waited another 20 minutes before venturing downstairs again. She could see Malachi in the crowd, dancing with this sister as if they were in a world of their own. They seemed to be moving in slow motion as they held on to each other, foreheads together as they moved up, and down, in time to the lover's rock music filling the hall. They might as well have been making love on the dance floor.

She felt disgusted. "How could he invite me out and then go off dancing like that with another woman?" she thought to herself.

Enough was enough. She decided to leave. How was she going to get home now? She was all the way on the other side of the river. She asked at the bar if they had any cab numbers. They did, so she called a cab and asked if she could stop off at the cash machine on the way back. By the time she got back home, she wasn't just angry at *him*, but upset with herself for not trusting her gut feelings.

****

Suzanne came to the conclusion that regarding relationships, *she* didn't know what was best for her, so she would leave the choice with the Person Who knew her best – her Creator.

So she stopped trying to attract what *she* thought she desired in a man because surely, God had prepared (or was preparing) someone just for her.

She ditched the idea that Pisceans were her best match; she had now been out with *three* Pisceans, and none of them had been 'The One' in the end!

Now that she had released her will to God where her soulmate was concerned, she decided to focus on other things instead. She still desired to buy her house with cash and to make a career out of writing and performing her poetry, so she focused on going out and performing, and saving the profits she made from the sales of her books and CD's to put towards her house.

It was a slow process.

Suzanne had thought that within a year, she would have saved enough for a deposit at least. She was toying with the idea of getting a mortgage that she could pay off within 5 years, instead of the 25 year life sentence.

But so far, she hadn't even saved up to £5,000. She was almost tempted to blow it all on a holiday, but she decided to stick to the plan. The holidays would come soon enough, too.

In the meantime, she continued visualising her Self and her family living in their dream home, taking fabulous holidays, and being successful in her chosen career.

One day she found herself backsliding into her old ways of thinking as she sat alone at home;

"If I had more money and I was in a fulfilling relationship, I'd be happy" she thought.

"Why not just BE HAPPY NOW?" her inner voice advised.

She remembered that it was important to get to the point where she felt as if she already HAD the things she desired; that she didn't WANT or NEED them.

"How would you FEEL if you already HAD what you were wishing for?" her inner voice asked again.

"I wouldn't feel anxious, I'd be at peace. Actually, I'd be *ecstatically happy*. I'd start planning how I was going to spend the money..."

"Well BE/DO that NOW!" her inner voice counselled.

'LET GO AND LET GOD'

Suzanne realised she was to let go of her NEED to see money made manifest, and just be open to the abundance of the universe.

She didn't NEED love, she didn't WANT money. She already HAD everything she needed. It was all within her, all she had to do was tap into the Source. *She* was the Source! By feeling abundant NOW, feeling love NOW, feeling happy NOW, she would attract love, happiness and abundance.

She recognized that the more she tried to GET money, the more she was sending messages out into the universe that she didn't HAVE it. And the universe could only reflect back her thoughts and feelings about a thing.

Once she had planted the seed of desire, all she had to do was water it and nurture it with positive thoughts, words and actions.

The 'problem' with the manifestation process is that it takes *time*...

Time is neither here nor there as far as the universe is concerned, but in the physical realm where we live, 'time is of the essence'. Its fundamental nature is like a seed; when a seed is planted, you can't see it. For months it remains hidden from view, underground, in the dark soil. But all the time it is growing, germinating, splitting itself millions of times, until the shoot breaks out, and it begins heading towards the sunlight. Even when the seedling breaks through the soil, it still doesn't look like much. But it continues to grow, and soon leaves and buds begin to appear on its stem. Yet it still doesn't look like the beautiful flower on the packet, so what do you do, dig it up and throw it away? No, you leave it to continue growing. Eventually, the buds begin to open and you see the full beauty of the blossom:

'Black Orchid' by Cezanne

– But it doesn't stop there; after the flower has bloomed and it *dies*, it bears thousands of *new* seeds, which in turn grow into millions of *new* flowers!

Now what would have happened to that seed if you kept digging it up to see if it was growing?

Suzanne learned that words of doubt, 'negative affirmations' and disbelief in the process 'dug up' the seeds she had planted in the garden of her mind. Her job was to keep her affirmations *positive*, regardless of what the situation looked like.

She decided to take heed to the little voice inside that was always telling her "Trust the process! Trust the process!"

****

Attitude of Gratitude

Every morning before getting out of bed, Suzanne would think about all the things she could be grateful for, and then express thanks with deep feelings of gratitude. This set her on the right vibration for the rest of the day.

She would then pray by speaking her affirmations out loud, referring to the notebook in which she had written long lists of positive affirmations. Pacing the floor, she spoke them out loud with power and authority. She even recorded them so she could play them to her Self just as she was about to fall asleep at night, and first thing in the morning, when she was in a relaxed state.

She spoke *life* into her health, finances, relationships, business, family, new home, and every area of her life. She also prayed for her community, and for help to do her part in healing the world.

She prayed over her son's lives, and thanked God for the promise He had made regarding them. When she had been pregnant with her first son and was contemplating terminating the pregnancy, God had told her that He had a *plan* for her unborn son, before the scan had confirmed that she was indeed carrying a boy.

After the birth of her second son, God showed her another promise in His word:
'I will pour out My Spirit on your offspring, and My blessings on your descendants. They will spring up like grass in the meadow, like poplar trees by flowing streams: One will say "I belong to the Lord" still another will write on his hand 'The Lord's'" (Isaiah 44: 4-5).

Suzanne reinforced these scriptures over her son's lives and thanked God for the Promises in His word.

She made sure she only thought good thoughts about her sons, especially when they were away from her. With all the gun and knife crime prevalent within her community, she knew that if she entertained such thoughts of it affecting her sons, it could become a reality. So instead, she used scriptures like *'a thousand shall fall at their side, and ten thousand at their right hand, but it shall not come near them'* to keep them safe, and always imagined them coming home safe and well. She taught them never to fear, and that they will always be safe because they have their angels to protect them.

She spoke over her own life:
"I am the Proverbs 31 Woman; I work willingly with my hands both day and night, and my work brings good fortune to me. My name is known because of my work, and I always remember to give God the praise. I talk with wisdom, and speak only the law of kindness. I give to the poor and needy. Strength and honour are my character, and I will rejoice in time to come because I kept them...I walk after the Spirit and I do not fulfil the lusts of the flesh...I have (or have made) fine clothes for my Self and my children, and I make things to sell, and I see that whatever I make is good....my husband is well respected; he keeps company with the wise and elderly. He has full confidence in me that I bring him good, not harm, all the days of my life...I use the talents that God has given me, and I act on my gifts in order to reach my goals..."

Now that she knew she could *think* her life into existence, Suzanne no longer chose to be poor. Why be poor when you can be rich?

As Wallace D. Wattles had put it:
'Whatever may be said in praise of poverty, the fact still remains that it is not possible to live a really complete or successful life

unless one is rich. You cannot rise to your greatest possible height in talent or soul development unless you have plenty of money. For to unfold your soul and to develop talent you must have things to use, and you cannot have these things unless you have money with which to buy them'.

There are some who would argue that you don't need plenty of money to 'unfold your soul' or to develop your talent, but judging from her *own* experience, Suzanne knew that she would have done a lot more for her Self and her sons if she'd had more money. From her *own* experience she had realised that the more money she had, the better she felt, and the less money she had, the worse she felt.

So she started telling her Self "I am rich!" "I am abundant!" "I am limitless!"

****

Sacred Woman

As Suzanne continued her Self-development journey, she attracted another book called *'Sacred Woman'* by Queen Afua. She wrote the 12 Principles of a Sacred Woman into her journal:

1. "As a Divine, Sacred Woman I am the highest physical and spiritual projection of woman-consciousness; I represent the abundance of life in health, wealth, love and beauty".
2. "I embody grace, dignity and majesty at all times"
3. "I nurture my Self through the nurturing of others"
4. "I manifest the highest principles of spirit, mind and body, through transformation of thought, word and deed".
5. "I can never be abused by man, woman or child, for I represent the active presence and power of the Almighty Creator".
6. "I have the power to heal with a glance, smile or word".
7. "I am the Original Healer, who calls upon the Creator's creation (the elements of air, fire, water and earth) to heal physically, mentally and spiritually, for I am the great grand-daughter of Mother Nature Herself!"
8. "I beam and radiate my inner divinity, by adorning my outer being with garments befitting my royal form".

9. "I am a vegetarian-fruitarian by nature; my foods contain the breath of life..."
10. "I endeavour to transform my domestic atmosphere into a PARADISE!!! My environment radiates my inner tranquillity..."
11. "I am ever striving to resurrect and exalt the divinity of my mate and counterpart..."
12. "I epitomize the highest aspect of the feminine principle in my great love of being a *woman*!"

Suzanne began incorporating the principles into her daily living, and learnt to respect her *Self* above everything, because she realised that to love and respect her *Self*, was to command love and respect from *others*.

'Shine, You Brilliant Woman, First Mother, Healer, Lover of the Universe!'

****

Year Seven: Love Attraction

Suzanne settled down for a quiet night in with a glass of red wine, and one of her favourite DVD's. She hardly ever watched telly, preferring to watch films she'd chosen her Self with the little free time that she had. She spent most of her time reading, listening to audio books or music, and meditating – that is, when she wasn't writing. She also preferred watching films with characters reflecting her own colour. Tonight, she was watching *'Dreamgirls'*. She identified with the main character Effie White; Effie was a single mother. All she could do was sing, and that's all she wanted to do. Her dream was to become a famous singer. All *Suzanne* wanted to do was to write and perform her poetry; her dream was to put out a best-selling poetry collection and help make 'Poetry' a popular genre.

Just as the film was about to start, Suzanne's message alert went off on her mobile phone. She glanced at where it was lying on the arm of the sofa, and was surprised to see a text from Charles. She hadn't even been thinking about him. She smiled as she opened the message; "Hi Suzanne, it's been a while I know, how are you and the boys?"

Suzanne pressed the pause button on the remote control.

"We're all fine thanks, and you?" she texted back.
"Very well, thank you. How's the poetry going?"
"Great! My first collection is finally out!"
Suzanne waited for the next text from him, but instead, her mobile phone started ringing. Composing herself, she answered it.
"Hi Charles"
"Hi – I hope you don't mind me calling?"
The sound of his deep, seductive voice always gave her butterflies.
"Not at all, why should I?"
"After the way we broke up, I wasn't sure you'd want to hear from me again."
"That's in the past. Let's forget about it, shall we?"
"Well...it's not as easy as that"

"What do you mean?"

Charles paused before replying; "...I'm a father now."

Suzanne remained silent for a few moments....after the initial shock of his revelation had passed, she asked "So is it a boy or a girl...and are you still with the mother?"

"She's a girl, and no, I'm not with her mother anymore. We broke up a few months ago"

"Does *she* know that?" Suzanne asked in a patronizing fashion.

"Suzanne I tried to make it work, I wanted more than anything for us to be a family, but it just didn't...*couldn't*...work"

"Why not?" Suzanne quizzed. She was on the woman's side on this one. Here was another brother walking out on his responsibilities as far as she was concerned.

"Don't make this hard for me, Suzanne".

"Well if you'd rather not talk about it..."

"She wasn't *you*!" he blurted out. "...That's what it boiled down to. As much as I tried to put my feelings for you to the side and concentrate on my family, I realised I just wasn't being true to my *Self*."

"Well were you being 'true to your Self' when you pissed off and left me for her?" Suzanne couldn't help shooting out. Her Scorpio sting wasn't in her *tail*, it was in her *tongue*.

"No...it was a big mistake." Charles replied quietly.

"Well you've made your bed, now lie in it!" Suzanne cussed, slamming down the phone, as the wound of the break-up re-opened.

As she sat there heaving with tears brimming in her eyes, another text came through from him. She opened it.

"Please, we really need to talk" it said.

"About what? You have a family now" she responded with shaking hands.

"We are not a family. I love my daughter dearly and I will always be there for her, but it's you I want"

Suzanne sat staring at the last phrase in his text. She didn't know what to say in reply. Just hearing his voice again after all this time had set her emotions off again. 'And a baby! Charles had not only had *sex* with another woman, but fathered a *child* with her! And now he wants to come back to me! How *dare* he?' she thought Self-righteously. But her inner voice was urging her to give him a chance.

Five minutes passed, and then another text came through from him.

"Can we meet up? I'd really like to talk to you in person"

Since she was learning to be guided by her inner voice, she decided she would hear what he had to say. 'But he's not coming here, if that's what he's thinking!' She knew that the chemistry between them would be just as strong as ever, so if they were going to meet up, it would have to be somewhere public. She remembered she was out performing that Saturday night so invited him to meet her there.

"We can meet up on Saturday..." she sent him the address of where she would be, but told him to meet her there after 11.00pm, by which time she estimated she would have finished her slot.

****

Love Attraction

Suzanne was in the habit of writing down her desires, as this seemed to solidify them somehow. Sometimes she used her songs and poems to express her feelings and wishes.

Every time she went out to perform, she always took note of the amount of single sisters in the crowd who were either out with their friends or alone – but without a man. Maybe he would turn up later that night when she got back home, or maybe she was just another sister without a man. She wanted to attract *her* perfect partner, but she also wanted to help her single Black sisters attract *theirs* too. So she felt inspired to write a poemsong and dedicate it to them. She would be performing it for the first time that Saturday, so she rehearsed all week in front of the mirror to get it right.

When she arrived at the venue, once again she noted the amount of single Black sisters in the place. Some she knew personally from the poetry circuit; so she sat with a group of them and enjoyed watching their performances. Soon it was her turn.

As she began singing, she tried her best to emotionalise the words, which wasn't difficult:

I've been on my own too long
And I'm tired of spending my nights alone
I'm looking for a love that's true
Someone to call my very own.

Lord can you help me please
To attract the man of my dreams?
Tell me what I have to do
To attract a love that's true
Please...

Oh Lord, show me the way
To find the perfect One for me
What steps must I take
To bring the man from my dreams into reality?

(Inner Voice)
First, I must heal my Self from the emotional damage caused by past relationships
The hurt, the pain, the wounds that keep opening up again and again
Each time I'm reminded of a negative experience it starts a chain reaction;
I lash out, shout and scream, say words I don't mean
And before I know it, I'm alone again!

Please...

Oh Lord, show me the way
What steps do I have to take
To find the perfect One for me
Who'll give me the commitment that I seek?

(Inner Voice)
I must learn to drop the emotional baggage I've been carrying around for years
Let go of all my insecurities and fears
Releasing bitterness, hurt and pain
Forgiving, so I can heal from within
And learn to love and trust again...

Even though the poemsong was over six minutes long, Suzanne had memorized it so well, she made no mistakes. It was like a teaching tool to help women prepare themselves for their soulmate. It hadn't so much been written *by* her – it had more come *through* her. She recited the last lines;

Now I trust and let go because I know that
DREAMS DO COME TRUE.
_(Track 11 on the CD 'Seeds of Love')

As Suzanne left the stage to a resounding applause, a familiar figure approached her.
"You again."
"Me again."
They hadn't seen each other in nearly two years. He couldn't believe how much she'd changed.
"Damn, you look good enough to eat!" he exclaimed impulsively. She smiled, thinking that all her efforts had paid off.
Suzanne had by now, gone from wearing the wigs and weaves, to wearing her hair natural. It was more work and almost just as expensive to maintain, but somehow, it gave her a new sense of pride and Self-identity. For this occasion, she'd had it done in a Bespoke Hairstyle; cornrow twists going up off her face into an elegant bunch on top.
Her clothing style had changed, too. She no longer wore man-made fibres against her skin, but stuck to natural cloths like cotton, wool, linen, hemp and silk. Her clothes were comfortable, soft and flowing; she tended to avoid understated clothes, preferring prints with an ethnic feel, which made her look more daring and exciting

in appearance. There was grace in her movements, reflecting her keen sense of harmony and refinement. Her makeup was natural-looking, enhancing her features rather than changing them completely.

'She definitely seems to be going through some sort of transformation' thought Charles '– for the better'.

What Charles was seeing was her true natural *inner* beauty shining through.

"Can I buy you a drink"? He asked, taking her by the elbow.

"That would be nice" she replied, thinking 'Why did he have to touch me?' He *knows* what his touch does to me!" It sent an electrical current right through her whole body.

As they stood by the bar talking, invisible sparks were flying everywhere.

They couldn't really hold a proper conversation because of the noise, so Charles suggested they go somewhere quieter. Suzanne recommended the lounge bar upstairs. She left her books and CD's with her sister Janice who was still promoting her Black History artefacts, saying she would be back soon. Janice looked at Charles and said "I remember you!" and gave Suzanne an approving smirk.

As they sat on the comfortable leather sofas, a waiter handed them both menus.

"Would you like anything to eat?" Charles asked.

"No thanks, it's too late for that" Suzanne responded "But I wouldn't mind a cup of peppermint tea, if they have any".

He looked through the menu, and then said "Yes they do, I think I'll have one too".

Charles signalled to the waiter to come back over, and ordered a small pot of peppermint tea.

"Ok I'm ready, fire away" Suzanne said, looking him straight in the eyes.

Looking back at her regretfully he held her gaze as he said "Suzanne, I'm really sorry for any hurt and pain I may have caused you"

"*May* have?" Suzanne replied sarcastically. "*May* have?" she repeated.

Sarcasm is the lowest form of communication, and it failed to help the situation.

Ignoring her remark, he continued; "...I know I did wrong Suzanne, but all I'm asking for is another chance. I know now that it's *you* I want to spend the rest of my life with"

"What about your baby mother?" Suzanne quizzed. "How would *she* feel about this new arrangement of yours?"

"I don't want to talk about her too much or put her down in any way, but all I can say is it's over. I'm never going back. It's you I want" He repeated. "I've missed you so much Suzanne, all the time I was with her, I've been wishing it was *you*. I thought I could make a life with my new family, but I was only lying to my Self. As much as I love my daughter, I have to take *my* needs into consideration as well. I don't just *want* you Suzanne, I *need* you...I was wrong. I'm sorry, please forgive me?"

His words played with her heart strings, but she tried her best to stay in control.

"What about the mother of your child?" she asked.

"Look, we'd only known each other about six weeks and before I knew it, she was telling me she was pregnant. I tried my best to do right by her, but it wasn't long before I knew I'd made a big mistake. But does that mean I have to suffer the rest of my life for it? I'll always be there for my daughter, but I'm not interested in being in a relationship with her mother anymore. I want *you*. I'm still madly in love with you Suzanne"

This was the first time Charles had told her he loved her out of his own free will, not before, during or after sex, or with the influence of alcohol egging him on.

As she looked at him from across the table, he smiled sheepishly with that boyish grin, and a pleading look in his eyes.

"When did you break up with her?" she continued to question him.

"I moved out a few months ago. She was making my life a living hell – I couldn't do anything right"

"Well it's your daughter I feel sorry for. *She's* the one who has to suffer in all this" Suzanne stated bluntly. "How old is she?"

"You're right. She's only sixteen months old. She's adorable, but I *will* be there for her and have her as often as I possibly can" Charles claimed.

"Do you have a photo of her?" Suzanne asked.

Charles brought out his mobile phone and showed Suzanne the picture on his screen-saver.

"Oh, she's beautiful!" Suzanne exclaimed.

"How's your relationship with her mother now?"

"Maria? Not good. But it hasn't been good for months, even before Ebony was born. She seemed to switch on me the minute she got pregnant" Charles sulked.

Suzanne remembered how she had been when *she* was pregnant. Those hormones had played havoc with her emotions; she remembered the time she ripped her son's father's jacket clean off his back.

"Are you sure it's not just her hormones?" she asked in defence of the woman.

"What do I know? All I know is that I'm not in love with her, I'm in love with *you*".

As they sat staring at each other from across the table, Charles reached over for her hand.

She knew that if they got too close, touched skin-to-skin, she wouldn't be able to control herself. She withdrew her hand before he reached it.

He looked down at the table, feeling almost defeated.

"Please Suzanne, give me a chance to make it up to you. I'll do anything to have you back in my life. Just name it, and I'll do it."

This was too much for Suzanne to take in. Getting up she replied "This situation was not caused by me, and it's not for me to try to fix it"

As she walked away, he rushed after her.

"How are you getting home?" he asked.

"My sister has a car"

"Let me drop you home – come on, that's the least I can do."

Suzanne exploded.

"The *least* you can do? You go off and make a baby with another woman and then come telling me the least you can do is give me a f***ing ride home?"

Charles took her by the arm to slow her down. She stopped, spun around and glared at him. Trying again he pleaded;

"It would give us a chance to talk some more. Look Suzanne, We Belong Together but if you're too angry too see that.....I mean, if you're prepared to let your hurt and anger at my mistake keep us apart then I'll have no choice but to walk away and we'll spend the rest of our lives wondering what could have been...or we can take this opportunity to examine what's in our hearts. Let me drive you home and we can just...... talk."

Suzanne paused before replying "...Okay"

By the time they arrived back downstairs, the event was over and Janice was packing up the stand.

As they walked to the car, Charles tried to put his arm around her shoulder to protect her from the cold wind blowing, but she refused his gentlemanly gesture, pulling her coat tightly around her instead.

They drove in silence for the first five minutes, before Suzanne asked if he could put some music on. As soon as he pressed the play button, one of the CD's Suzanne had compiled for him some years earlier began to play. They looked at each other and smiled. Memories flooded back to her.

"I have to admit, I *have* missed you" Suzanne said reluctantly.

Charles reached over and took her hand. He placed it on the gear stick *of the car* and put his hand over hers, so she could help him change gears, like they used to do.

Silent tears began to fall down her cheeks. Looking out of the window, she wiped them away before he could notice.

As much as she wanted to be strong, she knew she was powerless to resist him.

****

Re-united

They arrived at Suzanne's house. She turned the key and opened the door gently, hoping the boys would have gone to bed by now. At 11 and 13, they were old enough to stay at home by themselves now, but whenever she was going out, she always told them to be in bed by 11pm the latest. Sometimes they stayed up late playing video games. It was half term, so there was no school the next day, and no reason for them to go to bed early. It was dark and quiet, so they had obviously been obedient. She checked in on them just to make sure. Charles asked if he could take a peek too; he had been like a father to them, and he felt slightly guilty about his sudden exit from their lives.

He followed her into the living room.
"Would you like a cup of tea or anything?" Suzanne asked.
"I've had a cup of tea, so I'll take the 'anything' if that's ok with you" Charles said with a boyish smirk.
"Ha ha, very funny" she scoffed.
As she joined him on the sofa, they sat staring at each other from opposite ends for what seemed like ages.
He was thinking about how beautiful she looked - even more so if anything - and she was thinking about how stupid he'd been for going off and making a baby with another woman.
"I can't believe I'm actually here with you again – I didn't think it would happen" Charles finally said.
"Me neither" Suzanne replied " – But I'm not jumping back into another relationship with you, if that's what you're thinking!" she added.
"I know I hurt you, but I'm going to do everything I can to make it up to you" Charles said, reaching over for Suzanne's hand again. She withdrew.
"It's like you said, it's not as simple as that – you have a baby and a baby mother to think about now" she reminded him.
"I know...but can you forgive me?" he asked.
"I've *already* forgiven you. I did it for *my* sake, not yours"
"That's one of the things I love about you Suzanne; you find it so easy to forgive" he said, sliding slowly over to where she was sitting.
"*Forgiveness is the fragrance that the violet sheds on the heel that has crushed it.*" She recited.
He paused, taking in what she just said.

"Beautiful, did you write that?

"I wish...no, it was Mark Twain"

As he continued to shift his way over to her she asked anxiously "Where do we go from here?" After 8 months, her body had ceased to let her know she desired a man, but she could feel the passion re-awakening within her again.

"Well I've never been one to beat around the bush, so I'm just going to lay my cards on the table" Charles asserted, placing his arm on the back of the sofa behind her.

"I want to be with you, Suzanne, I don't want anyone else. I know I have a baby to think about, and that's complicated matters, but I've never been more sure about anything in my life"

Suzanne still wasn't sure if she should give in to him. It had been a long time since they were last together; she hadn't even told him about Solomon yet, and she wasn't sure how the boys would feel seeing him back here again.

"We really need to talk before deciding whether this would be a good idea" she said.

"...It's not just about me and you, there's your daughter, and my sons to consider, and your baby mother..."

"I know, I know..." Charles whispered, laying a finger on her lips. He kissed her gently. If she hadn't been sitting down, her knees would have given way.

She kissed him back, wholeheartedly. As they embraced passionately, their tongues played with each other while their hands re-discovered each other's bodies. She could feel her temperature rising; there seemed to be a ball of fire between her legs.

"I don't want to have sex with you, not tonight" she said weakly.

He kissed her on the neck, and as he slid her top up, he slipped his hands around her back and undid her bra, exposing her bare breasts. Cupping them in his hands, he slowly began sucking each of her nipples. She writhed underneath him; by now she was wet, but it didn't seem to put out the fire.

He slipped his hand up her skirt, stroking her inner thigh as he searched for the elastic in her knickers. Finding it, he pulled it to one side and began massaging her wet clitoris with his finger while he continued sucking her nipples.

"Oh my god, I've missed you!" Suzanne whispered.

"I've missed you too" Charles mumbled between mouthfuls.

Suddenly, she pounced on him like a lioness, tearing his clothes off. He willingly helped.

As he sat on the sofa naked with Pride standing to attention, Suzanne stripped off too, saying "I'm starving, so you'd better know what you came here for!"

She stood on the sofa with feet either side of him looking like a Nubian Queen, and his *face* was her *throne*. As she sat on it, he grabbed hold of her bum cheeks, pushing her into his mouth. He ate her yoni like it was his favourite fruit. She looked down at him and he looked up at her, and in that moment, they re-connected again.

When he had finished, Suzanne re-acquainted herself with Pride, sucking as if it was her favourite ice lolly, trying to finish it before it melted in the hot sun.

Charles lay her on the sofa and lay on top of her. As he entered her slowly, they both exhaled deeply.

"You're just as I remembered", he murmured in her ear.

It was pure lust as they laughed, joked, and talked openly as they re-enacted some of their favourite positions.

"Go deeper!" she commanded. He didn't think he could *get* any deeper, but upon her request, he found another half an inch to put inside her.

As they approached the finishing line, he made his signature deep-throated groan of gratitude, while she let out her signature sigh of relief.

Just as they both climaxed Suzanne was sure she heard the sound of the door creak shut, and the boys sniggering to themselves as they ran back to their bedroom.

****

Reflections

The following morning Charles told Suzanne that he hadn't had sex with his daughter's mother since a few months into her pregnancy. She believed that if she had sex, she might lose the baby. And then after the baby had been born, she was always 'too tired'. He had been starved.

"So what attracted you to her in the first place?" Suzanne asked.

He was about to tell her that it was her beautiful features and golden, flawless skin, but thought the better of it. Sometimes, when conversation dried up – which was quite often – that's what he would focus on. But instead, he told her that they didn't have as much in common as he had originally thought. They were both professionals (she was a barrister), they both owned their own properties, they both liked going to the theatre, and doing things 'buppies' liked to do. But they didn't have *chemistry*, like he did with Suzanne, and he didn't feel like he could talk with her about anything, like he could with Suzanne.

Suzanne told Charles about Solomon. It didn't seem to bother him, especially since Solomon had decided not to keep in contact with Suzanne – he'd said it would be easier for him to get over her if he had no contact with her.

As they lay entwined in bed, they talked about the events that had led to their break-up. Charles explained how he had felt shut out, like she didn't need him anymore. Suzanne explained to him that there were going to be times when she needed to spend time on her own, in order to do what she did.

"Relationships have their seasons" she explained; "Mother Nature really has shown us this. Just as there is Summer, Autumn, Winter and Spring, relationships also go through their seasons too; it can't always be Summer. There are also the cold winter months, when it seems as if everything has died, but in Spring, everything starts to blossom, and before you know it, it's Summer again! The problem is, most people give up during their winter period, thinking the relationship has died. That's just what *you* did, Charles. If you had just hung on, you would have seen it start to blossom again."

Charles thought about what she had just said; "You're right. I must remember that next time we're going through our 'winter season' again".

Suddenly, he got up, swung his legs round and sat on the edge of the bed, as if he had just remembered something. Placing his elbows on his knees and his head in his hands, he closed his eyes, as if he'd just taken the weight of the world on his shoulders. Suzanne came up behind him and wrapped her arms around his chest, her nipples grazing his back. Slow, silent tears began to fall down his face. Turning to look her in her eyes, he whispered "I'm sorry". She started to cry too. In that moment they both realised their relationship would never be the same again. Now there was a baby and a baby mother who would always come between them.

Just then, his mobile phone started ringing in his jacket pocket. He looked at her as if seeking approval to take the call. She nodded, un-embracing him as he got up to answer it. She could hear the woman's voice from where she was sitting.

"Is Ebony ok?" he asked anxiously.

He relaxed at her reply, then tried to calm her down, as she appeared to be ranting and raving down the phone.

As he ran his hand from his forehead to the nape of his neck, Suzanne knew that the woman was transferring her negative energy unto him, and that *she* was going to have to be the one to remove it again.

****

"She wants to go out tonight, and she wants me to babysit" Charles told Suzanne.

"Why don't you bring Ebony here?" Suzanne suggested.

"She said it's better if I look after her at *her* house, that way she'll be safer"

"That's ridiculous!" Suzanne exclaimed.

"You're her father! Tell her you want to take her to meet your family"

"I'd rather just keep the peace"

"Are you sure she's not just trying to get you to sleep over there?" Suzanne asked suspiciously. "What if she wants you back?"

"Well that's not going to happen, is it?" Charles assured her, taking her by the hand and pulling her close to him. "It's you I'm in love with, just remember that".

"Well you're going to have to let her know that you have a woman, and that you can't keep staying over there – you should start having your daughter at weekends so she can have her break too".

****

Introduction

It was a beautiful Saturday afternoon. The sun was shining brightly, with not a cloud in the sky.

It was Charles' first time having his daughter for the whole day. Ebony's mother Maria hadn't agreed to him taking her for the whole weekend, instead insisting that he needed to 'build up' to it.

It was now 11.25am. He had dropped Suzanne off on the High Road to do some 'retail therapy' while he went to collect his daughter. It took a while before Suzanne's mobile phone rang.

"Hi babe, I've got her, where are you?" he asked.

"I'm in the indoor shopping centre"

"Oh good, I've just parked in the car park, can you meet me there?"

"Ok"

By the time Suzanne reached the car park, Charles was already approaching carrying his daughter and the bag her mother had packed for her. She was wearing a beautiful sleeveless floral print dress with frilly ankle socks and pink sandals. Her hair was styled in two big puffy bunches with colourful bobbles to keep them in place. She was the spitting image of her father. She had taken most of her dad's mocha skin colour, and even her eyes and nose resembled his. No doubt, she was a daddy's girl.

Suzanne felt nothing but love for the little girl.

"Suzanne, meet Ebony, Ebony meet Suzanne" Charles introduced them.

"Hello Ebony!" Suzanne cooed.
Ebony reached out her hands for Suzanne to take her.

"Oh, my goodness!" Suzanne exclaimed, taking Ebony from her father while he took her bags.

They took to each other straight away.

"She's gorgeous!" Suzanne said to Charles.

"Yes...sometimes I find it hard to believe I helped create something so beautiful" he replied, looking at his daughter adorably.

They spent the next two hours shopping for clothes and toys for Ebony. Suzanne enjoyed picking out little dresses, cardigans and hair accessories, almost as much as she enjoyed shopping for herself. And it made a change from buying boys clothes.

They found a nice restaurant to have lunch in, and while Charles ordered their food, Suzanne looked in the bag that Maria had packed for Ebony. Finding her lunch, she asked a waitress if she could warm it up. She put a bib on Ebony, and watched in amusement as Charles fed his daughter. By the time he was finished, Suzanne was glad they had bought another dress she could change her into. After Ebony had her juice, Suzanne took her into the women's changing room and changed her nappy and dress. By now, Ebony was tired.
Carrying her back into the restaurant she asked Charles "Where's her pushchair?"

"Oh...I forgot it" he said looking embarrassed.

"Oh, never mind, just remember it next time, ok?" she said laughing.

****

Suzanne wanted Charles to do right by his daughter just as much as he did, and she supported him in spending as much time with Ebony as he possibly could. So twice a week, Charles would go to Maria's straight from work and spend a couple of hours with his daughter, returning to Suzanne's after Ebony went to bed at 8pm.

Maria would often offer him dinner, but he always made sure he had a snack before he got there, and waited until he got back to

Suzanne's before having his dinner. He didn't want Maria to feel that he needed her in any way.

***

Sharing Space

Charles and Suzanne decided to move in together, for practicalities sake more than anything. If Charles was going to start having Ebony regularly, he would need Suzanne's support. Plus, he spent most of his time at her place anyway. He had a three-bedroom house already, so to him, it made sense for Suzanne and the boys to move in with him, but when he suggested it to her, she objected.

"It's too small. Micah and Elijah are getting big now and will soon need rooms of their own. Plus Ebony will have to have her own room, and we need to set up an office if we're going to start this business. We need more space."

Charles thought more carefully before replying "You're right. Five of us in a three-bedroom house *would* be a bit cramped. Right, I'll sell my house and buy something bigger, ok?"

***

It didn't take long for Charles' house to sell; it was in perfect condition, and in a desirable location. Everything seemed to work out for the good; he had a cash buyer so there was no long chain. In three months, the sale was complete. During that time, Charles, Suzanne and the boys spent most weekends and some evenings looking for a house that they all liked. They finally found one in Croydon near a park and good school. It was slightly over Charles' budget, so he sold one of his investment properties to put towards the house, and towards setting up their business.

Suzanne gave up her council property and sold or gave away most of her possessions, advising Charles to do the same. This was going to be a new start for them all.

Wings of an Eagle

Charles woke from a vivid dream. Suzanne had been watching him sleep.

"What were you dreaming about? You seemed all jittery" she asked, stroking his face.

"Oh man...I was having this weird dream...I was standing on the ledge of this high-storey building" he closed his eyes, reliving it.

"I looked down...I must have been at least 100 floors up, and my feet could barely fit on the ledge – I was scared shitless. Then I noticed a guy standing to my left on safe ground, watching me. He had these huge wings, like eagles. My foot slipped, and just as I was starting falling, next thing I knew, he was right there, catching me. He placed me where he'd been standing – then he was gone. I didn't even get a chance to thank him".

"...Then another scene; I was looking for him. I really wanted to thank him for saving my life. As I walked down a crowded street, I met another man. I seemed to instinctively know that he was another angel. He gave me a cheque for a lot of money – then he disappeared too"

"Wow, what do you think it means?" Suzanne asked.

"I don't know...but I've been thinking a lot lately about giving up my job and pursuing my art instead. That's a BIG leap of faith. I guess subconsciously, I'm afraid I'll fail"

"You won't fail, Charles! We're in this together now; two heads are better than one" Suzanne did her best to convince him.

"Yes but it's not just me now; there's the mortgage to pay, Ebony, you and the boys to support as well. How will I manage?"

"Trust the universe Charles, the universe is abundant, the universe will supply – come on, I learnt all this stuff from you!" Suzanne reminded him.

"...And the sooner you get off the plantation, the better!" she added.

He laughed.

"You're right. I should know better. I'm seriously going to work out the maths and see if it would be a viable option to give up my job"

"Well you don't have to do it straight away – let's get this business off the ground first"

****

Friends?

The house phone rang.
Suzanne answered it. It was Maria.
"Is Charles there?" she asked.
"Hi Maria, how are you?" Suzanne responded.
"I'm fine, thanks"
"Is everything ok?"
"...Yes, I just need to speak to Charles"
"He isn't here at the moment, can I take a message?"
"Yes, can you tell him to call me as soon as he gets this message – actually, I'll just call his mobile, thanks"

Suzanne caught her before she hung up;

"Maria?"

"Yes?"

"I think it would be really nice if we could at least be friends. Ebony will be spending time here, and it would be much better for her if we both got along, don't you think?"

"*Friends?*" Maria sneered.

"You steal my man and then come telling me you want to be *friends*?"

"I didn't steal your man, Maria. Charles and I had a history long before he met you. I'm sorry things didn't work out for you, but I didn't *steal* him from you"

"Well as far as I'm concerned, we were still together when he started seeing you, so what do you call that then?"

"But I thought he had moved out?"

"Well he had, but we didn't say we weren't *together* anymore"

"Oh...so you *were* still together?"

"Yes!"

"You mean (whispering now) you still had a sexual relationship?"

"What business is that of yours? Is sex everything?" Maria stated bluntly.

"Oh, so you *weren't* still having sex" Suzanne breathed a sigh of relief.

"Whether we were or we weren't, you still stole my man!"

"Listen Maria, somehow we have to get past that. Charles and I are back together again. He has a daughter with you. I love Ebony as much as I love Charles, and I'd like us all to get along, if possible"

Maria hung up.

"Well at least I tried" Suzanne thought.

****

Settling in

Charles began having Ebony every other weekend; they arranged it so that Ebony came the same weekends the boys were there. That way, they had alternate weeks to spend together without any children.

Suzanne and the boys looked forward to when Ebony came. She was a great addition to the family. She had her own room which was decorated in pink and purple, and the boys each had their own rooms as well. On those weekends, they did things together as a family. Due to the age gap between the boys and Ebony, it was difficult to decide what types of films to watch at the cinema, but they enjoyed doing things together like going to the monthly *Kemet Market*, eating out, going to the park, and swimming.

The boys doted over their 'little sister' as they liked to call her. Everywhere Ebony went, one of the boys followed to make sure she was ok.

Suzanne enjoyed having a little girl to dress and comb her hair, and play dolls with. It was definitely different to having boys!

Some weekends the boys would go to their cousins, so Suzanne and Charles would do things with Ebony on their own. Sometimes Suzanne left Charles to spend Quality Time alone with his daughter.

All of them seemed to settle into the new routine effortlessly. The only thing Suzanne had a problem with was the added laundry, cooking and cleaning.

"Do you think we could get a cleaner?" she asked Charles.

"Even if it's just to clean the kitchen, bathroom and toilets once a week – that would really help"

"I don't see why not. The time we spend cleaning could be put to better use – we have a business to set up, so go right ahead and find one"

****

Planting the Seed

When Suzanne woke before dawn, Charles had already left the bed. 'Where could he be so early?' She wondered. 'Maybe he's gone to use the toilet'. She waited five minutes. When he hadn't returned, she got up to look for him.

Bleary-eyed, she headed downstairs. She could hear what sounded like chanting coming from the living room. As she approached, she realised Charles was doing – affirmations!

When she opened the door to the living room, he stopped. Turning to greet her he said

"What are you doing up so early babes?"

"Looking for you" she said, making her way towards him.

"Wow, I didn't realise you did those too!" she added.

"What, affirmations? Of course, how do you think I've achieved so much in life? I speak it into being!" he smiled at her assuredly.

"Well maybe we should start doing it together" she suggested.

"That's a great idea!" he agreed.

Suzanne locked the door.

Taking him by the hand, she led him to the sofa.

As she was only wearing a short night dress and he was wearing loose-fitting pyjama bottoms, when he sat down and she straddled his lap, it was easy for her to just slip it in. Once he was all up inside her, she told him not to move, but to close his eyes and focus on his breathing. She did the same. By focusing on their breathing, she told him that they would be better able to control their natural desire to begin thrusting.

Sitting upright, she placed her left hand over his heart, and instructed him to do the same to her. As their breathing slowed right down, they reached a deep state of relaxation and entered the Alpha state, where their subconscious minds were in touch with Universal Mind. Suzanne followed her inner guide as she took Charles through a guided visualisation, asking him to describe *in detail* how his life would be if it was perfect.

"I'd be running my own business instead of working for the white man, for a start"

"Doing what?"

"Working with you, creating products using *my* artwork and *your* poetry"

"What would that look like?"

Suzanne encouraged Charles to paint a vivid picture in his mind of how the business would run; she nurtured his seed by asking him the relevant questions that would help him build a clear image. As he began sharing his vision with her, she built up a clear image in *her* mind too.

He explained that it would be a *creative* business, not a *competitive* business, and explained the difference between the two. He wanted all their employees to be able to climb the ladder of success, and to make them feel as if it was just as much *their* business; they would get *out* what they put *in*. He wanted to offer monthly bonus plans, yearly bonuses, and incentives to keep them happy so they work-played at their best. His aim was to attract the best employees and *keep* them.

Charles understood that some people are *day* people and some are *night* people, so he wanted the office hours to reflect this; he said the office should open at 10am rather than 9am to give parents time to take their children to school first. He believed this would prevent their employees arriving at the office feeling stressed before they even started work. He wanted greater flexibility in working hours, especially for working parents, whose obligation should be to their children, not their employer. So instead of the office closing at 6pm, it would close at 8pm for those who wanted to start later and work later. Suzanne agreed; Micah, who had been born in the morning always rose early, whereas Elijah who had been born at 12.20am seemed to prefer staying up later the older he got.

Charles shared his dream of owning a High Street shop, with offices above it. They would sell their greeting cards, prints, and other inspirational products featuring artwork and poetry by artisans of African descent, and would also sell their goods from the shop around the world via their website. The shop would also offer a personalised greeting card and a framing service to walk-in customers.

"That's fantastic" Suzanne kept her voice slow and rhythmic as she continued to water the seed;

"How much money would you have to be earning for you to leave your job?"

"At least £50,000 a year" he replied.

"Do you believe it is possible for you to earn this, and more, by running your own business?"

Charles thought for a moment before replying "Yes"

"How will you earn that money?"

"I'm not sure, but I believe it's possible" he replied.

"That's all that is needed"

Suddenly, a surge of sexual energy rose up their spines; by resisting the urge to thrust, they were able to bypass the four lower chakras and feel their sexual energy rise straight to their crown chakras! As their third eye opened, they were able to see straight into the non-physical world...

"Yes, I can see it!" she exclaimed as he ejaculated a spiritual seed, planting it within her.

Neither of them even realised it was a New Moon.

'Thoughts impregnated with Love become invincible'

~ Charles F. Haanel

****

The Joy of Co-Creating

Suzanne and Charles began working on setting up their business together. They stuck with Suzanne's slogan *'Touching the Heart...through Art'* as it seemed quite appropriate, but renamed the business.

While Charles was at work during the day, she drew up a Business Plan, leaving him to do the Cashflow Forecast and Budgeting in the evenings.

She wrote down the vision; to use *his* artwork and *her* poetry to start off a brand new range of inspirational Black greeting cards and prints, and to continue to develop the range by buying-in original artwork and poetry from other artists and poets of African descent. This would not only enable them to diversify the artwork and poetry used, but help brothers and sisters in their community to benefit financially from their God-given talents too.

With Charles' accountancy skills and Suzanne's admin skills, it didn't take long to have everything in place. He paid for a website to be built and they worked together to create products, with the intention of adding to the range later.

Charles had his paintings scanned to get the best possible quality, and Suzanne worked on editing some of her poems to fit inside the greeting cards.

It all came together nicely!

Micah and Elijah also got involved in the business. At ages 12 and 14, they were old enough to take personal responsibility for certain jobs. Micah was assigned the job of helping Suzanne with the admin, and Elijah had the job of helping Charles maintain the website. Charles also started teaching Elijah basic accounting with a view to him helping with the accounts when he was older.

The boys seemed happy that their mum and Charles were back together; they had missed him more than Suzanne had realised. The four of them carried on just where they had left off – the only difference now was that most weekends, they included Ebony, who the boys absolutely *adored*. Micah and Elijah played the 'big brother' role, helping Charles and Suzanne look after her.

****

Over the next year, things seemed to progress at lightning speed.

By combining *Faith, Love* and *Sex*, the irresistible force of the Law of Attraction was formed. Suzanne was a force to be reckoned with on her own, but when she joined forces with Charles, they became invincible – there was nothing they couldn't accomplish!

Charles left his job and they both worked together to launch the business. They advertised in newspapers and magazines, and did stands at various events to promote Suzanne's poetry book and CD along their greeting cards and prints. All their products complimented each other.

By visualising their desires in detail, and speaking *life* into them, Charles and Suzanne were surprised at how quickly their desires began to manifest. They regularly spoke life into their business using positive affirmations, and prayed a special blessing over all the people their business would affect. Two heads really were better than one.

Suzanne was grateful to be with someone like Charles, who also knew how to speak things into existence. They spent time visualising their business empire, drawing up plans, writing down their goals, and discussing the fine details of how to run the business.

They developed a following of repeat customers, who also recommended their products to friends and family.

Orders flooded in from all over the world.

Within a few short months, they had found the perfect location to set up shop and offices, right on the busy high street in Brixton.

'When LOVE and SKILL work together,
Expect a MIRACLE'
~ John Ruskin

****

Year Eight: In Deep

Within the space of one short year since launching their business, Charles and Suzanne made their first million. The products they created using his artwork and her poetry, as well as the sales of Suzanne's poetry CD and book of lyrics were an immediate success. They had worked hard promoting their products, doing stands at various events and handing out their flyers. Suzanne's poetry performances also helped. They used social media sites to further promote their products, as well as advertising in a variety of newspapers and magazines.

Their continued use of prayers/affirmations sent out a positive vibe into the universe, which was reflected back as their life.
They had a set 'formula for success' which they repeated in unison every day, which went something like this:
"...I am so happy and grateful now that I am in perfect health; mentally, physically and spiritually. I willingly use my gifts to help others become whole too. I am financially free, and I am helping others become financially independent too. I let my light shine, and I allow others to let their light shine too, I can do anything I put my mind to, I am an inspiration to many, I am unlimited, I am abundant, I am fruitful; I am like a tree planted by the rivers of water that brings forth its fruit in due season, I receive a constant supply of ideas which I put into action, and whatever I put my hands to prospers! Ashé!"
It was their *combined* forces of thoughts, words and actions that helped to catapult their business to success so quickly.

£1,000,000.00 might sound like a lot of money, but with the plans they had, it was just the beginning! Their plan was to build a Business Empire; a large Black-owned Corporation that would not only help them gain financial independence, but would also provide training and employment for those of African descent who had been impoverished by 'the system'.

After paying off their mortgage and taxes, they looked for ways to make their money grow and share their good fortune, so they began planting money-seeds.

They set up a Benevolence Fund where they put at least 10% of all their profits. This would help those who couldn't find work to set up their own businesses, learn new skills, and work towards financial freedom too. This was one way they could 'give back' to their community.

They also began buying-in original artwork and poetry which reflected the mission of their business. This enabled the contributing artists and poets to benefit financially from their God-given talents, as well as helping to increase the diversity of the designs.

As their range of products increased, so did their reputation for producing high-quality, inspirational, motivational Black greeting cards and prints using original artwork and poetry, which left an indelible impression on the recipients.

Neither of them believed in 'profit without purpose' and both were clear that their business wasn't just about making money; its purpose was to help heal their community.

****

Their high street shop was an immediate success; their goods sold to walk-in customers as well as to people all over the world via their website. They employed five staff from their own community to work in the office, and another five to work in the shop below.

Before recruiting, Charles and Suzanne sat down together and wrote out Job Descriptions for each of the positions they wanted to fill. They discussed what type of person would best be suited to each job, and used their knowledge of Numerology and Astrology to decide what *type* of person would best fit the positions.

Once they had a clear picture of what type of people they wanted to fill each position, they then advertised, believing they would *attract* the right people. And they did.

Their employees were selected by their numerological birthdates, gender (as they wanted to achieve an equal balance of male and female energy in the office), heritage, whether Charles and Suzanne 'took to their spirit' when they came for interview (she always checked her gut feeling), whether they were spiritually-minded, and lastly by their skill level, since they were prepared to train the right person for each job.

Being on the same wavelength mentally made a big difference not only to the smooth running of their business, but to their home life. There were no big arguments, no long silences (unless of course, when they were meditating), and there was generally a good vibration in and around them both. This feeling of unity flowed from their home into the office, providing a peaceful and nurturing working environment.

They agreed to focus their attention on the business during the week, and on the children at the weekends, not doing any work from Friday evening to Sunday evening – that was Family Time. The only exception they made to this rule was if Suzanne had a paid performance to do, in which case they would all go as a family, or if it was too late in the evening, Charles would stay home and look after the children.

Both were quite happy putting all their energies into building their business empire. Suzanne trusted Charles implicitly. Even when he returned home late from visiting Ebony during the week, she never questioned him. She had by now learnt not to entertain worst case scenarios in her mind, imagining the things she *didn't* want to happen. The more trust she put in him, the more he was determined not to break it.

They agreed that even though they were now living together, they would still take time out individually to continue their *personal* development, so that when they came together, they would be stronger.

Occasionally, they would reach a point where they both had a build-up of sexual energy, and relished the weekends when they didn't have the children. Every other weekend was their special weekends together, and they looked forward to them with anticipation.

****

Her Own YONI-verse!

It was Charles who taught Suzanne about the sacredness of her Yoni – in fact, he had even named it for her.

He told her that her Yoni was the gateway to her personal solar system – her Yoniverse, and that he, the Black Man, was the gatekeeper. He explained that the man plants the seed, but it is the *womban* who nurtures the seed, and brings forth life. He said babies are *souls* that come through the *womb*man from the spiritual realm, but that her womb also has the power to create *other* things, not just babies.

Suzanne didn't have a clue what he was talking about at first so she meditated, focusing her attention on her yoni and womb. Gaining insight, she discovered that her womb was a *powerful dynamic creative force*, able to bring forth *anything* from the non-physical realm into the physical, and that her yoni was the *gateway* that connected the inner womb of gestation with the outer world of human life. The liquid that came from her yoni held within it a strong transference of power. It is therefore sacred.

Charles was aware of this, which was why he happily and gratefully engaged in cunnilingus.

He told her that whenever he opened her gateway and their fluids infused together, he was *also* taking on the ability to bring things from the spiritual realm into the physical, which is why he had a deep love and respect for his Queen/goddess and the **inher**ent powers of her yoni and womb.

Suzanne went online and discovered that some Eastern cultures even believe that if a man focuses on the yoni while meditating upon his desires, it had the power to grant his wishes – but this all depended upon the woman the yoni juice was coming from. If a woman was *aware* of her powers, her flower would naturally emit a 'fragrance' which provided the attraction **inher**ent in it.

Suzanne was grateful to have Charles as her King. She realised that many gods and Kings didn't understand the importance of finding their goddesses and Queens, for the gateway that leads to paradise within her.

All men are gods, but not all men are *Kings*; to reach Kingly status, it is necessary for the god to raise his level of consciousness to his *crown* chakra, located at the top of his head. This is the same for the goddess; for her to become a *Queen*, she must also raise her level of consciousness to her *crown* chakra. If a god has reached his highest level of consciousness and becomes a *King*, he has the ability to use his 'key' to open the goddess's gateway during their Sex Ritual, even if she isn't a Queen. But it doesn't work the other way round for the goddess; unless the god has become a King, the two can only go as far as *his* level of consciousness, and he may not even be able to open the gateway for them to be able to bring things from the non-physical realm into the physical.

Therefore it is imperative that all gods raise their level of consciousness to their crown chakra, and become Kings.

Once a god has achieved Kingly status, he should then find his goddess or Queen. Without her feminine energy, it would be difficult for him to **man**ifest anything on the physical plane, since the gateway to bringing things from the spiritual realm into the physical is found ***in her***.

In finding, protecting and serving her well, she will in return love, nurture, protect and heal him, opening the gate to infinite possibilities.

It is therefore necessary for the Black Man to understand that before he can lead, he must first allow his Queen to sit on her throne...in allowing her to do so, his own immortality will be heightened.

> *Above the yoni is a small and subtle flame,*
> *whose form is intelligence.*
> ~ Shiva Samhita, 15th century

****

It's All in the Skin

Suzanne was now able to cut down her time spent in the office, and only worked part-time in the business. This enabled her to achieve a more balanced lifestyle of devoting more time to her writing and the family. Most of what she needed to do could be done from home anyway, like choosing which poems were going to be used for the greeting cards. So after she had trained the admin staff, she left Charles to manage the day-to-day running of the business, only checking the books and financial reports with him on a weekly basis, and attending the office once a month to have meetings with the staff.

So with Charles in the office and the boys at school and college during the day, she had more time for her Self. She could go shopping, but it was kind of ironic that now she had the money to 'shop 'til she dropped', she had no desire to. Expensive clothes, designer handbags and shoes could never validate her worth. She much preferred to get her clothes made-to-fit with fabrics that she had chosen, anyway.

She attended African yoga classes two mornings a week, went to the sauna once a week, and spent the rest of the time focusing on her writing and meditation. Today she was doing research, and became fascinated when she began to learn about what makes Black people Black: MELANIN.

This biochemical pigment, she discovered, was actually a *blessing* to Black people!

She learnt that Melanin is secreted from a small gland in the middle of the brain called the Pineal Gland, also known as the 'black dot' or 'third eye'. The Pineal Gland is a known link between the *physical* and *spiritual* worlds, and provides the connection to higher consciousness, creativity, spiritual awareness and being able to manifest in the physical world. An *activated* Pineal Gland creates a stronger connection between the individual and the Creator, increases the body's ability to hold more light, and expands clarity.

Brown to black in colour, Melanin can be found in the skin, hair and eyes, and is more evident in dark-skinned people and

Caucasians with brown eyes and hair. It plays an important part in the function of the brain and nervous system, and is said to help elevate consciousness, and is what makes Melanin-dominated people more spiritual. In Black people, it is concentrated in the genitalia.

Melanin can also be found in nature e.g. plants, springs, lakes, soil, animals and in the air (ether) as well as the dark matter that permeates the universe. It is therefore *Melanin* that causes a person to be more in tune with nature. Now Suzanne could plainly see why those who were Melanin deficient were causing the most amount of damage to Mother Earth and her inhabitants.

She also learnt that Melanin provides a *natural barrier* from harmful UV rays reducing the risk of skin cancer, and because it maintains moisture in the outer layers of the skin, it prevents long-term signs of aging, which is why dark-skinned people generally look younger than their age.

The darker you are, the more Melanin you have.

Melanin also has the ability to absorb all types of energy including harmful ultraviolet rays, electromagnetic, and music and turn them into energy for the body to use. She smiled as she thought that must be the reason Black people like to have the music so loud until it resonates throughout their whole beings!

"If only Black people understood the power of the Melanin in their skin they would wish they were darker, not lighter!" Suzanne exclaimed. She wondered how it had been possible for those who lacked Melanin to make everyone else believe that the lighter you are, the better you are!

Suzanne also learnt that Melanin is kept healthy by the sun's energy, eating healthily and by what goes in the eyes and ears, e.g. music. When a Melanin-dominant person is deprived of natural sunlight and their natural environment, it can cause them to function in a less civilised way.

Melanin becomes toxic through bad eating habits (e.g. junk food), lack of natural sunlight and chemicals in the body such as drugs, nicotine, alcohol and steroids. If these substances are consumed, they will affect the psyche of the individual. Suzanne could also see that negative 'programming' through the media and music, especially modern-day hip hop, were also having a devastating effect on the psyche of Black people, causing them to act in ways contrary to their true nature. But she also learnt from Dr Llaila Afrika's book *'Melanin: What Makes Black People Black'* that vitamin B helps keep Melanin clean. A natural diet for a Melanin dominant person is the food that Mother Nature provides; fruit, vegetables, herbs, water, nuts, seeds, beans, sprouts etc.

Up to this point, Suzanne would occasionally 'treat' the children to 'take away', but now she was becoming more aware of the effects of food on the mind, she decided to cut out unhealthy foods like burgers, fried chicken and chips, and incorporate more of the above into her cooking. When she told 'the family' she was going to stop buying meat and include more fruit and veg into their diets, there was practically an uproar. The boys said they needed meat to get their protein. Even Charles said he had to have chicken. So she agreed to cut out red meat but continue buying chicken, opting for organic rather than the processed chemically-filled ones.

It was hard trying to get the boys to eat greens straight off the plate, but she found that if she blended them and added them in to the sauces or gravy, they hardly noticed.

She began doing more research into how different foods affect the mind, and came to the conclusion that the way for Black people to heal themselves was to get back to their natural environment, eat the right foods, and stop allowing themselves to be 'programmed' negatively.

There seemed to be a definite all-out war on fully Melanated people, to separate them from themselves, their Motherland, and their spirituality. Suzanne believed the issue wasn't just because of richness of the Melanin in their *skin*, but the richness of their *land*.

This brought Suzanne right back to Adam and Eve. She'd read somewhere that the Garden of Eden was in Africa, and it had already been scientifically proven that the hue-man race originated in Africa, so surely Adam and Eve must have been *Black*?

On her Black History course, she had learnt that Cauc*asians* were originally Black, but after going through the Ice Age, over time lack of sunlight and the cold environment had calcified their Pineal Gland, which caused them to become Melanin deficient. In

Suzanne's mind however, this still didn't account for the change in their eye colours or hair textures. Perhaps there was more than one type of Original Black Person, she reasoned. Maybe there were Black people with *straight* hair and Black people with *woolly* hair?

There were even theories that Cauc*asians* evolved from Albino Blacks, who had been ostracised from their community because of their 'leprosy'. They were taken to live in the caves in Europe, where they became 'cavemen'.

'This might explain why they hate their parents so much now', Suzanne reasoned on their behalf.

In any case, what was more important was the fact that today Black people with woolly hair were the ones at the bottom end of the 'food chain'. Somehow, those with the weakest genes had managed to convince everyone else that 'the whiter you are, the more superior you are'. Even some *Asians* were bleaching their skin.

Suzanne wondered how it had become possible for Black people who had such a rich history, to have ended up so low down in society, looked down upon by white supremacists as the lower class, or 'caste'.

She remembered reading about the way Europeans had treated Blacks during the Slave Trade, as if they were less than animals. They had justified their actions by saying that Black people had no soul, when it is *Melanin* that makes a person more spiritual.

They had in fact demonstrated their *own* lack of spirituality, by treating other hue-man beings in such a brutal way, with no conscience to their own actions.

What *makes* a person spiritual? When Suzanne meditated on the word 'Spiritual' it was revealed to her as;

'Spirit-ritual'

...in other words, to be 'Spiritual' is to perform ceremonial *ritual with Spirit*.
And whose tradition is it to perform rituals? Africans.

Yet Africans have given up their own rituals of making offerings to their ancestors and to Mother Nature, and taken on a form of spirituality that only kept them hidden from themselves.

Suzanne wondered how her ancestors would be feeling now if they were looking down and watching their descendants. Would those who had fought for their freedom be glad to see that their descendents although physically free, were still in mental slavery, and worse still, they didn't even realise it?

'The worst type of slave is the slave who believes he is free'

Suzanne made a conscious decision to trace her roots back as far as possible, and change her name by Deed Poll back to an African name in honour of her ancestors. She believed that as long as the descendents of slaves *kept* their slave master's names, they still had a spiritual hold over them – if not *physically*, then *psychologically*.

****

The Black Womban

The more Suzanne realized her own divinity, the more she carried her Self with virtue, dignity, grace and Self-discipline.

She discovered that the Black Woman carries The Mother of All Genes –Mitochondria DNA; mDNA is only found in *women* (not men) and since it has been *scientifically proven* that all races can trace their DNA back to the Black Woman, she is rightfully known as the Mother of All Nations.

She also learnt that ancient African cultures were matrilineal, meaning that one's lineage was traced through the *mother*, not the father. Women were the most important element of the society, and queens didn't become queens because they were the daughters of kings, they had queens that succeeded queens. They had religious leaders who were women too.

In Ancient Kemet (meaning 'Land of the Blacks', renamed 'Egypt' by the Greeks) the rulers were often pictured with their mothers and ruled equally with their queens. It was the custom among the Nubians that when a king died and only left a son, if he had a nephew, the son of his *sister*, the latter would reign instead of his own son. In other words, **inher**itance came through the *woman*, not the man.

Yet somehow this had all been turned around. The Sacred Feminine Principle had been removed from the Creation Story in the bible, and the first woman (Eve) had been accused of causing the downfall of all mankind, which had resulted in women generally throughout the bible and other religious texts being forced to become subservient to men. The genealogy of Jesus and other prominent men in the bible didn't even acknowledge women. It was even said that the Gospel of Mary, who was the closest 'disciple' to Jesus, was omitted from the scriptures.

Suzanne recalled Charles explaining to her that the Christian cross is a direct derivative of the Ankh cross. Now she learnt that the loop of the Ankh represented the *womb*, and the elongated bottom part represented the *phallus*. The line in the middle represented the two coming together, which creates Life.

With Christianity being a patriarchal religion, the loop (representing the Feminine Principle) was removed and replaced with another (smaller) phallus, and it became the symbol of death, instead of Life.

Throughout various forms of religion, the male energy then became dominant, forming a patriarchal mindset which allowed men to dominate women. As the Masculine energy became more prevalent, it took over religion, politics, law, education, business and agriculture, causing extensive damage to Mother Earth and her inhabitants. This was the *cause* of all the problems in the world today. Without the Feminine Energy there was no balance. According to the universal law of duality, both male and female energies are needed to create equilibrium.

Suzanne believed that because men are generally less intuitive than women and less in touch with their inner feelings, they tend to act out of *ego* rather than *emotion*. Their need for power, status, and control causes them to oppress the one thing they cannot live without – the woman.

Even certain words in the English language gave men dominance, like *man*kind, *man*ifest, and *man*datory.

To be fair, it wasn't *all* men who had this mindset; it was a particular group of white supremacy elitists who wanted to rule the world, including the Black Man who they feared. They were aware of the power Black Men and Black Women had when they came together in a high state of consciousness, so in order to take over the world, their strategy was to break down their psyche.

As Suzanne sat thinking about all of this the key turned in the door, and in walked in Charles. She glanced at the time; it was nearly 10pm. She hadn't realized it was so late; the boys had already gone to bed.

"Hi babes, what are you doing?" he asked as he hung up his jacket.

"Well I thought I'd have a go at writing an article, so I'm just doing some research for it" she answered cheerfully.

"Oh! What's it about?"

"Adam and Eve"

"Ok…" he sat down beside her. "What about Adam and Eve?"

"Well, when I used to go to church, the whole Adam and Eve story never really sat comfortably with me. I didn't like the way Eve was blamed for tempting Adam to eat the forbidden fruit which brought a curse on the whole of the human race, and ever since then, women have been oppressed by men, especially in different religions. So I decided to write an article to show how the story is flawed"

"Yes, well don't forget to mention the X and Y chromosomes"

"What's that got to do with it?" Suzanne asked with a puzzled expression.

"Well you just said it your Self – the *story* of Adam and Eve. I'm sure we've had this conversation before babe? Adam and Eve aren't literal people, they're *metaphors!*"

"Yes I know…but for what?"

"I'm starving, can I eat first?" He knew this was going to take time.

"Your dinner's in the oven honey. The salad's in the fridge" Charles headed for the kitchen and seeing his covered plate of food in the oven, set the timer and switched it on. Returning to the living room, he carried on the conversation.

"If I remember correctly, Adam is a metaphor for the Y chromosome and Eve for the X chromosome"

"Really…Where did you learn that?" she half-laughed sarcastically.

"Think about it; the bible says Eve was made from Adam's rib, right?"

"Yes…"

"Well look at the X and Y letters" Charles grabbed a piece of paper and pen and jotted the letters down.

"Ok…" Suzanne watched intently. She loved learning from him.

"Now the X is a female chromosome, and the Y is a male chromosome. Two XX's make a girl child, and an XY makes a boy child. You following this?" he continued to draw the letters on the paper to prove his point.

"Yes…"

"Well according to the bible, God took a 'rib' from Adam to create Eve, right?"

"Yes…."

"Now watch this; Adam is a male, so he must be an XY, right? If you take away a 'rib' from the X or the Y, you'll either end up with YY, or XV (he scribbles out the bottom right branch of the 'X' and the bottom part of the 'Y' to illustrate). But if you take away a 'rib' from the XX, what do you end up with?"

"Oh my god, XY! …But what does this prove?" Suzanne looked up at him and asked.

"That it is *scientifically impossible* for women to be created from men. Men come from women, women do not come from men! So many things are hidden in the English language, and this is just one of them. Adam and Eve are *metaphors* for the X and Y chromosomes."

Suzanne sat in astonishment. But why was she even shocked by this revelation? She suddenly remembered her poem *"I Am What I WILL to Be!"*. Some parts of the poem had come as a 'download', where she had felt like all she was doing was taking dictation. She believed the ancestors spoke through her sometimes. In one part of the poem she had written; *'The ancestors speak through me, so listen carefully...'* She remembered waiting to see what 'they' were going to say, and the next lines were;

"I am the Original Woman; I was here first! MAN came out of WOMAN, HE came out of SHE, MALE came out of FEMALE and HE came out of HER, See it's hidden in the words!"

She thought about how far she and her sisters were from re-membering themselves, and wondered how they were ever going to regain their positions in the world.

The timer went off on the oven.

****

Be the Source

Suzanne, Charles, and their three children spent a lovely weekend together.

On the Friday night, Charles had suggested they go to the cinema, but Suzanne had proposed he take the boys, as little Ebony wouldn't be interested in anything they wanted to watch.

While they were out, Suzanne cornrowed Ebony's hair and seasoned the fish for dinner the next day, since they would be out.

They held their usual stand at the monthly *Kemet Market* on the Saturday where they sold their products. Suzanne performed, and afterwards enjoyed walking around with Ebony looking at all the other stalls. She stocked up on natural hair and skin care products, and also bought some beautiful African-inspired soft furnishings and carvings for their home, some jewelry for herself, and a little African print dress for Ebony. Whatever money they had made on their stand, Suzanne had spent it again!

On the Sunday they entertained family members; Suzanne's siblings came over with their children and her mum, and Charles picked up his mum and brought her over too. Each family member brought a dish or dessert, while Suzanne cooked the rice and peas, chicken, fish and salads. The boys played video games with their cousins, and the adults caught up with each other's lives.

Before they knew it, it was time for Ebony to go home. Everyone kissed her goodbye, and since Charles was taking his mum back home too, the rest of the family started getting ready to leave as well.

When they had gone, Suzanne sat thinking about how great her life was now.
She had the perfect partner (for her), two lovely boys who gave her no trouble, a successful business, an adorable step-daughter, and they lacked for nothing.

Charles was by no means perfect, but by focusing on the positive things about him instead of the negative, she seemed to be able to draw more of that out. The more things she found to love about Charles, the deeper her love for him grew. It worked the same with the boys; she found that if she rewarded them with praise anytime they did anything 'good', they wanted to do more good things.

Looking back at her life, she recalled how not that many years ago, she had been struggling to make ends meet, looking for 'The One', and experiencing mental frustrations because she believed she needed more in life to be happy. It was only when she learnt to 'let go' of all her striving to be, do and have, and learnt to be grateful for what she already had, that things began to flow her way. She had stopped asking her Self questions like "Do I deserve to be happy?" or "Have I earned it?" and reached a place where nothing was wanted, nothing was needed, and nothing was missing. She was complete and whole in her Self, in each moment called NOW.

It was only when she realized her life was not about becoming better, higher or greater, or of acquiring 'things' but to simply *experience* who she was, that life began to open up to her. She began to feel joyful just because. She began to love her Self fully and unconditionally for the first time.

The secret was in learning that she was not here to acquire anything, but to *give*. She had learnt that if she desired to experience more love in her life, she had to *give* more love. If she wished to have more money, she was to demonstrate that she already *had* it, and give. If she aspired to have more wisdom, she had to express the wisdom she already *had*.

She was surprised at how quickly things had begun to change once *she* began to 'be the Source'.

When Suzanne began showing her divine Self by demonstrating Who She Is Right Now, there was nothing else for her to do. Instead of believing that she was 'born in sin' and that she had to achieve some state of perfection, she believed that she came *into* this world in a state of perfection. Every time she looked into a baby's face, she knew this was true. Now all she had to do was simply *experience* who she was:

"I am loving. I am peaceful. I am joyful. I am patient. I am kind. I am whole, perfect and complete, in each moment called now".

It was only when she began showing more love to her Self and to others that love came back to her in abundance. It was only when she chose to be happy all the time, that experiences came to *keep* her in that state of bliss. When she decided to remain in perfect health, she began to learn about the right types of food to eat and exercises to do to help her stay healthy.

So whenever she found herself wishing for more, or wanting more of anything, she would ask her Self "I wonder if there's anyone else out there who wants more of this too?" She would then choose to be the Source in *their* lives; it could be a friend, family member or complete stranger.

She would think to her Self "What if I had *so much*, that I could afford to give some away?" It didn't matter what it might be, she began giving away anything and everything that she thought she didn't have enough of. Whether it was patience, love, wisdom, compassion, money or friendship; when she wanted some, she found other people who wanted more of the same and gave it to them.

The feeling of giving to another and making *their* life better gave her such an energy lift, that her whole life purpose changed. She no longer began trying to get things for herself, but began having things so that she might give them away!

And she discovered that the more she gave, the more she received. As she began to fulfill her life's purpose of *giving*, the universe began to open up an unlimited supply, because the universe knew that there were a lot of people now depending on her to be the Source of it.

****

Sharing the Love

Even though she and Charles were well off and had a nice home, Suzanne didn't separate her Self from her people, and didn't think of her Self as better off than they were. As far as she was concerned, they were all in this together. She wanted to do whatever she could to help her brothers and sisters free themselves mentally and physically. Luckily for her, Charles was in full agreement.

Being a Black brother, Charles had experienced first-hand how difficult it was to navigate through the system and come out whole. From school, college, university, to finding work, he'd had to fight the subliminal messages which told him he would never be as good as his white counterparts. But he had received a strong foundation in the home, and was able to fight the system all the way – to the top. Now he was in a position to make a difference.

Charles was sympathetic towards his brothers who were still fighting the system daily. He had often seen images on T.V. of angry black men, or heard stories of them being jailed for dealing drugs. What had *not* been explained was how they had been forced into these positions due to the lack of jobs, and to jobs not paying them a high enough salary to support their families. He could just imagine the psychological effect on a Black man who cannot find work, and who cannot support his children. What were they supposed to do? Of course they are angry – angry at a system which was against them!

And Suzanne had empathy for her sisters who longed for a decent black man but couldn't find one. The media seemed to be sending out the message that "Black men are either in prison, unemployed, gay, in mental institutions or with white women, so you might as well 'Try Something New'". If all Black women were to start believing this, where would that leave the Black population?

The message being sent out to Black men was that Black women were angry, bitter, h**s and b****es, and that white women were prettier, had nicer hair, would give them better-looking children and 'status'.

They discussed what they could do to help their people heal, and agreed to start putting on their own events, aimed at helping black singles to meet, and black couples to stay together.

Now that they had achieved love, peace and harmony within their *own* relationship, they were better able to spread it to their community.

****

Year Nine: Another Level

It had been over a week since Charles and Suzanne last made love. They had been so busy, they'd hardly even noticed.

Charles was in the office when he received a text from Suzanne.
"Tomorrow is the night X" it said.
Charles smiled.
"The night for what?" he texted back
"It's a surprise ;-)"
She knew she had to give him advanced notice because he wasn't as spontaneous as she was, although he was learning to be. Tomorrow would be Saturday night and it was their free weekend without the children. She didn't really have anything planned; she'd just sent the text on the spur of the moment – but now she had to think of something!

She quickly called her hairdresser to see if she could get an appointment for the following day, and also decided to go for a manicure and pedicure.

Tomorrow was going to be busy so she did the food shopping, returning home in time to help the boys get ready to go to their dad's for the weekend.

****

"So what do you have planned?" Charles asked the following morning.
"We're going out later" Suzanne responded casually.
"Oh! Ok, where?"
"It's a surprise, remember?" Suzanne smiled mischievously.
"Ok...so what's the dress code?"
"Traditional"
"Wouldn't you rather have an early night in?" he asked with a glint in his eye.
"...Mmmmm....there'll be plenty of time for that when we get back!" Suzanne replied jumping out of bed.
"Hey, where're you going so early?"

"To the gym for a quick sauna and steam, then I have an appointment at the hairdressers!" she replied, unwrapping her silk scarf from her head.

"Oh, ok...I might as well come with you then"

Charles had been hoping they were going to have a lie-in. He stumbled out of bed and dragged on a pair of jogging bottoms. He still looked good, but he'd put on a bit of weight around the middle as he wasn't going to the gym as regularly as before. On top of that, he was eating better. A work-out would be good for him.

As they were leaving, Suzanne informed Charles that they would need to be ready to leave that evening by 6.30pm. They agreed to be back at home by 5.30pm the latest.

Charles did his workout then came straight back home, had a quick shower and spent the rest of the day relaxing, reading and sleeping. He'd had a busy week at the office, and was happy for the peace and quiet.

****

Suzanne arrived back home just before 6pm. Charles greeted her at the door with a hug, kiss and a stiffie.

"Put that thing away!" she laughed.

"Come on, we've got time for a quickie before we go" he murmured in her ear.

"No we don't, look at my hair – I'm not messing it up!"

"It's lovely..." Charles said, turning her around in a full circle.

"I had my nails done, too!" She showed him her own French-manicured fingernails.

"Mmmm...nice!" he commented. But really he only had one thing on his mind.

"Right, I'm going to have a quick shower and then we'll be off – are you hungry?" she asked.

"Starving"

He didn't know what she had planned, so he'd been saving his stomach since lunchtime.

"Good, because there's food where we're going"

"What kind of food?"

"Oh...you'll see"

Suzanne carefully placed a plastic cap over her hair and had a quick shower. When she re-entered the bedroom Charles asked "What are you wearing?"

He always liked to match the colour of his shirt or tie with her dress. They even had a few matching outfits.

Suzanne walked into her wardrobe and chose one of them; a Vintage 70's Dashiki Tunic dress with bell sleeves. Laying it carefully on the bed, she unwrapped the towel and began oiling her body down.

Charles stood watching with a huge bulge in his pants as she lovingly caressed the oil over her body, admiring herself in the mirror. Seeing his reflection she turned and asked "Aren't you going to get ready?"

Walking towards her he replied "Yes, in a minute"

Taking the bottle from her, he began oiling her back slowly.

"Oh, thanks!"

He pressed himself against her from behind so she could feel his hard-on.

"Charles...." she warned. "If we don't hurry up, we're going to be late!"

"Oh, ok" and like a scolded school-boy, he sulkily made his way to the bathroom.

When he returned from his cold shower Suzanne was already dressed, and was carefully applying her make-up. She only wore enough to enhance her features, not to change them completely. She applied lime green and gold eye-shadow to match the colours in her dress, then carefully applied a lip-liner and lip-gloss to accentuate her lips. She placed small hairclips with little red roses attached to them to jazz up her hair.

"You look stunning" he commented.

"Thank you darling!"

Charles went to his walk-in wardrobe and chose his matching dashiki top, chino jeans, a brown belt and shoes. He unwrapped the cellophane sheet from the dry-cleaners, laid them on the bed and pulled his tight white boxers on.

"I'm thinking about starting a martial arts class" he announced as he got dressed.

"Really? Which one?"

"Well I was coming out of the train station at Seven Sisters and someone handed me a flyer for Mashufaa classes"

"Mashufaa? Is that a form of martial arts?"

"Yes, it's *African* martial arts. It sounds really good, I'm thinking of taking the boys for the free taster session next Friday. What do you think?"

"Sounds great! That would be really good for them"

"The only thing is, the classes are on a Friday evening so if we *do* start going regularly, you'll have to look after Ebony – is that ok?"

"That's fine by me – it's a good swop actually!"

****

Dance in Trance

They arrived back home in high spirits from the evening's entertainment.

Suzanne had taken Charles to an African restaurant called 'Back to Africa' where they had sat on mats on the floor eating pounded yam, egusi soup and other West African delicacies with their hands, while enjoying watching the live African bands playing. The Kora player had been the highlight of the evening for Suzanne.

The djembe drumming, African dancing and singing had gone to straight the core of their beings, reminding them of their roots.

They had bought the band's CD and played it all the way back home, and by now, Suzanne was beginning to feel something awakening that had been buried deep within her DNA.

Taking off their shoes at the door, they headed straight for their bedroom. Suzanne brought the CD with her, put it in the stereo, pressed the 'play' button, then lit some candles. Charles took off his dashiki and jeans and sat on the bed as he watched her enter her wardrobe again. He knew Suzanne well enough by now to know that he was in for a treat.

He thought perhaps she was going to re-appear in some sexy lingerie, so wasn't mentally prepared for what he saw when she *did* finally emerge.

Suzanne seemed to have transformed her Self into some kind of Exotic Dancer/Sexual Healer/Temple-Priestess. She was wearing a white see-through flowy dress-thing which plunged into a V-shape at the neck-line down to her navel. It was fitted at the waist, with long, flowing bell-sleeves that almost reached down to the hem of the dress, which dropped in multiple folds down to her knees. He could see right through it – and she wasn't wearing anything underneath; her nipples jutted through the sheer material, begging him for attention. Around her temple, she wore a gold chain with various symbols hanging from it – he'd never seen it before. She was barefooted, showing off her manicured feet.

As she began moving her body to the rhythm of the drum beats still playing on the CD, the spirit of her ancestors seemed to take over. With arms swaying like leaves in the breeze, she twisted and twirled, gyrating her hips in a sensual, sexual manner, as she sent forth her Inner Womb Message. The whole atmosphere in the room changed.

Charles became aroused, moved almost to tears, and concerned all at the same time. The look on her face was such as he'd never seen before. She wasn't focused on him; she looked as if she was in a trance, totally caught up in the moment. The elongated shadows on the walls behind her created by the candle-light looked like spirits dancing along with her.

Perhaps she was calling on the spirits of her ancestors...or was it the Holy Spirit? He couldn't tell – all he knew was that it was a force of Love. He felt at peace as he watched her; he'd never seen her move like that; was she possessed? 'Where did she learn to dance like that?' He wondered.

When she had finished, she gracefully walked towards the bed where Charles was sitting propped up on one elbow.

"Is there no end to your talents?" he asked, awestruck.

"I can do whatever I put my mind to!" she replied smiling, as she sat next to him on the bed.

Charles stared at her intently as he watched her come back to her Self. As they sat in silence Charles appeared to be in deep contemplation. He finally asked "If there was anywhere in the world that you could go, where would it be?"

Without having to think about it, Suzanne responded;

"My Motherland, Africa".

"Africa's a big place, which part?"

"All of it, but I'd most like to visit Egypt"

"Mmmm...." Charles pondered, as if in agreement. Then tracing a finger over the lump where her nipple was protruding through the dress, he looked her in the eye and asked "Can I take this off now?"

Suzanne held her arms up and helped him remove it. Noticing that the music on the CD was still playing, Charles got up, started it from the beginning again and turned it up loud. He removed his boxers and socks as he made his way back to the bed.

Both of them were by now bursting with passion.

That night when they made love, it was as if all the heavens, God, the angels and their ancestors were all watching and cheering them on. It felt like nothing they had ever experienced before. Suzanne cried from the bottom of her heart, and afterwards, Charles clung on to her for hours, remaining inside her long after he had ejaculated, as if not wanting to break the newly-created bond between them.

****

Announcement

A few days later, Charles got home from work early.

"Oh! I wasn't expecting you home so soon!" Suzanne greeted him with a kiss.

"Hi Charles!" Elijah and Micah greeted him too.

"Hi boys, what are you up to?"

The boys were sitting around the dining table.

"Just homework" Elijah said.

"Ok, I'll wait 'til you've finished"

The boys looked at each other then said to him in unison "We've finished!"

"Oh no you haven't!" Suzanne interrupted. Then turning to Charles asked

"Why, what's up?"

"Oh nothing...I just have an announcement to make, but it can wait until later"

"Are you sure?"

"Of course. What's for dinner?"

"I haven't even started cooking yet! I seasoned some fish earlier, I was just going to sauté some potatoes and make a salad to go with it, is that ok?"

"Sounds good to me"

As Suzanne headed for the kitchen, Charles followed her.

"Did you tell the boys about the Mashufaa class this Friday?" he asked her.

"Oh, I forgot! Why don't you tell them now? I'm sure they'll be up for it"

Charles returned to the living room and told the boys about the class. They were definitely up for it; they loved doing activities with him. Returning to the kitchen, Charles asked Suzanne if she needed any help.

"No it's ok, all I have to do is wrap the fish in foil and stick it in the oven, while that's cooking I'll do the potatoes and salad. It won't take long...then we can hear your announcement!" she said smiling at him as she wrapped the bream.

****

After dinner, the boys cleared away the plates from the table and loaded the dishwasher. As they all sat around the table; Charles placed two tickets on the table and said "Suzanne, pack your bags, we're going on holiday"

"On holiday? Where?" Suzanne asked, not quite believing what he was saying.

"To Egypt, of course!"

"Egypt? But...*how*?" she asked, still in disbelief.

"What do you mean, how?" Charles questioned, amused. "You have a passport, don't you?"

"Yes...but what about the boys? And Ebony?"

"It's all been arranged. The boys are going to stay at Janice's for the week, and I've already told Maria I'll be away for a week...I'll make it up to Ebony when we get back"

"Yes but... I don't feel comfortable about leaving them behind...you know my goal was always to be able to afford to take them on holiday during every school break"

"Mum it's ok" Elijah offered. "We'll be fine"

Charles had already discussed it with them fully before he booked the tickets, and it was their idea to stay at their auntie's, so they could spend some quality time with their cousins too. When Charles explained to Janice why he wanted to take Suzanne on holiday, she was happy to have the boys. They were teenagers now; all they needed was feeding.

"Ok let's do it like this" Charles suggested; "We'll take this holiday together, and organise another family holiday after the boys have finished their exams. How's that?"

Suzanne closed her eyes and listened to what her inner voice had to say about it.

"Ok....But promise me you'll keep up your studies while we're gone?" she said to the boys.

"Yes mum" they both said.

When it actually sunk in, Suzanne exclaimed in delight, "Oh my god...we're actually going to *Egypt*!" flinging her arms around Charles' neck.

****

Ancient Kemet

Suzanne and Charles arrived in Cairo in the early hours of the morning after a short flight from Gatwick airport.

Arriving at the hotel around 6am, they slept for a few hours before heading down to the 5* hotel's restaurant for breakfast. They then spent the rest of their first day making full use of the hotel's excellent spa facilities, swimming in the outdoor pool, relaxing in the Jacuzzi, then having a steam and sauna, before having full body massages. Charles even treated Suzanne to a seaweed facial. By the end of the day, they were totally relaxed and rejuvenated from their trip.

They undid all the pampering when they made passionate love that night.

Suzanne had put her hair in braids so she didn't have to think too much about what to do with it while on holiday, and because she wanted to go swimming with Charles.

On the second day, Charles had arranged for them to go scuba-diving; it was like being in another world! Suzanne was awestruck at the beauty of God's underwater creation; the intricate designs He had 'painted' on the all different types of fish... and the plants seemed to have a life of their own as they swished and swayed in the currents!

Charles was a much better swimmer than Suzanne, and offered to take her even deeper underwater so she could see more. Even though she would have probably drowned if she was on her own and ran out of air, she trusted him.

They picked some shells from the bottom of the ocean to bring back home. Her only regret was not having the boys with her to share the beautiful experience, but she promised herself that she would do this trip again with them, and make it longer next time.

That evening, they got dressed up and went down to the hotel's plush restaurant for dinner.

As they searched for a free table, an older West-Indian couple beckoned them to join them at their table. It turned out they were celebrating their 32nd wedding anniversary!

Mr and Mrs Jones were still happily 'in love' after being together for 33 years; their children were now grown up, and they were enjoying having 'quality time' with each other again.

Suzanne wondered if they still had a sex life, but was too embarrassed to ask. They certainly *looked* as if they were still attracted to each other in that way. She wondered if she would still be attracted to Charles when they reached their 60's.

Mrs Jones looked at Suzanne's left hand and noticed she wasn't wearing a wedding ring. She asked if they were just on a casual holiday as lovers or if they were actually in a committed relationship.

"No, we live together, and we're very happy with the arrangement" Suzanne informed her.

"But you look so good together, why you don' get married, wha' do you, you scared fe commit?" Mr Jones questioned Charles.

Charles cleared his throat;

"No, no, we're not scared, we've been thinking about it, haven't we?" he looked at Suzanne for support. But Suzanne stood her ground.

"I don't see how getting married would help us stay together. If I'm happy in a relationship and I see it has the potential to last, I'll do my best to make it work. A wedding ring wouldn't do anything to change that" she stated.

"What, you mean you wouldn't get married?" Charles asked her in a shocked tone.

"Well....*maybe*. I'm just saying, a wedding ring wouldn't make any difference to me"

Charles breathed a sigh of relief.

****

The Pyramids

On the third day they left the hotel at 7am to join an excursion to visit the oldest and only remaining of the Seven Wonders of the Ancient World – the great pyramid of Giza. The largest of the three main colossal monuments was originally built as a burial tomb for King Khufu in the 4th Dynasty. Seeing the real thing was nothing like the pictures. But then, photographs could never capture the true significance of their existence. Their Egyptologist guide gave them much information about the pyramids, like the fact that the Great Pyramid of Giza had originally been covered in a smooth limestone casing, which had allegedly been stolen.

"Wow, it seems *everybody's* been *r*aping Mama Africa!" Suzanne thought.

There were a few casing stones still remaining at the base of the pyramid; one of the largest was nearly 5 feet high, weighing about 14 tons. The sheer magnitude of the Pyramid meant that a *lot* of limestone had been removed. Suzanne asked the tour guide what had been the purpose of the casing in the first place? She was told that the casing had acted like a mirror, causing the Pyramid to reflect light.

Suzanne and Charles were both interested to learn more about the pyramids, the Sphinx and their history. They decided to do more research together when they got back home.

The guided tour only left more questions in Suzanne's head, like "who built them?", "how were they built?", "*why* were they built?"

Charles had paid extra for them to enter the great pyramid, but their tour guide was not permitted to accompany them.

As they entered the tunnel, bending down to follow the long low passage leading to the Queen's chamber, an unexplainable chill ran throughout Suzanne's body.

"Can you feel that?" she asked Charles.

"Feel what?"

"I don't know...I can't explain it, I just feel...strange" she replied.

As they entered the chamber, an overwhelming feeling came over Suzanne. She began hyperventilating.

"Are you ok?" Charles asked in a concerned tone.

"Yes...I don't know..."

Her inner voice advised her to go and stand in a particular spot. As she did so, she felt what she could only describe later as a 'download' and passed out.

****

"Are you ok?" Charles asked with a concerned look on his face. By now, some of the other tourists had also gathered round.

"Yes, I'm fine" she responded as he helped her back to her feet.

"Maybe we should go" he said, looking around.

"No it's fine, I feel at home here"

As they walked around admiring the sarcophagus, walls and ceiling carved out of the thick granite stone. They both felt a residue in the air of a people who were once a great civilization.

Leaving the Pyramids, they took a short camel ride through the desert until they reached the great Sphinx.

At one point it had once been buried up to its neck in sand, but now, it stood 200ft long, 65 feet tall with its face measuring 13 feet wide, looking towards the rising sun. It had been so revered by the ancients that they had built a temple in between its massive paws. It had the body of a lion(ess) and the face of a human – but was it a male or a female, and was it the face of a Black person? The tour guide informed them that the nose and lips had been vandalized, but they weren't sure who by, or for what reason.

But to Suzanne and Charles, the reason was obvious.

****

Souvenir shopping

On the fourth day, they hired a local tour guide to take them to a traditional market where they bartered for souvenirs. Charles bought Suzanne a silver ankh necklace to replace the Christian cross she'd stopped wearing. She bought the boys one each as well, and a silver bracelet for Ebony, as well as gifts for family and friends.

When they arrived back at the hotel in the late afternoon, Suzanne decided to have a nap before getting ready for dinner. Charles lay down beside her, but was too excited to sleep, so once he was sure she was out, he left the hotel room and headed down to the bar...

****

Surprise?

This was their last evening in Egypt. They had arranged to meet Mr and Mrs Jones for dinner again. As they left their hotel room, Charles discreetly slipped something into his trouser pocket.

Linking hands, they made their way over to table 28 where Catherine and Sydney were already waiting for them.

Charles was dressed in a pair of cream linen slacks, a white loose cotton shirt, and beige canvas shoes. Suzanne wore a knee-length dress that was fitted at the bodice and waist, and white high-heeled sandals. Her skin seemed to glow against the white material. She had styled her braids away from her face, and finished it off with a butterfly clip. Her only make-up was a bit of eye-liner, mascara and lip-gloss, giving her an au-natural look.

"You look like the perfect couple!" Catherine complimented as they reached the table.

"Thank you!" Suzanne said, while Charles helped push her seat in as she sat down, before sitting down himself.

"Today is a special day!" Charles announced.

Sydney winked at him.

Just then, two brothers approached their table playing violins. Tapping Charles frantically on the arm Suzanne whispered excitedly "Charles look, it's *Nuttin' but Stringz!*"

"Yeah, I know" Charles replied calmly.

That's when she realized what he was up to.

Turning and giving them a grateful look, Charles took his cue and said to Suzanne smugly;

"I think you'd be very happy married to me"

'Is this his way of proposing?' She wondered, '...or maybe he's using reverse psychology; maybe what he really means is he thinks *he'd* be very happy married to *me*!'

"Are you sure about this?" She questioned him "...Besides, what makes you think I *want* to get married?" She had stopped expecting him to pop the question years ago.

Charles fumbled with his words;

"Well I wouldn't ask unless I was sure within myself. Life is short, so if you were to turn me down I would totally understand and try to assert what you needed to feel the same as me. In life one can only make choices, and I choose to be happy at all times, if possible."

She realised that despite his outward show of Self confidence, deep down, he still needed reassurance.

"Do you think you'd be happy married to *me*?" she asked him.

"I'd be the happiest man in the world" he replied spontaneously.

"So are you proposing?"

"Would you *want* to marry me?" he asked reservedly.

"This is getting ridiculous! Are you proposing or not?"

He paused and took a deep breath, then slowly slid unto the floor and unto one knee. Taking her by the hand, he said solemnly;

"Suzanne, it would make me very happy if you would accept my proposal to be my wife"
Staring down at him in disbelief she responded

"Is that it? *Why* do you want me to be your wife?"
Caught off guard, he shuffled unto the other knee;

"Well... I think I've met my match, I think we have something very special between us, and I think what we have can last a lifetime" he smiled up at her, pleased with his reply.

He's right, it worked. Warming to his offering, she gave him a big hug and replied "Charles, I would LOVE to be your wife!" with tears of joy in her eyes.

He reached inside his trouser pocket and took out a black velvet box. Opening it, he took out the ring, took her by her left hand, and placed the ring on her index finger.

Suzanne stared at the large single solitaire diamond ring in the shape of a love heart with a small ankh cross flanking either side. Inside were inscribed the words 'For Life'. She exclaimed "Good heavens! Charles, it's...*beautiful*!"

She couldn't have chosen a better ring herself. Instinctively, she removed the ring from her left hand and placed it on the index finger of her right hand, then flung her arms around his neck.

The two brothers changed their violin melody to a lively upbeat tune, and everyone in the room got up and started clapping and dancing to celebrate, including Charles, Suzanne, Mr and Mrs Jones, and the staff. At the end, Charles asked the brothers to join them at their table for dinner, but they had to leave.

"Oh, before you go, can we get a photo with you please?" Suzanne jumped up with her camera. She knew her boys wouldn't believe this had happened without proof. Mr Jones offered to take the picture.

When *Nuttin' but Stringz* had left, Suzanne exclaimed "Charles, don't tell me you flew them all the way over from the US? That must have cost you a *fortune*!"

"Nah" he responded laughing, "I met them in the hotel lobby earlier – I recognised them from one of the boys' CD covers, got talking to them, and when I told them I was planning on proposing to you this evening, they offered to play"

They had told Charles that a wealthy family had commissioned them to play at their son's 21st birthday party, which is why they were there.

"Phew, that was a stroke of luck!" Suzanne said, relieved.

"It was meant to be" said Mr Jones.

****

The Secret

Charles asked Mr and Mrs Jones "What's the secret to your long and happy marriage?"
The couple looked at each other before turning back to him and replying:

(Husband) "Always go to bed with forgiveness in your heart – never carry hurt or begrudging over to the next day"

(Wife) "Pray together. Having God in the centre of our marriage is what keeps it strong"

(Husband) "I make sure I tell her I love her every day – and I mean it!"

(Wife) "Make time for each other, even when the children start coming – do you have children?"

"Yes, three" Charles responded.

"Well that's wonderful to see you're still taking time out to spend time together. That's important in a relationship. Ever since we got married, we've always had one weekend a month to ourselves, without the children. Either they would go to his sister's, or mine. We would 'share the care'; we would have their children once a month so they could have *their* Time Out too. And they're still married as well!" Catherine enthused.

(Husband) "Yes, it's important to have a good support network around you, either friends who are also married, or couples like us who have been happily married for years, who can give you advice during the rough periods – because they *will* come. It's inevitable. But you've got to have *stick-ability*. Remember why you decided to get married in the first place. Remember the vows you made to each other".

Suzanne asked "Will *you* be our mentors?" and looking at Charles added "I'd love to think that *we*'ll still be in love after 30 years of marriage, like you are".

"We're not so much *in love* as in *commitment* to each other" Mrs Jones corrected. "If you fall in love, it's just as easy to fall out of love again. But it's our *commitment* to each other that keeps us going, more than our love for each other."

Still, Charles joined in; "I agree, will you be our mentors?"

In unison the couple reply "We would love to!"

Excitedly, they exchanged email addresses and home phone numbers so they could keep in contact.

****

When they reached back home, they couldn't wait to show the boys the photos and start doing research on the Pyramids, the Sphinx, and other places of interest in Ancient Kemet –
and to inform family members of their decision to officially 'tie the knot'.

****

Breaking News

Charles arrived at Maria's at 6.30pm as usual. It was a Wednesday evening. When he arrived, Maria already had her coat on, and announced she was going out.

"She's had her dinner and bath, all you have to do is play with her and when she's ready for bed, make her a cup of hot chocolate" she said as she hurried through the door. She was looking rather ravishing, in a tight black sleeveless mini dress. 'Where's she going dressed like that?' Charles wondered as he headed for the living room. Ebony was sitting on the floor watching one of the classic Sesame Street DVD's he'd bought for her.

Seeing him come through the door, she got up and ran towards him with her arms raised, crying out "Daddy, daddy!"

"Ah, come here my girl!" he said, scooping her up and giving her a big hug and kiss.

He spent the next couple of hours playing with Ebony, reading to her, and singing songs with her before she finally fell asleep in his arms after her milk. Charles looked at his watch. It was 8.30pm. He should be leaving now, but Maria wasn't back yet.

He carried his sleeping beauty upstairs and placed her gently in her bed.

Returning to the living room, he opened his briefcase and took out some papers. 'Might as well get some work done until Maria gets back'.

Another hour passed with still no sign of Maria. He called her mobile...no reply. He didn't bother to leave a message, thinking she'd call him back as soon as she saw his missed call, no doubt.

Another half an hour passed. Suzanne called.

"Where are you?"

"I'm still at Maria's, babe. She went out and I'm still waiting for her to get back"

A sudden feeling of panic gripped her, but she chose not to entertain the negative thoughts that would make her doubt Charles' integrity.

"How's Ebony?"

"She's perfect. She's fast asleep now; as soon as Maria gets back I can leave"

"Ok, well be home as soon as you can, I'm waiting up for you"

"As soon as she's back, I'm out of here"

"Ok babe, see you later. Love you"

"Love you too".

It had gone 10.30pm before Charles finally heard the key turn in the lock.

He had dozed off, but the sound of the door opening woke him up again. Maria entered the living room looking ravishing and slightly dishevelled at the same time. She had obviously had one or two drinks; she was never a drinker.

"Hey, you still here?" she slurred.

"Where did you expect me to have gone, my daughter's here, remember?"

"It's not *me* that needs to remember, it's *you*" Maria stated, removing her high heeled shoes as she moved towards him.

Charles stood up, putting himself on guard.

"Look Maria, I'm really sorry things didn't work out between us, but you know I'm doing the best I can by you and Ebony"

"Well, your best isn't good enough; I'm a woman, I'm the mother of your child, I have needs, I want more Charles...I want you back!"

He knew this was coming. He had to fight to resist the temptation.

"Now listen Maria, that's not gonna happen" he said, holding her by the arms as she tried to fling them around his neck.

"Why not? Look at me!" she backed up and began removing her clothes.

"No Maria, stop!" Charles rushed forward to stop her from going any further.

"Why? Don't you still want me?" she asked seductively, stepping out of her dress. All she was wearing was the red Victoria's Secret bra and pantie set he'd bought her before she had Ebony. She still looked great in it. Charles felt a stirring in his nether regions as he struggled to look away. He remembered Suzanne telling him that he was free to do as he pleased, that she had no expectations of him...but that if he cheated on her, she would know. Was it worth the risk? No, he decided.

Taking his mind off her body and sex, he covered his eyes and said sternly;

"Listen Maria, I've got something I need to tell you"
Hearing the serious tone in his voice, Maria stopped making advances.

"What is it?"
"I'm getting married"
"What? *Married*? To who?"
"Who do you think? Suzanne of course"
"But...WHY?"
"What do you mean, *why*?"
"Why would you marry *her* when you can have *me*...and your

daughter is here...we could be a *family*..."

"Stop right there Maria. We tried that, remember? It didn't work"

"Yes, but I was still getting over having our baby, I wasn't myself, you could see that..."

"Maria...please don't make this harder for us than it has to be. You know we were never really compatible. I'm glad we have Ebony, and you *know* I'll always support you both in the best way I can, but it's Suzanne I love. We're getting married Maria. I just wanted you to know".

Without another word Maria picked up her clothes from the floor, and turning away from him, headed slowly out of the room, as if in a daze.

"Maria!" Charles called after her.

Not replying, she continued heading upstairs towards her bedroom.

He gathered his things together and left quietly.

****

Best Man

Charles calls Dave.

"Long time no hear! How's things, bro?" Dave asked.

"Oh man, life just seems to get better and better!" Charles replied enthusiastically.

"Wow, what's that woman *doing* to you?" Dave asked in an amused tone.

Charles laughed. "I've met my match, that's all I can say. Actually, I'm calling because I want you to be Best Man at my wedding"

"You're getting *married*?"

"Yeah"

"Damn, she really has you hooked, hasn't she? What about Maria?"

"What about her?"

"Well, how did she react when you told her you were getting married?"

"She wasn't happy as you can imagine, but life goes on, you know. Besides, technically, I was with Suzanne before I was with her"

"Yes but *she's* the one with your child – Suzanne already has two of her own – are you planning on having one with her too?"

"I dunno – we'll see" Charles had always imagined himself getting married before he had children, and now the thought of having two children for two different women didn't really appeal to him, or reflect his character. But he knew he had to be true to him Self.

"Did you get your ring back from her?" Dave asked.

"Of course not!"

"You mean you had to buy another ring?!"

"What, you think I'd take the ring off Maria and put it on Suzanne? You're crazy, man!"

They both laughed.

"Well, I'm happy for you bro. So when's the big day?" asked Dave.

"Next June – and we're getting married abroad, so you'll have to book the week off work!"

****

Year Ten: A Spiritual Union

Suzanne left Charles to deal with all the legalities of getting married abroad, while she dealt with organising the wedding venue, booking the hotels, sending out invitations, and getting their outfits made, etc.

The last thing they wanted was to get married abroad and then find out their marriage wasn't valid in the UK, so they hired an overseas wedding planning agency to make sure everything was in order. Their plan was to keep it simple; no more than 50 guests, a small ceremony, with wedding and honeymoon in the same location! However the more they planned, the more complicated it got; family members not being able to afford the airfare, friends not being able to travel on the dates, other friends demanding to know why they hadn't been invited, parents complaining that the price of airfares were nearly doubled around that time as it was a school holiday and that they would have preferred to take their children out of school... Then when Charles asked Maria if Ebony could be bridesmaid, she point blank refused, saying there was no way she was going to allow him to take her out of the country. But when he offered her an all-expenses-paid trip to accompany Ebony, she finally agreed.

Charles' mother, now in her late 60's, was usually firmly against getting on an aeroplane. But as soon as he told her he was getting married abroad she somehow overcame her fear of flying. There was no way she was going to miss her only son's wedding!

With the money they saved from having a traditional white wedding in England, they contributed towards airfares and accommodation for their guests.

****

"It's time for me to change my coil" Suzanne announced.
Charles didn't know what she was talking about.
"What coil?"

"Don't you remember? I told you I'd had a coil fitted when you asked why I wasn't getting pregnant!"
"Oh! Oh yes...sorry, I forgot. So it's time for what?"
"To have it removed. I can either get a new one fitted, or we can try for a baby" she said sitting on his lap.
Charles rested his hand on her stomach.
"A baby sounds nice" he replied.

****

Build-up to the Big Day

Their wedding was scheduled for the 25th June, which was a Wednesday.
Most of their guests were due to arrive on the Tuesday, but Suzanne and Charles, Dave his Best Man, Janice (bridesmaid), and the boys arrived in Cairo on the Sunday to make sure all the preparations were going according to plan.
It was so hot that they had to spend the first day inside the air-conditioned villa acclimatising to the heat. Suzanne had planned it so that all the men closest to Charles would stay in one villa with him prior to the wedding, and all the women closest to her would stay in another villa. Other guests would stay in a nearby hotel.
They had agreed that not sharing a room the days leading up to their wedding would only add to the excitement and anticipation. They both wanted their wedding night to be extra special.
Both Charles and Suzanne were aware that something had happened the night they made love after returning from the African restaurant, and ever since then, their love-making had gone to another level. It was as if they could transport themselves to another dimension quite easily each time they made love, which is why they made a point of preparing themselves for each sacred sexual encounter. Charles had agreed not to eat any meat that week, and they had also agreed not to consume any dairy products or alcohol.
Suzanne had brought all the things they would need for their Sex Ritual, including incense, candles, massage oil and music.

****

Pre-wedding Celebrations

Charles had made sure that Maria was on the same flight as his sisters and mother so they could all travel together, and hopefully build stronger bonds. His sisters thought Maria was a stuck-up bitch, but they loved Ebony. Mrs Ankrah (Charles' mother) took Maria in as one of her own and by the time they arrived in Cairo, they were all like family.

The day before the wedding, Charles and Suzanne spent the afternoon and early evening entertaining their arriving guests in the hotel lounge. It was good re-uniting with old friends and family members, especially the ones they hadn't seen in years. Mr and Mrs Jones, their mentors, also came for the wedding, saying they wouldn't have missed it for the world.

Charles introduced them to both his and Suzanne's mothers, and the older generation formed a little clique of their own.

Dave took Maria under his wing, under Charles' request. He was attracted to her, but he could see that she still had feelings for Charles, so as it was, he just made sure that she didn't feel isolated.

Micah and Elijah asked Maria if Ebony could play with them and the other children. She said yes, but asked them to stay away from the swimming pool with her. They said ok, even though they knew five-year-old Ebony was a great swimmer, since Charles had been teaching her to swim since the age of three.

Suzanne decided to use this opportunity to make another effort to befriend Maria, but as she approached, Maria got up and walked off, mumbling something about needing a cigarette. She passed a silent blessing over her and carried on mingling with the other guests.

By 6pm she was ready to head back to the women's villa for an early night. Tomorrow was going to be a long day.

****

Men Talk

That night, Charles and his group of men relaxed in their villa.

"I still can't believe you're finally getting *married*!" commented Dave, glugging from a cold can of beer.

"Why's that such a big shock to you?" Charles asked his Best Man.

"Well look how long we've known each other Charles; you've always been really particular about the women you date, and now here you are getting married to a woman with *two kids*!"

"They're not kids Dave, they're young men, and they're great. I'm proud to be part of their lives. Besides, when love strikes you're powerless to resist and the circumstances don't really matter"

"So what's so special about Suzanne?" Peter, one of their old schoolmates asked.

"Yeah, why choose her over the woman you already have a child with?" asked another.

"...And she ain't half bad looking either!" commented Dave, referring to Maria.

Charles looked around to make sure no-one else was within hearing distance.

"Promise me this won't go any further than these four walls?"

The other brothers crossed their fingers over their chests in half-solemn oaths.

"Well it's like this...Suzanne and I...when we make love, it's like nothing I've ever experienced before...seriously...it's like we're entering another world – I mean, we literally get transported into another dimension!"

The other brothers looked at each other before bursting into fits of laughter.

"That sounds like some freaky kinda sex, man!" one commented.

"So when you enter this 'other dimension', what do you see, angels, aliens, or what?"

Charles remained silent.

"Aw, don't take it to heart, we're just messing with you bro...but are you serious about the aliens?" he asked again.

"I didn't mention aliens" Charles responded, getting up to refill his glass of water.

"How can I explain it? This woman of mine, Suzanne, she's like my soulmate, you know? If you seriously want to know what I'm talking about, I suggest you find your goddesses and Queens too. Until you do, you won't be able to enter the gateway that leads to heaven on earth."

****

The Big Day

The wedding was scheduled for 11am. Suzanne had wanted it to take place early since they were both early risers, and she wanted them to be away somewhere quiet by 6pm the latest.

She got up at 6am and went out into the pool area to sit and meditate. An hour or so later, Janice joined her.

"Morning!"

"Oh, good morning Janice! Where's Keisha and Annette?"

"They're still sleeping. What are you doing up so early?"

"I *always* get up early" she informed her sister, beginning her yoga stretches.

"Ah, it's so peaceful here!" Janice turned her face towards the sun.

"Yes, it's lovely"

"So how do you feel? Today's the big day!"

"I feel...happy and grateful. God couldn't have chosen a better man for me"

"Yes, Charles is a nice fella – and he's got money too! I hope I find someone like him"

"Yes, well money isn't everything. Money can't buy happiness, or love...and besides, when you meet the right person, there's nothing you can't achieve anyway. Money will be no object"

"Is that so?"

"Of course!"

"Well you two seem to have figured it out...so how did you attract someone like Charles, anyway?" Janice asked.
Out of all the sisters, Suzanne had been considered the least attractive when they were growing up, since she was the darkest.

"Well first of all, it starts with your Self. Whatever you desire to see manifest in your outer world, you must first create it *within*. So if you're looking for say, unconditional love, first love your *Self* unconditionally. See what I mean?"

"Yes but I *do* love myself, and I *still* haven't attracted anyone like Charles – all the guys I seem to meet are full of themselves! Why can't *I* meet someone who's rich, handsome and spiritual?"

"Well you both have to be on the same wavelength mentally, for a start. I developed an abundance mentality, so I attracted someone on that same vibration, and we were able to achieve our goals together. I actually believe God was preparing us for each other long before we met"

"Really? So what about Ebony...and Maria?"

"Yes...God can have a plan for you, and you can go off track from that path. But you can always get back on track again, it's never too late"

"So where does that leave Maria?"

"Maria will attract the right man for her, someone who's on her wavelength. The universe is abundant. She'll be fine"

Just then, Annette, Keisha and the two mothers appeared.

"Good morning! Did you have a good sleep?" Suzanne asked, hugging them all.

"Yes thanks!" they replied.

"So are you ready for your big day?" asked her mum.

"Definitely! Keisha, if I get in the shower now, can you style my hair when I come out?" she asked her sister, a hairdresser by profession.

"Of course! I brought some extra hair to make a beehive style for you..."

"No thanks, if you can just style my *own* hair that would be great. I brought some hairpins and a tiara, that should do, shouldn't it?"

"Ok it's *your* hair!" Keisha gave in.

"I'll do your make-up!" Janice offered.

"Ok, but not too much, I want it to look as natural as possible"

"Aren't you going to have some breakfast before you start getting ready?" asked mum.

"I'm going to make a smoothie a bit later, nothing too heavy" she answered, pouring a glass of water for herself.

"How is that going to sustain you for the day?" replied mum in a concerned tone.

"I'll be fine mum, don't worry. When you're ready, call the hotel and order your breakfast, they'll bring it over. I'm getting in the shower now"

****

Two Become One

It was an open-air wedding, held in the hotel courtyard where a marquee had been set up. Beautiful flower arrangements with white and red roses decorated the walkway leading down to the altar where the ceremony would be taking place. Two purple and gold cushions lay at the altar, along with a large white pillar candle standing upright, and two long thin candles lying on either side of it.

All the guests took their seats. Charles and Dave stood at the front in their purple suits facing their guests while they waited for Suzanne. She was due to enter from the back and walk down the aisle to meet her groom. Micah and Elijah sat at the front on either end of the rows of chairs, alongside Charles and Suzanne's mothers, and their mentors Mr and Mrs Jones.

Soft organ music played in the background. The guests talked amongst themselves quietly while they waited for the bride to arrive.

Suddenly the music became louder, and all the guests turned to see little Ebony walking down the aisle dropping white rose petals from the basket she was carrying.

Suzanne followed about two feet behind her, with Janice close behind. Suzanne had decided to do the walk alone, since her father had passed and she didn't feel anyone could replace him.

She wore a traditional white wedding dress, but had refused to wear the veil over her eyes, saying she was going into this (marriage) with her eyes wide open!

She walked down the aisle slowly and gracefully at first, carrying her bouquet of white and red roses in front of her – then suddenly broke into a 'hallelujah!' dance, mixing African and contemporary dance steps together as she waved her bouquet high and low, giving God thanks that this day had finally arrived! Everyone started laughing and clapping as they cheered her on.

Charles looked on in admiration, as visions of her dancing for him the night he made the decision to marry her came back to him. He suddenly left his position and began walking up the aisle to meet his bride, kissing his daughter along the way. As he approached her, Suzanne realised that the dream she'd had the year they met, of him walking towards her on their wedding day, was actually coming true! He offered her his arm, and they continued back down the aisle together, Charles with a proud look on his face. By this time everyone was standing and clapping, including Micah and Elijah.

The only person who wasn't happy was Maria, who rushed out in tears. Sarah, one of Charles' sisters, followed her. Both Suzanne and Charles were so caught up in the euphoria of the moment that they were oblivious to the situation.

As they reached the priest, they turned and faced each other. After the priest had performed the traditional part of the ceremony to make it legal in Egypt, they incorporated their own ritual into the rest of the proceedings.

Kneeling on the purple cushions, they each picked up one of the long thin candles lying at the altar. Micah and Elijah got up and lit them before returning to their seats.

Holding the glowing candles, they took it in turn to make their vows to each other based on Conversations with God:

"I purposefully agree to use this relationship as an *opportunity* for mutual growth, full Self-expression, and for ultimate re-union with God through the joining of our two souls"

"I recognise that while we are one, we still have our individual paths to follow; I will allow you the freedom to walk your own path"

"I will not impose my will upon you, or try to manipulate your mind"

"I will not lose my Self in this relationship, but will use it as an

opportunity, not an *obligation*, to decide Who I Really Am"
"The test of our relationship will not be how well I live up to *your* ideas, but how well I live up to *my own* ideas"
"I promise to give you my love and energy without expecting the same in return"
"I will always keep in mind that whatever I do to you, I do to my Self, and whatever I do *for* you, I do for my Self"

As they looked into each other's eyes making their vows, the crowd's attention was diverted by the flicker in the candle's flames;

"I acknowledge that there *will* be challenges along the way, so I commit to doing whatever I can to make this relationship work, to always see the God (good) in you, and to constantly remind you of Who You Are through my actions"
"I will do my best to remember that winning or losing is not the test, but only loving or failing to love"
"In any challenging situation, I will always ask my Self: *"What would Love do now?"*

When they had finished making their vows to each other, they simultaneously lit the large pillar candle together, then blew out their individual candles, symbolising the two becoming one.

Micah and Elijah then presented the rings; after Charles had placed Suzanne's wedding ring on her finger, she removed the engagement ring from the index finger on her right hand and placed it on her left finger to join her wedding ring. She then took the second ring from Micah and placed it on Charles' finger.

The priest announced "You are now husband and wife!"

As Charles kissed his bride long and slow, their guests stood up again, and applauded.

****

At the reception, Charles made a moving speech telling the story of how they met, and the strange feeling that had come over him, as if he had known her from somewhere before – perhaps in a previous lifetime? He shared how every time they split up and got back together it always felt like 'coming home', and that his inner compass had always seemed to point back to Suzanne. He re-lived the night he had finally made the decision to marry her, the night she had danced for him. He said he was happy to have inherited two wonderful boys like Micah and Elijah, and that he would do his best to be a good role model for them, then thanked Suzanne's family for adopting him into *their* family.

He then addressed Maria personally, thanking her for blessing him with a beautiful daughter, and asked her to forgive him for following his heart, saying he was praying that God would provide the perfect partner for her too.

Tears streamed down her face as he spoke to her from his heart; even Suzanne was finding it hard to hold back the tears. Little Ebony left her seat and went up to her father who scooped her up with his left arm. Holding the mic with his right hand he continued with his speech;

"I want to thank you all for coming out here and sharing this special occasion with Suzanne and I, and making today such a beautiful day. To all you single women, keep visualising your Self with your perfect partner; think about what you want, not what you *don't* want in a relationship, and then ask your Self, "if that man came along, would I be the type of woman that *he* would want?" Use your single time to develop your Self and prepare your Self for your mate. And men, raise your consciousness levels, there are many Queens out there waiting for their Kings. They need you, and you need them. Find each other".

With that, he sat down with Ebony on his lap, to a resounding applause.

When they had all settled down again, Suzanne stood up and walked to the centre of the floor space. The backing track to her poem *'True Love'* started playing, and she recited the poem she had written based on 1 Corinthians 13:

What is the true meaning of the word 'Love'?
The thing is, 'Love' has so many meanings!
So when you say to me "I love you"

Do you mean you're in love with the way I look
Or the way I make you feel
Or you love the way I walk, talk, laugh, smell or appeal?
Is it my smile that captivates you?
Or the way I wear my hair?
Or is it the clothes I wear that makes you stop and stare?

Is it that you love ME because of how I treat YOU,
With Tender Loving Care?
I cook for you, I clean for you, I massage you
I dote on YOU.

Or do I love YOU because of what you can give ME
A nice home, fancy car, a lovely family

Security...

Do I love you with all sincerity
Or am I just thinking of me?

What is the true meaning of the word 'Love'?

*True Love is a commitment of the **heart**;*
Right from the start it says
"I CHOOSE to love you
Whether we're together, or apart"

Love never fails.

*True Love says "I'm going to be **patient** with you –*
When you try my patience, I'll <u>still</u> love you"
Love never fails.

*True Love is **kind**; it sows a seed*
It's helpful, merciful and benevolent to those in need

Love never fails.

*True Love is **never envious** of what I have,*
But it inspires you to reach your <u>own</u> goals,
And doesn't boast when it does.

Love never fails.

*True Love **isn't proud** –*
Pride comes before a fall! (giving Charles a knowing look)
But in Love you can stand tall.

Love never fails.

*True Love **isn't rude or selfish***
And doesn't feel the need to be loud,
Or to always have centre stage in a crowd.

Love never fails.

*True Love **isn't easily angered**,*
*It **forgives and forgets***
Even when it's difficult,
And it leaves no regrets.

Love never fails.

*True Love **always protects***
And when I'm down in the dumps
***Never rejoices in** my **downfalls**,*
***Only in** my **triumphs**.*

Love never fails.

*True Love **always trusts**, never accuses,*

***Always hopes**, never doubts*
***Always perseveres**, never gives up.*

Love never fails.

I love you, unreservedly
And can you say you love me, unconditionally?

LOVE NEVER FAILS. *(Track 12 on the CD 'Seeds of Love')*

After she had finished her poem, she turned to Charles and mouthed to him "I LOVE YOU."

And he mouthed back "I LOVE YOU TOO".

****

The reception was held in an elaborately decorated hall inside the hotel.
For the opening dance, Charles chose *'Here and Now'* by Luther Vandross, while Suzanne chose *'Always and Forever'* by Heatwave. They danced as if they were the only two people in the room, reminiscent of the day they first met.

Maria left the celebrations and went into the hotel lobby. Dave followed her.
"Hi Maria, how are you?"
"How do you *think* I am?" she answered coldly.
"Hey listen, I'm on your side. I know this is painful for you.
 You're a brave woman, Maria. Not many women would have attended their ex's wedding"
"Yes well I'm only here because of Ebony. I wish I hadn't come now...this is so unfair!" she broke down in tears. Allowing her to sob into his chest, he put a hand around her bare shoulder.
"Listen, if it's any consolation, I think Suzanne has nothing on you"
"Really?" she asked looking up at him with her big, hazel eyes.

"Nah...I mean look at you...you're beautiful, intelligent, you know how to dress, you're strong...I know who *I'd* be with if I was Charles" he said, admiring her lemon yellow mini dress against her bronze flawless skin.

"Ok ok, I know you're just saying that to make me feel better" she said, dabbing her face dry with a handkerchief from her bag.

"No, I'm serious! I tried to get him to see sense, but he wasn't having any of it. I mean, Suzanne's a nice woman, don't get me wrong, but if I had to choose, I'd choose you every time."

Maria paused, taking in the compliments before suggesting "I need to get out of here...d'you fancy a walk on the beach?"

****

The Challenge

Suzanne and Charles left the wedding reception at 5.30pm and took the short limousine ride to *Le Méridien Pyramids Hotel* on the other side of Cairo.

The 5* hotel had a breathtaking view of the pyramids of Giza. They were due to spend 3 days there, before rejoining their guests. While they were gone, Suzanne left a list of excursions that would be running each day for the guests to book if they chose to. She also left some information based on the research she and Charles had done about the pyramids and Sphinx.

She wrote a short essay for their guests to give them a deeper understanding of the places they would be visiting. In it, she explained that before Egypt was raided by the Arabs and Europeans it was occupied by *Africans*, and that it had originally been called Ancient Kemet which meant 'Land of the Blacks'. She informed them that ancient wisdom, knowledge and understanding of Universal Laws had been stolen from Ancient Kemet, and that this knowledge was now being kept within the hands of a select few.

She said that this small group of rich white men liked to call themselves 'the Iluminati' which meant 'enlightened ones', due to the knowledge they had acquired when they raided the tombs, pyramids and universities. They had hijacked symbols like the Pyramid, Eye of Horus and cross and were now using them against their original purposes. Instead of sharing the knowledge of the sciences practiced by the ancient Egyptians, they were now using them to control the masses. They had even plagiarised the original concept of religion and twisted it to create *other* religions, also used as forms of control. Suzanne explained how these people had tried to wipe out any knowledge that Egypt had originally been occupied by Blacks, and that its ancient secrets were developed by Black people, and had tried to claim Egypt as *their* history, even though it's in Africa!

She gave their guests the task of looking for clues that Egypt had originally been built by Africans during their stay. She told them the writing was on the walls. She said to look closely at the Sphinx; was that the face of a Black person or white person? Even though the nose and lips had been vandalised, it was still plainly obvious, she claimed. She invited them to spend the next few days looking for clues that Egypt was in fact, a Black land, and not to be fooled by its present occupiers.

Their guests rose to the challenge. They split into two teams and set about finding out how much of what Suzanne had said was true. Whichever team came back with the most information after the three days, had won.

Maria and Ebony were due to leave the day after the wedding, but Maria decided to extend their stay, so Ebony could bond with her new grandmother, aunties and cousins, she said.

****

A Marriage of *Minds*

Suzanne and Charles spent their first night together as a married couple. Their sexual union was too sacred to mention here – let's just say that for the first two days, no-one saw or heard from them.

On the third day, they emerged from their hotel room looking more in love and united than ever.

They had breakfast in the hotel's courtyard where they had a breathtaking view of the pyramid Giza.

"I wonder what it would look like if it still had its original limestone casing" Suzanne thought.

"Wow, yes I can just imagine!" Charles answered, gazing up at it.

That was when they both realised they could communicate without actually speaking to each other!

They both sat visualising the pyramid in its full original glory and splendour. They imagined it beaming angles of light so bright that they could be seen from outer space.

Later that day they went sight-seeing on the way to re-joining their guests. As Charles stood staring up at a great obelisk carved with hieroglyphs, Suzanne took a picture. When they reviewed the image on the camera, it looked as if Charles was catching a sphere of light in his hand...

"Wow, how did you do that?" he asked Suzanne.
"I didn't do it, you did!" she replied.

They both looked more closely.

As Charles had been paying homage to his ancestor, it was as if the soul of Imhotep had come down to greet him. It sent a chill up their spines.

It was a picture Charles would treasure forever.

****

Blessings

When they arrived back that evening, their guests greeted them excitedly. Charles was surprised to see Maria and Ebony still there.

"Daddy, daddy!" Ebony ran up to greet him.

Picking her up, they made their way into the hotel where they would be staying in the Honeymoon Suite that night.

"Did you miss me?" Suzanne asked the boys.

"Mum, look at us, we're not babies anymore" Elijah answered, giving her a hug.

They had one final get-together with their guests in the hotel's banqueting suite. They would all be leaving the next day.

As they all took part in the last supper, Dave pulled Charles to one side.

"I've got something I need to tell you" he said.

"Ok I'm all ears"

"Man... I don't really know how to say this" Dave stuttered.

"Hey, this is me – besides, I have a feeling I know what you're going to say anyway"

"Really? Try me!"

"You've taken a liking to Maria, haven't you?"

"How did you guess?!"

Charles laughed.

"It's kinda obvious, bro. You want to know if I approve, right?"

"You've got me all sussed, haven't you?" replied Dave coyly.

"Dave, how long have we known each other? You're practically my *brother*. Of course I could tell you like Maria!"

Dave replied "It's just that...well, no-one has ever made me feel the way she does Charles. I've fallen for her hook, line and sinker. I'm sorry."

"Well, you have my blessing"

"I do?!"

"Of course...what better step-father could I possibly want for my daughter than my best friend?" he answered, giving Dave a man-hug.

****

Year Eleven – Double Celebrations!

'Love Bump' by Cezanne

As Suzanne lay across her husband's lap doing her pelvic floor muscle exercises, she thought about how happy and grateful she was to finally be living the life of her dreams: She was happily married to the man of her dreams, they were financially independent and running a successful business, and were in a position to help others in their community. On top of that, they had three wonderful children, with another one on the way.

They relaxed together on their large purple sofa with *'Fertile Ground'* playing softly in the background; *'Let's build our home from this empty nest...'*

It reminded Suzanne of how long it had taken to build their relationship into the solid structure it was now. It had been a lot of hard work, laying the foundation, and painstakingly building upon it bit by bit. But it had been worth the effort, and now nothing could tear it down again unless they themselves chose to, and they had both worked too hard to want to destroy what they had built together.

The roses on the cushions decorating their sofa made a positive affirmation of their love, stronger than thorns. One of the reasons their love was so strong was that they both took time out to develop themselves individually. By giving each other the space to grow, they had allowed their love to blossom, like the roses on the cushions.

On a glass table beside the sofa stood a framed picture of their wedding day; Suzanne's trophy.

She had also been inspired to collate ten photographs of herself and Charles in their happiest moments, and using Photoshop, had typed each of the vows they had made on their wedding day unto each photo. All 'Ten Commitments' were then framed and displayed around their home, acting as a constant reminder of the promises they had made to each other.

Personally, Suzanne didn't believe in the 'institution' of marriage, believing it was a spiritual union that only God could sanction, not a man-made ceremony. But Charles had convinced her that it made life easier legally if they officially married, plus it provided greater stability for their children, and would set a good example to the boys. There would be no divorce, splitting of assets or fighting over money, he had promised her. Suzanne knew Charles was committed to her whole-heartedly, and so despite her own personal viewpoints, she had happily married him.

And now here they were, celebrating their first year of wedded bliss. They had reason for double celebrations too, since they were also expecting the imminent birth of their first baby together!

Charles slid her top up, revealing her huge, ripe belly, tight like a drum.

"Let me see if I can hear the heartbeat" he said, breaking into her thoughts.

Laying his head gently on their 'love bump' (as they liked to call it) he linked hands with hers as he tuned into his unborn child. They had agreed to wait until the birth to find out the sex of the baby; they already had two boys and a girl between them, so they thought it would be nice to keep it a surprise. Secretly though, Suzanne was hoping for a girl of her own since she already had two boys, yet on the other hand, she thought it would be nice to give Charles a son of his own.

Over the years, Charles had become a father figure to her boys. Whenever they had 'man issues' to discuss, rather than go to their dad, they would go to Charles. When they reached puberty, it was he who did the 'pep talk'. He took them to football matches with him, and they would often go out together, just 'the men'. Suzanne didn't mind, in fact, she appreciated it, as it gave her time to her Self.

Now aged 16 and 18, the boys had stopped wanting to go to their dad's every other weekend, preferring to stay at home and entertain friends instead.

So now here they were, one big happy family.

They had just moved into a beautiful 7 bedroom detached house on the outskirts of London which they had bought a year ago in a state of disrepair, and had renovated to their own specifications. The house was arranged over four floors; in the basement they had built a state-of-the-art cinema room and a games room where they entertained friends and family. There was also a mini studio for Suzanne to record her poetry. She had also planned to help other Black poets record their poetry too; she felt that the wealth of literary talent within the Black community had to be recorded so it could go down in history. She would have to put that project on hold and wait until the baby was a bit older now.

Charles liked to use the basement whenever he had his friends over, as it gave them privacy.

On the ground floor, they had designed a large open-plan living room with floor-to-ceiling sliding doors leading to their beautifully landscaped garden; its main feature was the exquisite water fountain. Large comfortable L-shaped leather sofas were placed near the glass doors, where the family sat together most evenings. A 52" flat-screen t.v. was built into the wall.

A large carved oak table and leather-padded chairs which could seat up to 10 people dominated one corner of the room. Their kitchen was directly off the main living room adjacent to the dining area.

Another wall was lined from floor to ceiling with their combined collection of books, but Suzanne kept her personal books in their bedroom, the ones which she had marked all her personal notes in.

In one corner, a huge fish tank with all kinds of tropical fish featured. Big tropical plants were also placed strategically around the bright, airy room.

Although they had the money to buy more elaborate furnishings, they were both content with the minimal look. As long as Suzanne had her fresh-cut flowers in every room replaced weekly, she was happy.

Charles' mother was getting on in age, so they had moved her in. Her living space was also on the ground floor so she didn't have to climb any stairs. She loved cooking, and had taken this on as her daily task, while Suzanne continued to make smoothies and fresh juices for the family every day. She wanted to make sure they were taking in a high content of Mother Nature's foods, which would help them to operate at a higher frequency.

The first floor was dominated by the boys; they called it the 'boyzone'; Micah and Elijah each had their own bedroom with en-suite shower rooms, and a 'chill-out' room where they could relax and watch D.V.D's or play video games. The entire top floor belonged to Suzanne and Charles. She had wanted to call it her Queendom (as she had always called her bedroom when she was single) but in the end, they had called it 'The Kingdom of Heaven'. You needed a key to enter, and only Suzanne and Charles held them. Entering their Haven was like entering another world – but that was their privacy. Ebony's room was also on the top floor, but she only slept there when she came at weekends.

The road they lived on was quiet, with lots of trees and greenery. In the morning, all you could hear was the sound of birds singing. Even though there was only one other black family on their road, they didn't feel out of place in the area.

Charles and Suzanne had created their own idea of 'heaven on earth'.

They could also now afford to go on holiday together as a family during every school and college break. And even though Suzanne could never understand why she had to pay extra for the 'luxury' of eating food the way nature intended it to be, at least she could now afford to feed the family with the best foods; *organic*.

Suzanne didn't have to worry about how she was going to cope with keeping such a large house clean *and* a new baby, since they could afford to pay a cleaner to do most of the housework, and her husband, sons and mother-in-law were also on hand to help.

She had achieved her goal of making a living doing what she loved; writing and performing her poetry. She had already published a book of poetry with its complimentary CD, and continued writing poetry for the inspirational black greeting cards and prints that their business produced. She was also working on her first book.

Their business was generating an income from both online and high street sales, and due to the uniqueness of their products, they were building a base of loyal customers from all over the world who placed repeat orders, while constantly adding new ones. Even as she lay there pregnant, money was still going into their bank accounts. All they had to do was advertise every month. They had started the business designing products featuring his artwork and her poetry, and were now increasing their product range by buying in artwork and poetry from other artists and poets of African descent. This enabled them to diversify their range, while at the same time providing a way for other 'artisans' to earn a living from their talents.

What more could she ask for? She was living the life of her dreams.

It was almost too good to be true, she thought.

Love is...a wonderful gift between two souls experiencing heaven on earth.

****

In the Beginning...

Now in the third trimester of her pregnancy, Suzanne kept herself mentally and physically active.

After her morning meditation and exercise classes, she would return home and write for a couple of hours a day, as well as do research. From the beginning of her pregnancy, she had made a conscious decision to keep her Self in a happy, healthy state, as she knew her moods would affect the baby. So she continued her yoga and meditation, and had also started aqua-aerobics. Charles' mother, 'Ma Ankrah as they had taken to calling her (short for 'grandma') often accompanied her; the classes were good for her too.

Even though she didn't *have* to work, Suzanne still felt a driving force within her to share the knowledge she had accumulated since asking God for 'the Truth'. What had started out as research for an article about Adam and Eve had turned into enough material to write a whole *book*!

She had already learnt that 'Adam and Eve and the Garden of Eden' story were simply metaphors, and now she was beginning to wonder if the whole *bible* was written in metaphors, including the story of Jesus. Historically, there was no evidence to prove that the man 'Jesus' ever existed. There were no official records, no artefacts, no works of carpentry, no Self-written manuscripts by Jesus, and no eye-witness accounts. Yet there were plenty of written accounts regarding *other* events that had taken place around the time Jesus was supposed to have walked the earth. And considering he had attracted such large crowds, was a threat to the reigning king and religious establishment, had healed the sick and raised the dead it was odd that no-one *at the time* had written about him, she contemplated.

The gospels that now make up the New Testament were written at least 40 years *after* when they say he was crucified – there was not one 'gospel' written during his lifetime, neither by his followers, authorities, or the 'scribes'!

So if Jesus is a metaphor, what is he a metaphor *for*? she wondered.

Suzanne also learned that the artist Michaelangelo had been commissioned by King James to paint images of a white Jesus, and had used his family members as models. Suzanne remembered being given a bible by her mother when she was growing up, with beautifully painted images throughout – of Caucasians. None of the images portraying any of the characters in the bible had been Black. What effect did that have on the psyche of African people, when all the images of the people they should look up to and worship were of white people, even Jesus, their 'Saviour'? Even the hand coming out of heaven representing God, was a white hand!

This challenged Suzanne's faith, since she had always believed she'd had a personal relationship with Jesus when she attended church. He had felt so real to her. She'd even written an inspired poem called *'Jesus Never Left You...'* But when she really thought about it, how damaging is it to a Black man's psyche to believe that a white man is his saviour? To sing songs of how much he loves Jesus, and to worship a white man?

Africans had been forced to forsake the honouring of their own ancestors to worship a white god through a religion that had been forced upon them through slavery and colonialism. Instead of them communicating with the spirits of their ancestors, as was their tradition, they were now spending their time trying to communicate with the dead of another race. Jesus himself had said his message was only for 'his people' – everyone else was considered a gentile, or worst still, a dog!

As she sat contemplating all of this, she remembered what Charles had told her about the missionaries bringing the bible into Africa, and Christianity being used to gain control over the wealth of the land. Looking at the state of Africa today, she could see that their plan had worked. They had the land, while Africans were mentally enslaved by their religions.

She also learnt how the 'missionary' position got its name, and why the Catholic religion liked their followers to call the priest 'Father' – not to mention the sexual perversion of their priests.

And now, her research had brought her from Adam and Eve, right through to the 'virgin birth' story of Isis and Horus.
She discovered that the story of Isis and Horus was very similar to the story of Mary and Jesus, yet it originated in Ancient Kemet, long before Christianity was ever contrived. The story had been plagiarised and used in many other religions, and apparently, Roman Catholics still worship the Black Madonna today, the original 'Mary' – Isis.

Suzanne was beginning to make a connection between the story of Isis and Horus, and the book of Genesis in the bible. She wrote them down like this:

Genesis
Genes/Isis

It seemed that the word 'Genesis' had been formed from the words 'Genes' and 'Isis'. What was the hidden meaning? She wondered.

Then there was the Council of Nicea. In a politically motivated move, the Council had been set up some 300 years after the alleged death of Christ, to put an end to the division between the various Christian churches. There were inconsistencies in the beliefs of the divinity of Jesus, when he was born, and what date his resurrection should be celebrated. So over 300 bishops from all over the world had gathered to finally agree on issues like 'was Jesus the Son of God?' 'When did he die?' and when his resurrection should be celebrated.

The bible is a collection of ancient manuscripts; some made it in, some didn't. The Council of Nicea made the decisions on what scripts should be included, and what should be left out. Any information that would teach the masses the real meaning of life and how to get their life to work, seemed to have been omitted.

Suzanne wondered if the knowledge of Universal Laws had been deliberately removed in order to keep the masses subservient. Was the creative power of our thoughts, our ability to speak things into being, to visualise and bring things into the physical from the spiritual realm deliberately shrouded in order to keep us in darkness?

Although the Council insisted that they hadn't changed anything from the original manuscripts, why had it taken them *three months* to make their decisions?

Suzanne was sure that the original manuscripts had indeed explained Universal Laws and how to get your life to work, but because the religious institution wanted to use the bible and other 'holy books' to control the masses, they had taken out the information that would empower people. She even doubted whether the scripture *'no man can come to the Father but through me'* was in the original manuscript. She believed that if it wasn't for this one scripture that made Jesus the only way to get to God, the Christian faith wouldn't even stand.

Without a doubt, there were *many* ways to get to God, as God was just too big to miss. The best way to get to God from her experience, was to go *within*.

The God she knew loved everybody, not just Christians, or Jews, or Muslims, or rich people, or blacks or whites. Every 'body' had an equal opportunity to get to 'heaven' through their thoughts, words and actions.

Suzanne watched the film 'The Matrix' again, this time with her third eye wide open. She could now see how this world *is* a 'matrix'; a perceived reality, a prison with no bars, a slave system. People get up and go to work, return home, watch 'programmes' on tell-lie-vision, go to bed, get up and do the same thing again the next day, like robots. They spend their hard-earned money on consumerism, which they have been told they *need* through adverts. They pay their mortgage or rent, bills, buy clothes to wear to work, and at the end of the month, might just have enough left over to be able to save for a holiday each year. If not, take out a loan or use your credit card, and pay twice as much for the holiday as advertised, with interest payments on the card. The banking system thrives on debt. The whole *world* is in debt, even Great Britain and America, who in turn have made Mother Africa, the richest continent in terms of natural resources, in debt to them.

"They will reap what they have sown" thought Suzanne. Not even they with all their money could escape Natural Laws.

'*...These people are not to be feared*' she wrote. '*They are a handful of white men who hide behind their massive wealth, stolen from countries in Africa, and from innocent individuals who are just trying to make a living for themselves and their families. They don't care whether people lose their homes or businesses, or of the psychological effect and stress it causes to the people. The more fear they can generate, the better. Fear is what their god feeds off*'.

'How can I really help my people to overcome and beat 'the system'?' she wondered.
The answer came to her immediately. Love.

Love?

"Love is the answer. Love is the complete opposite of fear, and banishes fear like a small candle lit in a dark room."

"Yes, but how does one apply that *practically*?" she asked again.

"Fill your Self up with Love, until there is no room left for fear"

She innerstood completely. Hating people was not the answer.

She allowed her Self to be guided as she wrote that instead of seeing people as the *enemy*, it was better to see all life's challenges as *opportunities* to decide Who We Really Are. '*We are naturally loving. We are naturally peaceful. We are naturally open to others. This has been our downfall in the past, yet now it was time to put our Selves first among those we love. If we put our Selves first, others won't be able to abuse us*', she wrote. She was hoping this message would especially reach leaders of countries and organisations that were oppressing their own people in order to help the white man achieve his objectives of taking over the Motherland, as well as those who were infecting the minds of the youth with lewd lyrics in their music, and the images they were portraying.

'To allow another to continually inflict damage may not be the most loving thing to do – for your Self or the other' (CWG Book 1)

Suzanne felt empathy towards those with a destructive nature, as she now realized it was due to their lack of Melanin. But her love for her people and the challenges they were now facing was more important to her. Her goal was to help them understand how to win the battle, and heal themselves.

She started off by drawing a diagram:

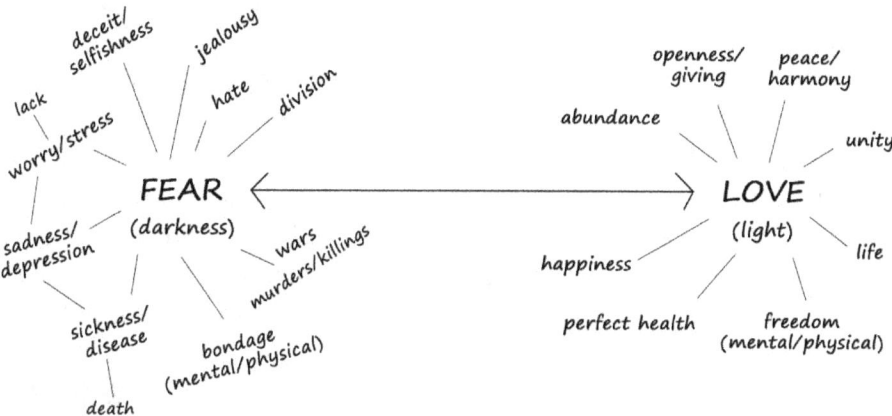

She then used it to explain that there are two forces in the universe; *fear* and *Love*. Both are needed in order to create the Universal Law of Polarity, which says that without one, you cannot experience the other. '*Without fear, you wouldn't know what Love is. It's just a natural Law of the Universe, like up and down, left and right, hot and cold*' she wrote.

She suggested that it was much easier and better to live a pure, simple life of Love rather than a complicated life full of fear.

She explained that since another Universal Law is '*what you focus on, you attract*', it's easy to see what you will attract by focusing on Love, and what you will attract if you focus on fear.

She described how the elitists who desire to control the world need our mass-consciousness to achieve their goals. They create fear-based religions, news reports, music, politics, 'programmes' on their tell-lie-vision, in order to generate enough fear to feed their evil objectives. "They understand the creative power of our thoughts. They are only a small percentage. It takes many *thoughts for something to manifest from the non-physical realm into the physical. But if we all stop allowing ourselves to be 'programmed' and focus on Love, abundance, peace, happiness and unity the world could change overnight, and the small group of elitists would no longer be in control".*

She said it was time to stop watching mainstream tell-lie-vision, start eating the foods our Mother Nature has provided so that our Pineal Gland can operate at its peak, stop listening to music that causes us to think and act in ways contrary to our true nature, and to focus on Love.

"There are those people who choose to worship the force of Love (God), and there are those who choose to worship the force of fear (Lucifer/the devil)" she wrote.

'It's interesting to note that there are those who THINK they are worshipping the force of Love, but in Truth, they are worshipping the force of fear. Pure Love has no fear. If you are worshipping God because you are afraid of what will happen if you don't, your love for God is fear-based'.

She described fear as a destructive force, while the force of Love is constructive, imaginative and creative.

She continued to write; *'It is the white man's FEAR of the Black Man and Black Woman that causes him act the way he does towards them. Together, the Black Man and Woman are powerful, and he knows it, which is why he does everything to try to keep them apart'.*

She added; *'The elitist white man fear Black Men and Women so much, that they are willing to kill off millions of their own, just to keep the Black Man, Woman and Child down. They know that ancient civilisations were built by Blacks, including knowledge of how the Universe works, sciences, mathematics, the arts, and that ancient wisdom is carried on through our genes. If we were to all wake up and remember Who We Really Are, they would no longer be in control. So they try to control us by removing us from our natural environment, mentally enslaving us through religions, mis-education, unhealthy food, corrupting music, mind-altering drugs, cigarettes and alcohol'.*

She explained that fighting fear-based behavior with more fear-based behavior was not the answer. *'The only way to defeat* fear-based behavior is by counter-attacking with Love-based actions. To act out of Love when someone is abusing you does not mean allowing the abuse to continue, on the contrary, allowing another to continually inflict damage may not be the most loving thing to do, for your Self, the other, or the planet, our Mother Earth. Operating in fear is not our true nature. When we take on other people's ways of acting and reacting, we're only defeating our Selves' she wrote.

'What is important to note was that all Africans need to unite in order to win this battle; those from the Continent, and descendents of the enslaved'.

'The way to counter-attack the demonic force is not with a negative mindset, but a mind and heart filled with Pure Love; beginning with love of Self, then love for your people, and love of your Mother, Nature. Let it start there before it branches out anywhere else – as they say 'charity begins at home'. She argued that Black people are the only people who seem to think that ensuring the preservation of their race is not important, and that doing things to uplift our community makes us 'racist'. Where did this mindset come from? She asked.

'To have love for your Self and your race doesn't mean hating anyone else. It simply means getting your priorities right'.

'Stop trying to be something you're not. Love your hair, your skin, in all its natural beauty. Stop the wig-wearing, stop bleaching. Return to your Source; Nature. Use natural products as much as possible, stop using chemically-ridden products on your skin, which enter your bloodstream. Stop eating processed foods and eat the foods Mother Nature has provided for you. Then you will begin to heal.'

Suzanne's goal was to help free her people from mental slavery, and protect them from further harm. The psychological damage which caused them to think it was 'normal' to act in ways contrary to their true nature was just as bad as the physical enslavement her ancestors had gone through, and worst still, would continue down through to future generations unless they woke up to the Truth of Who They Really Are.

She made a conscious decision to re-mind her Self daily Who She Was:

"I am love. I am peace. I am joy. I am forgiving. I am blessing. I am light!"

She believed that the more she took on her true, natural virtues, the more she would attract others who operated out of Love instead of fear. These would be the new army of warriors who would slay the dragon – with light and Love.

When the thought came to her that *'there is nothing to fear in the future'*, she made the intention that whenever she found her Self in a dark situation, she would re-mind her Self;

"I am the light!"

****

Breaking News

It was 9.45pm on a Friday night.

Suzanne lay heavily pregnant on the couch, while Micah sat on the floor in front of her as they watched a DVD together. Elijah was out with friends, 'Ma Ankrah had long gone to bed, and Charles still wasn't home yet.
There was a knock at the door.
"Who could that be at this time of night?" Suzanne asked Micah.
"Maybe Elijah's left his key at home" he answered getting up to answer it.
Micah returned with a concerned look on his face.
"Mum, it's the police - they want to speak to you"

Suzanne's mind immediately ran on Elijah.

'Don't tell me he's gone and gotten himself into trouble!' she thought as she heaved herself up from the sofa. But Elijah had never been in trouble, not in school or college, let alone with the police. And his friends weren't the type of young men to lead him astray either. She wondered what could possibly bring the police to her house.

Micah supported her as she made her way to the front door.

"Mrs Ankrah?" said the policeman.

"Yes, what is it?"

"Can we come in?"

"Is something wrong? Where's Elijah?"

"Elijah?" the policeman asked, looking puzzled.

"Isn't that what you're here about? My son?"

"Oh! No...I think you'd better sit down Mrs Ankrah. We have some bad news for you"

"What's this all about?"

Suzanne tried not to panic as she sensed the seriousness in the reason for their visit.

"It's about your husband...Charles Ankrah?"

"Yes...what about him?"

"I'm sorry to inform you, but about an hour ago he was involved in a serious car accident. He suffered multiple broken bones and internal injuries"

Suzanne gasped.

"No...you must be mistaken...surely?"

The policeman took a set of keys out of his pocket.

"Do you recognize these?" he asked, holding up the keys to Charles' black Mercedes with a key-ring showing a picture of Ebony on one side, and herself on the other.

"Y...yes, they're my husband's"

The policeman handed them to her.

"Is he ok? H...how did it happen?" she asked in a confused state as she took them.

"We're still investigating the cause of the crash Mrs Ankrah, but we're here to escort you to the hospital, if you like. He told us you were heavily pregnant just before he passed out."

"*Passed out*? He *is* still alive, isn't he?"

"Yes, but they don't hold much hope for him. Shall we go now?"

As Suzanne gathered her things together, she told Micah to call Dave, and to call Elijah and tell him to meet them at the hospital.

Micah took it upon himself to also call his aunty Janice to let her know her sister would need her.

****

The drive to the hospital seemed to take forever, but Suzanne remained positive within her Self that everything was going to be alright.

"When are you due?" the policewoman turned and asked.

"Any day now" Suzanne responded, taking hold of Micah's hand.

She saw a faint look of dismay flash briefly across the policewoman's face.

Just then, she remembered that she hadn't told her mother-in-law that her son had been taken to hospital. She called Janice and asked her to go and collect 'Ma Ankrah before meeting her at the hospital.

Arriving at the ward, Suzanne was unprepared for what she saw. Charles' broken body was barely recognizable as he lay lifeless on the bed. His head was wrapped in a large bandage, and he wore a brace to keep his broken neck in place. Tubes were attached to different parts of his body, which were connected to a life support machine.

When she caught sight of him, all the air left her lungs. Shock, horror and disbelief overwhelmed her. As her knees gave way, Micah and the policeman caught her, while the policewoman quickly pulled up a chair for her. As she sat down, a doctor came into the room.

"Doctor, please tell me…he will live, won't he?"

The doctor looked Suzanne straight in the eyes and told her gently "He's in a coma, Mrs Ankrah. Apart from his broken neck and internal injuries, a CT scan has revealed extensive damage to his brain. It's only the life support machine keeping him alive now"

"Oh my dear god...*CHARLES!*" Suzanne let out a blood-curdling scream as she got up and resting her hands on his chest, begged him "*PLEASE DON'T LEAVE ME!*"

Charles opened his eyes. He appeared not to be looking at her, but *into* her. There was no fear in his eyes, only peace, love and contentment, as if he didn't have a care in the world. It was only for a brief second, but in that moment, Suzanne saw straight through to his soul as if his body was just a veil, shrouding his true identity. As his true Self was revealed, his aura became visible to her. Suzanne felt as if she was being cocooned in love, light, peace, happiness and purity. The two police made their exit.

Just then Dave, Maria and Ebony arrived. They had spoken to the doctor and were aware of the graveness of the situation. Micah spoke to them briefly in whispered tones before taking the opportunity to go and call his brother again to find out what was taking him so long. As he headed towards the Main Entrance, he saw his aunties Janice and Keisha supporting 'Ma Ankrah in between them as they hurriedly walked towards him.

"Oh, thank goodness, there you are! Is everything ok?" asked aunt Keisha.

"It doesn't look good" Micah replied quietly, shaking his head at the ground.

"Where are they? Is Suzanne ok?" 'Ma Ankrah asked.

"They're in room nine" Micah pointed the way to them.

As they entered, the silent, healing sensation of love and peace that had filled the room enveloped them as well, connecting them all. It seemed to be emanating from Charles; it was obvious that he was dying.

Suzanne, Dave, Maria and Ebony were all holding hands around his bed, as if in silent prayer. Janice and Keisha joined them.

"Oh Lord, no!" cried out 'Ma Ankrah as she caught sight of her son. "Please I beg you Lord, don' tek me only son from me!"
She joined Suzanne in leaning over his body and praying.

Micah re-entered with Elijah. Up to that point, Elijah had been in total denial about the seriousness of the situation, so the look on his face was of utter disbelief. He immediately went over to his mother and put a protective arm around her.

Suzanne was leant over the bed, focused on willing Charles to live. She refused to believe that he was going anywhere. He was happily married. He had a beautiful daughter, two adopted sons who looked up to him, as well as the birth of his new baby to look forward to. He was the Director of a successful business. He was rich. He had everything to live for.

But she had seen something when he opened his eyes. His soul was liberated; it no longer had any interest in the body, or its roles and responsibilities. It had let go of relationships, and detached from all of the cares of this world. He had moved from *body*-consciousness to *soul*-consciousness. He was a free spirit.

She suddenly remembered two of the vows they had made to each other on their wedding day; to allow their souls to each walk their own paths, and not to try to impose their will upon each other. What was his soul trying to do? Did he want to stay, or leave?

The moment she let go of her need to keep Charles attached to this world, his spirit left his body.

Dave picked up Ebony and whispered "say goodbye to your daddy, princess". Ebony kissed Charles lightly on the cheek before turning away, burying her head in Dave's neck. Maria took her from him, as mother and daughter hugged each other crying. Dave tried to be strong as he put his arms around them both. Charles had been closer to him than any of his brothers.

As Charles crossed the threshold into eternal life, Suzanne began to sob uncontrollably; first quietly, then getting louder and louder as the realization of the situation sunk in.

Her and Ma's wailing brought the doctor and nurses back in, who turned off the life-support machine and began removing the tubes from his body.

The sight of the flatline was too final; Suzanne screamed out a blood-curdling "NOOOOOOOOOO!!!"

Any moment now, she thought she *must* wake up from what had to be a horrible dream.

But somehow she knew this wasn't just a bad dream. She could feel her heart breaking *again* as she experienced an overwhelming feeling of emptiness and sorrow. Her sisters did their best to comfort her as she began to cry loudly and uncontrollably.

She began hyperventilating, holding on to her stomach.

"Doctor, I think she's in pain!" Keisha called the doctor.

He looked over and exclaimed;

"Oh my gosh, I think she's going into labour! Are you feeling pain anywhere?" he asked her.

She nodded as she continued sobbing and hyperventilating.

"Where is the pain?" he asked.

She put her hand first over her heart, then her stomach.

He instructed one of the nurses to get a wheelchair.

"We must get her to the labour ward, quick!" he said.

"I'm not leaving Charles!" she cried out.

"Suzanne, you're in labour – you can't give birth here!" Janice spoke firmly as she helped the nurse force her into the wheelchair. From then on, everything became a blur for Suzanne. Not even she could tell if her loud wailings were from the labour pains or her grieving.

As they wheeled her up to the labour ward the nurse asked "Did you bring your notes?"

She shook her head.

Janice told the boys to go to her car and get the baby bag, which she had seen sitting by the front door when they picked up 'Ma Ankrah, and had instinctively picked it up too.

"I'm not leaving mum" Elijah stated bluntly.

"It's ok, I'll go" Maria suggested.

"Good idea" replied Keisha. "I'll come with you"

"I'd like to be here for the birth too...if that's ok?" Maria asked.

"It would be nice for Ebony"

"Are you ok with that?" Janice asked Suzanne, who nodded as she grimaced in pain.

Somehow, Charles' death had created a bond between them all.

"Mummy, I want to stay with you" Ebony pleaded.

This created a dilemma; Dave wanted to stay with Charles' body, and children weren't allowed on the labour ward.

"I'm sure if we explain the situation, they might make an exception" the nurse assured them.

For now, Dave stayed with 'Ma Ankrah and Charles' body, while Maria and Ebony left with Keisha to collect the baby bag and notes from Janice's car.

When they returned, the nurse had explained to the midwife that Ebony's father had just passed, and her baby brother or sister was about to be born.

"Can she stay? None of us want to miss it" Maria pleaded.
The midwife finally agreed, but insisted she would have to wait outside the ward until after the baby had been born. So Maria and Ebony remained in the Waiting Room.

From Suzanne's perspective, everything was just one big blur; she couldn't tell if the pain she was feeling was from her broken heart, or contractions. She had no will left to push, yet nature was taking its course anyway. She could vaguely make out her sisters bending over her urging her to push, while the midwife placed a gas and air mask over her face.
As she gave birth she continued wailing and sobbing with one long groan after another asking "Why me? Why now?"

Charles had attended every pre-natal appointment, and now he wasn't even here for the birth.

Within an hour and a half, she had given birth to a beautiful, healthy baby boy.

But when the midwife placed the baby on her chest, she couldn't even look at it. Her sisters took over, helping the midwife weigh and wash the baby, and dressing him while the midwife delivered the placenta.

Suzanne continued moaning with long, painful groans even after the labour was over.

The doctor was called again.

"I think it's best if I sedate her. She's in shock – she's been through a lot this evening"

As Suzanne appeared to be delirious and sobbing hopelessly, her sisters agreed. She was in no fit state to look after the baby she had just delivered.

After the doctor gave her the injection, she drifted off slowly into sleep…

****

As Suzanne entered her Alpha state, she became detached from her physical body and was immediately transported into a space of intense, bright light. Charles appeared as an ethereal form of pure love and light. As he walked towards her, he smiled with such a peaceful, happy expression. A powerful healing presence enveloped her.

He didn't speak in words, but she understood everything he was communicating to her perfectly. He let her know that he was alive and well, just not in his physical body. He told her not to worry about him, that he had fulfilled his soul purpose in that lifetime, and that it was time for him to move on. He had been on a mission of Love, which he had completed. He reminded her that he had left a precious gift for her to cherish, and that he would always be with her in spirit.

As he drew her close to him a divine presence filled every part of her being with pure, unconditional love, until she felt part of it. She felt warm, peaceful and happy...

****

...When Suzanne regained consciousness, the intensity of her grief had diminished considerably.

She had caught a glimpse through the spiritual window and had seen Charles' soul, and now *knew* that mortality is only an illusion, and death is only a separation of the true Self from the body.

She felt a new sense of hope knowing that Charles could never die, and that she could never be separated from him. Death truly had no sting; it was simply a *transitioning* of the eternal spirit from the physical to the spiritual realm, back to its Source, which was Love.

She finally realized that Love isn't a *feeling*, it's a state of *being*.

In her new state of enlightenment she remembered the true and original nature of her *own* soul: She was Love.   She was peace.   She was joy.   She was light.

Seeing the real Charles had reminded her of her own immortality. She now felt as if she knew her purpose and destiny; just as Charles' purpose had been to remind her of Who *she* was, *her* purpose was to remind others of Who *they* were.

As her consciousness expanded, she remembered the lesson of loving and letting go; of being detached from outcomes and having no expectations of other souls she was in relationship with, just as God had no expectations of her.

Suzanne had loved being able to call Charles "MY husband" but in Truth, he was not a possession for her to own or to keep, but had simply been on loan to her from the Divine, sent to help her achieve her goals in life.

In that moment she consciously set a *new* goal for her Self; to give Love free from expectations, and to detach from everything including 'her' children, because they were not her possessions, they were sacred souls on their *own* sacred journeys, who were just given to her as a gift from the Divine.   In Truth, nothing belonged to her; everything she owned belonged to God. When it was time for her to leave her body, she would take nothing with her.

As Maria handed her baby boy to her, the excitement of having created a new life mixed with the grief of Charles' death was a bitter-sweet combination.

But it was time to let go of her negative emotions, and realize that Charles was still very much alive.

As she looked into the baby's wide, alert eyes she thought she saw something familiar.

They say the eyes are the windows to a person's soul;

Could it really be…

"CHARLES?" she whispered with a trembling voice.

****

Afterthought...

I have to say, I'm just as surprised at the way the story ended as you are! The whole journey of writing this book has been filled with twists and turns; my original intention had simply been to write a 'black erotica' novel (I wrote the sex scenes first!) but I saw it evolve into something much more deep and meaningful.

The process of writing this book can only be likened to giving birth. I spent the whole summer of 2012 'in labour' pushing this book out with intense focus (it could easily have taken me another two years!). Having now given birth to this beautiful book, I must say, it was worth all the pain! I'm looking forward to seeing how it continues to grow and develop...

Some questions I've been asked:

"Why did you have to kill Charles?"
I have to apologize if you were expecting the 'happily ever after' ending. That *was* my original intention, so when Errol, the editor suggested killing off one of the main characters, my first reaction was a vehement "NO!" But the more I thought about it, the more I had to agree that the ending was too cliché (getting married and living happily ever after) and that Suzanne had to face the ultimate test.

On a subconscious level, it also symbolized the 'Death of a Dream' for me.

It took me a few weeks to fully internalize how Charles' death would affect Suzanne and the rest of the characters, before I could begin to write about it. I read *'A Mission of Love'* by Dr. Roger Cole who worked with dying patients (which I bought at Inner Space in Covent Garden). It really helped me shape the storyline. When Errol dropped a note in his edits to say that he was crying, I knew I'd achieved my objective. I cried as I was writing it, and I wanted my readers to feel the emotions too. Yet at the same time, I wanted it to end on a positive, hopeful note.

I know Errol probably won't appreciate me telling the world that he cried when he read it, but that's the point; *men, it's ok to cry*! Crying is a normal reaction to a given situation. It shows you have soul.

I've been told that the ending was an 'anti-climax', but if you read it again, you should see that in Truth, there is no such thing as 'death', and that Charles is still very much alive!

"Is the character Charles based on anyone I know?"

I created the character 'Charles' in order to impart the knowledge I've accumulated since asking God for 'the Truth' in 2007. However, his personality was based on someone I knew, who could be described as my 'twin soul'. The way in which the two main characters met was exactly how we met, and he gave his version of the (profound) event in Year Five: 'Flashback' (it was also his idea to throw it in randomly!). Unfortunately though, we never had any of those deep, meaningful conversations.

"So **does Charles really exist?**" I cannot truthfully answer 'no' to this question, since I believe in the creative power of my thoughts, words and actions. If he didn't exist before, he's in the making!

Charles also represents my masculine energy and how I like to think I'd be if I was a man – and that's the type of man I desire! Queens, if you built your hopes on meeting someone like Charles, I'd say 'go for it', and also prepare your Self for when he does come along. Learn the lessons in this book and put them into practice. I am the teacher *and* the student; I'm still learning how to master all *my* thoughts, words and actions in order to create the life of my dreams too.

"Have you ever performed a Sex Ritual?"

I only discovered 'the secret' of Black Male and Female Sex through the process of writing this book; I woke up one night and wrote the scene where Suzanne and Charles performed their first Sex Ritual (in Year Eight). It was as if I was 're-membering' stuff buried deep within my DNA, or subconscious mind. Then I came across the book *'The Secret Science of Black Male and Female Sex'* by T.C. Carrier, which confirmed what I had 're-membered' and which I recommend for reading. (See 'References')

When I learnt that my sexual energy is the same energy I can use to create, I stopped wasting it having sex willy nilly (excuse the pun!). I now focus on harnessing my sexual energy and transmuting it to create. Our ancestors built great civilizations and mastered the arts, sciences, mathematics and knowledge of the universe. The information is buried deep within our genes, and just needs to be re-awakened. We have been asleep for too long; my hope is that this book goes some way into helping us re-member Who We Are as a people. Our spirituality and sexuality is the key.

When the Black Man and Black Woman unite in a high state of consciousness, we can accomplish much.

It's funny, because when I was a church-going Christian and was told that sex before marriage was wrong, the thought of having sex was like an obsession. But now I know there's a higher meaning to a sexual union, I no longer desire to join my body-temple with any Tom, Dick or Howie.

Life's a beach.

That leads me to the next question:
"Is this your autobiography?" I've also been asked.
Although there are a lot of similarities between Suzanne and my Self, I'd say not more than 50% of the story is 'autobiographical'. I've drawn from some of my most profound life experiences, but I also used this book to stretch my imagination to its limit. I also wrote the best part of this book under Divine Inspiration – and Errol's suggestions have also gone some way into shaping the storyline too.

This isn't about me; this book has a greater purpose than just being a great story – it's a Self-help book with tools in it that can actually help transform your life!

This book is for my sisters, and if the brothers get hold of it and read it too, even better! We will be on our way to reclaiming our lost heritage even quicker. We have a large inheritance waiting for us, paid for by our ancestors. As we begin 'waking up' and opening our third eye to the Truth, there is nothing we will not be able to achieve, just like our ancestors.

In the words of our ancestor the great Marcus Mosiah Garvey:

"Up you mighty people, You can accomplish what you will!"

Namastu (I bow to the Divinity within you)

BOOK TWO:

As I was working on Years 10 and 11, I found my Self writing material that exceeded where the story was due to end. So I am currently in the process of writing the **Sequel** to *Single, Spiritual…AND Sexual!,* **'No Expectations'.** If you would like to find out how Suzanne progressed after the death of her husband, and the ultimate lessons she learns in her new state of enlightenment join my Mailing List by sending an email to: **singlespiritualandsexual@gmail.com** and I'll let you know as soon as it's due out! (Put 'No Expectations" in the Subject Line).

Acknowledgements

My first acknowledgement *must* be to **God**, The Great Creator, The Source, the Mother/Father Principle, Universal Mind, Love, my Higher Self (or whatever you choose to call Him/Her). I am so happy and grateful that You chose *me* as the channel for this book to come through. "Thank You!"

I must also say a big "THANK YOU!" to my friend **Errol McGlashan** for all the hard work and dedication he put into helping me edit this book. Although he doesn't consider himself 'the editor' and refused to allow me to acknowledge him as such (I did anyway), I wouldn't have wanted a 'professional' editor even if I could have afforded to pay one! Despite the fact that he was totally unprofessional in his approach to the way he identified with the characters (especially Suzanne), I knew he was the right person for the job (since he was the only person the Universe brought along!). His enthusiasm, dedication, passion, insight and creative input were invaluable, right down to the idea for the twist at the end of the story. He even gave the character 'Malachi' his yardie accent, and wrote the pastor's sermon in Year One (I just added to it)! There were times when his laptop broke and he had to go to the internet café to do the editing, or when he had to work through the night to meet my timeline, putting his own poetry-writing on hold.

I have truly enjoyed 'co-creating' with you Errol, I owe you big time.

I thank my mother **Melita** for bringing me into the world at this most important time in the history of Mother Earth, and for raising me in the Christian faith. God bless you, I love you. I also give honour to my late father Ralston Fletcher, my late grandmother **Lena** and all my ancestors and spirit guides.

To my siblings; Antoinette, Noel, David and Janet; although I no longer use my birth name and am not bound by any family obligations, I will always be your sister. To my sister **Jacqui** (Keasa Yaa) who is not only my blood sister, but my *soul* sister;

just think, a year ago you were telling me you didn't feel as if your life had a special purpose; look at how far you have come in the space of a year! In time, with your Astrology and my Numerology knowledge we will impact the lives of thousands!

To my three princes **Zaviere**, **Sanchez** and **Azagba**, the jewels in my crown! Thank you for giving me the space and time to not only write this book, but do the paintings and write and record the poems that accompany it. Ok, you didn't *give* it to me, I *took* it, I know, but thank you for being patient with me when I was acting dysfunctional as a mum. You've been great. If I'd had to worry about you staying out late at night, getting into trouble, and having to push you all the time, I wouldn't have been able to focus on my work. I am so proud of you! I love you. I didn't know why I was being led to give you all names with the letters 'A' and 'Z' in them. But now I know it stands for Alpha and Omega, the beginning and the end, the first and the last: Know that you are *gods*!

To their fathers **Lofton** and **Ewemade**, thank you for looking after them so I could focus on nurturing my *inner child*. I would especially like to say a big "THANK YOU" to the father of my youngest son Azagba for not only looking after him and being a great dad to him, but continuing to support me in *my* work, offering whatever help, advice and encouragement you could give. Without your support, I wouldn't have been able to achieve all I have over the last four years. This is one of the most recent texts I received from him which shows what type of person he is: "Hi C, I prayed for you today. I prayed that your success in getting your book published despite a journey of the pain, the doubts, and quiet despair will be rewarded through the destination that is this book and via profits of sharing your strength, wisdom, your hope, your positivity and generosity that you will leave with your thousands of readers. And when I prayed Mark 11:24 came to mind; '*Therefore I say unto you, whatsoever things you desire, when you pray, believe that you receive them, and yes you shall receive them*'. You deserve nothing less, best wishes, Maddy". At this point, I had only told him I'd written a novel – he didn't even so much as know the *title* of the book, or what it was about! Even after he downloaded the first chapter and read it, he enthusiastically helped with the marketing material. So I gratefully say *"thank you Maddy!"* for your support and admiration of what I do for a life.

I would like to thank my Facebook friend **Viv Ahmun** for allowing me to use your photo to illustrate year 10 – it fit into the story perfectly – and you could almost pass for Charles!

To astrologer **Israel Ajose**, thank you for advising me when it was the best time to 'plant the seed' for this book, when to do my book launch, plus other things! For information on his astrology classes and for readings email: **neteru@hotmail.com**

To all my friends who have supported me in the uphill struggle of my writing career, including **June Wiggan** and **Sandra Ambo** who took the time to read the very first draft of this book and offer their comments, fellow writer and activist **Margaret Aberdeen** who took me in when I became homeless for the second time, and where I first discovered the book *'Conversations with God Book One'* (www.margaretaberdeen.com), **Marlon 'Kush' Palmer** who gave me *'The Secret'* DVD for my birthday in 2007, which was where I first began learning about the creative power of my thoughts (he also gave me the film 'Sankofa' which traumatized me but inspired me to write the poem *'We Belong Together'*), fellow writer **Esther Poyer** who has offered continuous advice and support over the years, the 'IP Queen' **Nancy Mukoro** who as a lawyer specializing in the creative industry has offered me some great advice for free. Fellow poetess **Leafy Bee** for teaching me a new word *'innerstood'* from her collection *'Ghetto Poems'* (available on Lulu), 'Dynamic **Debbie**' **Bulgin, Kwame McPherson** who took me to The Millionaire Author's Bootcamp in June 2012 which was where I got the idea to publish this book on Kindle – if I hadn't started publishing it on Kindle chapter by chapter, I could have easily spent another year working on it at my leisure! But I am SO GRATEFUL for the kick up the rear end to get it out! Thanks also to journalist/researcher **Felicity Heywood** who also helped with the final edit of this book. Minty from **Nubia**

House radio (Tune into my show *'Pure Poetry'* every Monday 6-8pm GMT **www.nubiahousemedia.com**), **Buzzing Bee** on **SLR Radio**, and **Michael Hibbert** from **www.trustmeradio.com** (my book is featured on his site permanently!). Massive thanks also to **Mr P** for helping me market my book, **Althea Grant, Livingston Gilchrist, Andrea Enisuoh (Words of Colour), Ngoma Bishop, BEMA Network** and the **House of AMAU** Writer's Group.

I would like to say a very special "Thank you" to **Theo Calliste** who I stayed with during my last bout of homelessness. Thank you for allowing me to turn your living room into my art studio, and for putting up with my mess! For the first time, I had the opportunity to focus on my 'Self' and this is where I started learning to meditate. During the course of my stay at his house we developed 8 of the tracks on the *'Seeds of Love'* CD (more of the tracks we produced will be on my next CD). The lesson: *'In every failure is the **seed** to your future success."*

I would also like to give thanks to the musicians who went with my flow and contributed to the *'Seeds of Love'* CD; **Chi Bomani** (djembe drumming/vocals), **Ras Gad** (vocals), **George Dawkins** (sax), and of course **Theo Calliste** (acoustic guitar). The creative process working with Theo was this; Theo would get 'bursts of inspiration' and play beautiful compositions into his Dictaphone. I took them off the Dictaphone and uploaded them into a music programme. After listening to them over and over again I would be inspired to write words to go with them. Both his music and my words were 'divinely inspired'. And last but by no means least, my youngest son **Azagba**, who recorded *"Your Own Universe!"* on the track *'Conversations Within'* in 2009 when he was only five years old. The scream he did at the end was totally spontaneous, which he picked up from the vibe of Theo's guitar playing (he was sitting with us!)

I would also like to thank all those who have influenced and impacted my life in a positive way, which have helped shape me into the person I am today. Some I have met, and some I haven't (apart from through the material you have produced). You know who you are.

Last but not least, I would like to thank YOU, the reader for buying my first book! I hope you have enjoyed and learnt from it; if you would like to give me feedback, please leave a review at **www.singlespiritualandsexual.com** or on **Lulu**.

    5% of the Self-published author's job is *writing* the book, 95% is *marketing* it, and the best form of marketing is *word of mouth*, so if you know people who you think would benefit from reading *'Single, Spiritual…AND Sexual!'* join the 'Transformation Revolution' and share the link to the website with everyone you know!

With great gratitude,

Book References:

'*The Secret*' by Rhonda Byrne (I prefer the audiobook and DVD)
'*Conversations with God Book One*' by Neale Donald Walsche
'*The Master Key System*' by Charles F Haanel
'*The Science of Getting Rich*' by Wallace D. Wattles
'*When We Ruled*' by Robin Walker
'*Black Scientists and Inventors*' by BIS Publications
'*How Europe Underdeveloped Africa*' by Walter Rodney
'*The Mis-education of the Negro*' by Carter G. Woodson
'*Message to the People*' Marcus Mosiah Garvey
'*Heal Thyself*' by Queen Afua
'*Sacred Woman*' Queen Afua
'*African Holistic Health*' Dr Llaila O. Afrika
'*Melanin: What Makes Black People Black*' by Dr Llaila O. Afrika
'*The Secret Science of Black Male and Female Sex*' by T.C. Carrier
'*Feel the Fear and Do it Anyway*' by Susan Jeffers
'*A Mission of Love*' by Dr Roger Cole (on death and dying)
The Bible

Rebuilding the Black Community
(London, England):

Black History Classes with Robin Walker (author of '*When We Ruled*')
email: historicalwalker@yahoo.com

Black History Walks and Film Screenings in London with *Tony Warner*. www.blackhistorywalks.co.uk

Black History Classes with Onyeka www.onyeka.co.uk

Black History Studies www.blackhistorystudies.com

Yoruba classes: email Chief Kolade Ogunbayode: **mrkay@fsmail.net**

Mashufaa Classes (African martial arts): www.mashufaa.co.uk

African Yoga www.afrikanyoga.com

The Children's Cultural Film Club:
www.goldonyx.co.uk or call 07946 670 949

About the Author

𝒞ezanne is a Self-taught Visual & Spoken Word Artist and Self-published Author, guided by her in-tuition.

Her work is a creative expression of her spiritual journey.

"I remained a blocked writer and artist for over 20 years, unable to use my natural God-given talents of writing and art due to 'mental blocks' brought on by low Self-esteem and my religious upbringing. However since putting my Self through a series of Self-development programs (including working with Positive Affirmations and learning how to meditate) I am now writing and painting freely!

My poetry-writing journey began in 2001, starting with inspirational Christian poetry. The first one "Look to Me!" (Gods Reply) is featured in Year One of this story. You can listen to and download all the poems featured in this story by visiting: **www.reverbnation.com/cezannepoetess** (book of lyrics also available). Feel free to 'like' them, share them and Become a Fan!

Between 2009-10 I locked my Self away and painted 11 paintings (most of them are featured in this book). I hadn't painted in over 20 years, and never with oils on canvas before! I also wrote some of the poems featured in this story in collaboration with acoustic guitarist Theo Calliste.

Between 2010-12 I wrote this novel, only to find that some of the poems I've been writing and recording since 2001 could be used to illustrate the story, as well as my paintings!

My hope is that through my work, I will help my community to heal. I am happy to take part in and organize events that work towards building sustainable Black relationships."

To keep up-to-date on Cezanne's activities 'follow' her blog: **www.cezannepoetess.wordpress.com**

You can also join her Mailing List at:
cezannepoetess@gmail.com (putting 'Mailing List' in the Subject Line). You can also use this email address to book her for live performances, interviews and speaking engagements (no unsolicited mail please).

For products featuring Cezanne's artwork and poetry visit:
www.cezannesart.co.uk (including **signed copies** of this book – they make great gifts!)

Add her on **Facebook**: Cezanne Poetess
Follow her on **Twitter**: @CezannePoetess
Add her on **LinkedIn**: Cezanne Poetess

'Seeds of Love' CD & Book of Lyrics

'**Seeds of Love**' is a compilation of 13 of my poems which all feature in this story.   Musical contributions were made by acoustic guitarist **Theo Calliste** (spiritra@hotmail.co.uk) **Chi Bomani** playing djembe drums *(*he also *sings* on the track 'Trust'), saxophonist **George Dawkins** on the track *'Conversations Within'*, My youngest son **'Azzy'** also added "Your Own Universe!" (he was 5 years old at the time!).   And lastly, **Ras Gad** added some ooooo's and aaaaaaah's to *'The Preparation'* and *'Equilibrium'*.

You can listen to and download all 13 poems (mp3's) at:
www.reverbnation.com/cezannepoetess

Its Book of Lyrics **'Seeds of Love'** is also available as an e-book or paperback from Amazon and Lulu, or by visiting **www.singlespiritualandsexual.com**.

*'Be transformed by the renewing of your mind,
So that you may prove what is that good and acceptable and perfect will of God'*
(Romans 12:2)

NOTES

NOTES

www.ingramcontent.com/pod-product-compliance
Lightning Source LLC
Chambersburg PA
CBHW070725160426
43192CB00009B/1319